No. 819
$12.95

JOURNALIST'S NOTEBOOK OF LIVE RADIO-TV NEWS
By Phillip O. Keirstead

TAB BOOKS
Blue Ridge Summit, Pa. 17214

Contents

Preface

This book is designed to explain the basics of modern radio-television journalism. It can be easily understood by a beginner or by someone already working in broadcasting who wishes to become a newsperson.

My aim has been to instruct using the traditional values and techniques against a setting of steady technological change. Broadcast news is changing rapidly, largely because the electronic revolution has made it possible for broadcast journalists to put sound and pictures on the air more completely and quickly than ever.

As a result, broadcast journalism has become highly specialized. Its practitioners need a solid understanding of journalism concepts and techniques in addition to complete knowledge of the technology with which they work. Putting a broadcast news story on the air is a complex operation and one which totally involves the reporter. The broadcast journalist can never lose track of the fact that he or she is directly involved in the technology of getting a story and producing it in its final audiovisual form. All this must be done against the constant urgings of that demanding taskmaster: time.

News departments are becoming increasingly professional, and while employment rises and falls in relation to the relative health of the economy, there is steady improvement in the number and quality of broadcast news departments.

Before we move into the past and present of broadcast journalism, just a word of thanks to my wife, Sonia-Kay, for her inspiration, constructive suggestions, copy reading, and most of all faith that this book would be finished. Special thanks also go to Helen Cohen, Gladys Jukich, and Frances Kahn for doing dozens of tasks which made editing and organizing this book much easier.

And to the long list of people the author has met and worked with over some two decades: thanks for all you have taught me!

Phillip O. Keirstead

Introduction

There are almost 9000 radio and television stations operating in the United States and its territories. The majority of these stations present news in some form. The content may vary from a summary of campus happenings broadcast over a 10W (watt) college radio station to two-hour early evening television newscasts. which are currently being shown in several of the country's major markets.

Considering that broadcast news did not become a staple on the American scene until World War II. the country's broadcasters have made great progress in developing their own unique form of journalism to its present form.

A few years ago broadcast news was done by staff announcers who either read prepared scripts or ripped copy off of wire service teleprinters. Today newsrooms are staffed by people who have grown up in broadcasting and are trained in this unique form of news gathering and dissemination.

Some of the credit for the change goes to former Federal Communications Commission (FCC) Chairman Newton N. Minow. who in 1961 told a National Association of Broadcasters convention that the output of the nation's television stations was a "vast wasteland." Minow's speech led to a great deal of agonizing by industry leaders. While the FCC is powerless under the Communications Act to prescribe programing. it can apply forceful pressure to emphasize certain activities. This kind of pressure was put on broadcast news. Since the Minow speech broadcasters have felt increasing pressure to provide news and public affairs programing—not only in quantity. but with quality.

Parallel to this goading by the government. many stations found that doing a good job with news helped their image and increased their audiences and revenues. As result. in large and small markets around the country you can find professional broadcast journalists covering news first hand and producing their own unique presentation of the day's news.

They present the news in succinct and understandable form, while using pictures and sound to increase the audience's perception of what is happening. The unique quality of broadcast news is its ability to present events as they happen or shortly after, using the pictures and sounds of the events themselves rather than just the interpretive senses of a reporter.

Broadcast news is not necessarily the be all and end all, even though many people get the majority of their news from broadcast stations. Newspapers and magazines have the ability to cover stories in greater depth and to do certain other tasks that do not adapt well to broadcasting, such as reprinting the entire annual town budget or the like.

Today's ideal broadcast newsroom is headed by a news director who reports directly to the top management and is on

There have been instances of making a monkey out of an interviewee or interviewer, but I suspect this early picture was posed. (Courtesy National Association of Broadcasters.)

the same level as the heads of the program. engineering. and sales departments.

The staff will do news and news only—no commercials. The reporters will solicit. on the telephone and in person. their own news stories. In the case of television. the film or videotape will be shot by professionals. skilled in their unique art: the visualization of events.

The news department will have the electronic tools it needs such as radio communications facilities. tape recorders. cameras. and news services. The staff may be varied in background. but it will consist of proven broadcast news professionals who know how to report a story in the best manner to be understood by their audience within the confines of limited time.

Some broadcast news departments have reached a high degree of sophistication. Others suffer from such common ills as understaffing. low budgets. lack of freedom from sales and program influences. or insufficient professional standards.

When one listens to a good newscast on radio or watches an equally good effort on television. one finds it hard to picture a situation such as existed in the late 1950s when a metropolitan station employed two newsmen who did voice reports by calling each other on the office telephones. Other performances included excessive echo chambers. morse code sounds. reports from the (sound effect) "weather tower." and Hollywood gossip inserts in the newscasts. Fortunately. this sort of performance is now very much the exception in an industry which has achieved considerable maturity in its news presentations.

Some of the major challenges facing broadcast news professionals include consultants. Hollywoodism. and the press conference syndrome.

CONSULTANTS

In the past few years station managements. especially in television. have found their newscasts to be healthy sources of revenue. As a result management has sought to define just what makes a successful newscast. Success is now defined by the size of the audience estimated by rating services and the consequent income from selling advertising.

Today consultants can be found in newsrooms from the Pacific to the Atlantic telling managers and news directors to put more of this or less of that into their newscasts. From the viewpoint of many news directors, these consultants tend to want larger numbers of shorter stories oriented toward the basic emotions such as sex or fear.

A news director who is critical of consultants would say they want 20 television news stories in a half-hour (approximately 16 minutes of air time would be available in a half-hour), giving short shrift to content and concentrating on fires, robberies, and the basic emotions.

The consultants say they only advise and that it is up to the station management to decide how to use the recommendations. But the consultants also freely admit that they feel they can measure greater response to items of supposedly common interest such as violence and sex. So from the consultants' point of view, if you want to get the maximum number of people to watch or listen, you program the sort of material which is apt to appeal to the broadest spectrum of people.

There is so much controversy over the advice of consultants because of a view held by news professionals that part of the function of news coverage is to enlighten people: to give them information which may not be appealing to their emotions but may be important in the context of how their city is run, the amount of taxes they pay, or the quality of their schools. This sort of information can be pretty dull unless interpreted by skilled, creative people.

The move toward using the services of consultants has resulted in many stations—especially television stations —changing the nature and mood of their news presentations. The anchorpersons now tend to be more relaxed, and a certain amount of banter or conversation takes place among the people participating in the newscast. In television this is called the "happy talk" format. This has removed some of the pomposity which used to stultify newscasts. But some happy talk formats lose the point of the newscast, which is to inform the public, and become a sideshow with more of an entertainment than a news reporting approach.

HOLLYWOODISM

By Hollywoodism I mean the furthest extension of the happy talk idea. The newscast becomes an entertainment vehicle, choosing its stories and the form of presentation solely for mass appeal and for entertainment value.

12

Professional newspersons and responsible station managements universally decry this approach. Even some of the more severe exhibitors of this style have come back to the fold, using an informal, somewhat racy style but making an effort to put substantial content into the newscast. However, there are a few stations which use "tabloid journalism": loading their newscasts exclusively with flashy items such as sex crimes, murders, robberies, and accidents.

THE PRESS CONFERENCE SYNDROME

This is one of the most invidious problems plaguing broadcast journalism. In many major markets it is easier to schedule union reporters and crews to be at a certain place at a predetermined time. So we get a proliferation of press conferences in which all the media attend and get spoon-fed whatever the stagers have to offer. If all goes well, the session may include a fairly stimulating question and answer period.

The press conference has its place, but it should be only one of the activities of a good news department. The news director and the assignment editor should be thinking up their own stories in areas which need investigation and sending reporters to provide coverage rather than just taking whatever is available at a news conference.

One solution to this problem is to hire sufficient staff to do more than just skim the top off the daily press conference list. Another technique is to boycott less important gatherings and demand that key participants be made available to reporters on a one-to-one basis. Fortunately, there is a gradual swing away from reliance on set events as broadcast stations establish their own identities with sufficient staff to carry out their tasks.

We are in an exciting period for broadcast news. New breakthroughs in audiotape, film, and videotape technology have significantly increased the flexibility of reporters and technicians. The weight and bulk of equipment has nearly been wiped out as a hindrance to broadcast news.

Radio reporters are working with pocket-sized, battery-operated tape recorders and pocket-sized, portable, two-way radios. Film cameras are lighter and now contain built-in, transistorized, sound amplifier-mixers. Filming can be done under poor lighting conditions with the new film stocks or with lightweight, portable, illumination equipment.

Portable ENG camera with chest brace. (Courtesy Robert Bosch Crop.)

Videotape and television cameras are rapidly being miniaturized, although there is still much to be done with some of the backup equipment used in live and microwave relay of television pictures.

1
The History of Broadcasting

One of the first important discoveries which made radio broadcasting possible occurred over a century ago in 1864. James C. Maxwell, a Scottish physicist, developed a theory of electromagnetism. Maxwell suggested the existence of electric waves, which are now understood as basic elements in radio theory.

The father of modern electrical theory, Thomas Edison, developed a method of wireless communication between trains and railroad stations during the 1880s. But one of the most significant theoretical discoveries came in 1887 when a German, Heinrich Hertz, made rapid variations in electric current to show that current could be projected into space as radio waves. Modern radio is based on this discovery.

An Italian, Guglielmo Marconi, concluded in 1894 that you could use Hertz's waves to send telegraph signals without wires. By 1901 Marconi succeeded in transmitting the letter "S" in Morse code from England to a receiver in Newfoundland.

Once the wireless was invented, its use spread rapidly. One of the earliest and most important applications was for communications between ships and the mainland.

The next challenge was to figure out how to superimpose voice signals on radio waves. The key invention came in 1904 when John Ambrose Fleming, an Englishman, invented the vacuum tube. In the same period an American, Lee De Forest, developed the Audion tube, and a compatriot, Reginald Fessenden, invented the heterodyne system for transmitting speech on these waves.

In 1908 De Forest gave a demonstration of his system. He broadcast music from the Eiffel Tower in Paris. Reports indicate De Forest's music was received as far as 500 miles away.

The next year Charles David Herrold of San Jose, California built an experimental radio station and broadcast music and news to his friends, whom he had equipped with elementary crystal receivers. Herrold probably was not aware of his contribution, but he may actually have done the first radio news broadcast.

In 1916 De Forest broadcast election returns over his experimental station.

After a number of years spent unscrambling patent problems involved in manufacturing radio equipment, radio began to grow. During the early years one manufacturer might have the patent for one essential part while another would control a second essential part. Without some sort of working agreement, it became nearly impossible to manufacture equipment. It was as if Henry Ford had owned the patents to a gasoline engine and someone else controlled rights to the steering mechanism.

After World War One was over, the growth period began. In 1922 there were about 600 stations on the air in the United States. Two years later the count rose to 1,400.

In order to get people to buy radio receivers, the manufacturing companies and several major retailers put their own radio stations on the air. In later years most of these firms sold out, except for the Radio Corporation of America (RCA), which is the parent company of the National Broadcasting Company (NBC).

A number of historians use 1920 as the founding year for radio broadcasting as we know it. The University of Wisconsin physics department began broadcasting from an experimental station (WHA) in that year. In Detroit, the owners of the *Detroit News* put WWJ on during the summer of 1920. And on Election Day in November 1920, KDKA in Pittsburg began broadcasting by giving results of the Warren Harding presidential election.

The first programing was highly informal, with music being drawn from personal record collections. Amateur and professional performers did acts free just for the exposure. This did not last long, because the performers soon decided they ought to be paid for their work. (See Fig. 1-1.)

Fig. 1-1. In the days before television the big console radio used to dominate the living room. (Courtesy National Association of Broadcasters.)

As the costs of operating radio stations rose, many marginal efforts expired and stations went off the air or began to think about sharing programs. On January 4, 1923, the American Telephone and Telegraph Company (AT&T) station in New York, WEAF (now WNBC), did a simultaneous broadcast in conjunction with WNAC in Boston. Later that year AT&T set up a station in Washington, and frequent network sharing of programs took place between this state and New York. By the next year AT&T was able to put together a 23-station coast-to-coast network to carry a broadcast by President Calvin Coolidge.

Also in 1924 a network was formed to broadcast the Republican National Convention, and in 1925 President Coolidge's inauguration was carried over a 21-station hookup.

News on a regularly scheduled basis got a slow start. The majority of the news-type programing consisted of special broadcasts—the sort of thing we would call special events today.

The early news broadcasts were done by newspaper reporters. Bill Slocum of the *New York Herald-Tribune* started

17

doing 15-minute news summaries over WJZ (now WABC in New York) in 1923. Later that year, H. V. Kaltenborn, then a young editor at the *Brooklyn Eagle*, began a series of news programs over WEAF. Kaltenborn went on to be identified as one of the "greats" of early radio news broadcasting.

The early radio stations were forced to employ newspaper reporters for two reasons: there were no broadcast news specialists available, and the stations had not yet thought to set up their own news organizations. In addition, the wire services—Associated Press (AP), United Press (UP), and the International News Service (INS)—refused to sell their services to the radio stations. The wire services were responding to intense pressure from newspaper publishers who considered the new medium a competitive threat.

In 1928 representatives of the publishers met with the press associations to try to establish a policy which would restrain the activities of radio news. However, the wire services did permit radio stations to carry brief reports of Herbert Hoover's presidential election. These broadcasts were well received and aroused public interest.

In 1932 the infant CBS Radio Network signed a contract with United Press to receive results of the presidential election. A few days before the election, UP canceled the contract. But the cancellation was kept secret from AP and INS which, expecting a competitive threat, had jumped in and offered their services free to CBS and NBC.

The success of these broadcasts infuriated the newspaper publishers. A heated debate broke out at the 1932 meeting of the American Newspaper Publishers Association. However, some major publishers pointed out that printing radio program schedules would help their circulation and that short items broadcast on radio would increase the public's interest in reading more detailed versions in the newspaper.

But in 1933 the wire services ended their limited service to radio stations. CBS retaliated by starting the Columbia News Service (CNS). Paul White was hired away from his post at UP to run the new CBS project. White contracted with Dow-Jones to get its business news service, and he bought the British Exchange Telegraph service. White also set up bureaus in Paris, London, and Moscow for world news and in Washington, D.C., Chicago, and Los Angeles for domestic news. CNS produced a nightly 15-minute newscast.

NBC also expanded its news facilities, contracting with the Consolidated Press Service and establishing overseas bureaus. The publishers were up in arms. Fearing an outbreak of "hostilities" between the written and oral press, CBS and NBC arranged to meet with publishers in December 1933.

They hammered out a pact which called for discontinuance of CNS. NBC agreed not to compete in the area of news collection.

The three wire services and the publishers agreed to set up the Press-Radio Bureau to provide CBS and NBC with sufficient news copy for the two networks to do two 5-minute newscasts a day, one in the morning and one in the evening. The stories were not to exceed 30 words, and the wire copy was embargoed so it would not be released until the morning and evening papers had hit the street.

This agreement left the independent stations out in the cold, and they decided to do something about covering the news. One solution was Transradio Press (TP), an association of 20 members formed in 1933. By 1934 TP had 150 subscribers. The copy was written to be read aloud and was thus the precursor of today's broadcast wires.

UP and INS felt the pressure, and in 1935 they reversed their policy and offered to sell their wire services to any newspaper-owned radio station. Soon the requirement that a station be owned by a newspaper was dropped. The reaction was immediate. By 1939 UP has 293 radio subscribers, INS has 141, and TP had 177.

The Associated Press, which was owned by newspaper publishers, was prevented by its owners from selling its service to radio stations. The restriction was relaxed in 1940, and by the end of that year AP had 40 radio subscribers. Today AP operates the biggest radio wire service in the country.

The networks continued to have overseas reporters and began to emphasize their European coverage as the threat of war grew in 1938. During the period of the press-radio war some stations continued to present news as they had done in the early days, by using newspaper reporters. In the early 1930s New York newspaperman Walter Winchell began broadcasting on a local station and later moved to the ABC Radio Network. At the same time Edwin C. Hill did news broadcasts and another New York newspaperman, Elmer Davis, joined Hill on CBS. Lowell Thomas began his radio

Fig. 1-2. A control room during an early network radio news broadcast. (Courtesy National Association of Broadcasters.)

career in 1930, first on CBS and then on NBC. Later he returned to CBS.

Actually, broadcast journalism traces its real growth to World War Two. The clock on the wall at WOR in New York City read 2:26 p.m. on Sunday, December 7, 1941. The station was broadcasting a professional football game. Word came of the Japanese attack on Pearl Harbor, and WOR broke into the game to announce the news. Two minutes later a bulletin was broadcast on the full NBC Red and Blue networks. And at 2:30 CBS bulletined the attack during a station break and then immediately changed the regular half-hour news program which followed to tell the story of the attack.

During World War Two radio news programing was enlarged significantly as the public became increasingly interested in knowing what was happening in the United States and abroad. (See Fig. 1-2.)

The increase in news coverage took place despite an agreement between the broadcasters and the government which amounted to a form of censorship. Under the Censorship Code of 1942 the stations agreed not to broadcast weather forecasts except when a weather emergency threatened. They also agreed to broadcast only the military news released by the government.

Ironically, the press-radio competition which raged from 1933 to 1935 died out during the war, and newspapers began carrying listings of radio programs and printing special columns about radio. One tradition which traces its origin to World War Two is the scheduling of news once an hour.

During the war audio recorders came into use. The early machines used either spools of wire or paper tape. Both were a nuisance, but they did permit reporters to put the sounds of World War Two onto a reproducible medium. Some famous broadcasts took place during that period, and they are preserved today because those early recorders were available.

Radio also had some special events to report. President Franklin Delano Roosevelt's war message to Congress was broadcast on radio. And American radio listeners heard an eyewitness description of the signing of the surrender documents aboard the battleship *Missouri* while it was anchored in Tokyo Bay.

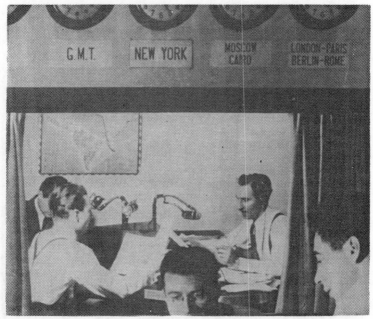

Fig. 1-3. An early network radio broadcast, showing the newscasters reading their scripts. (Courtesy National Association of Broadcasters.)

Radio reporters went on the D-Day invasion of Normandy and made many famous and heroic broadcasts. All of the events were available to Americans over some 900 radio stations. The networks played a major role in covering the war. (Fig. 1-3.)

The concept got its start back in 1923 with the linkup of stations by AT&T. In 1926 the National Broadcasting Company was organized, and on November 15 of that year NBC began programing over a 25-station network extending from the East Coast to Kansas City. NBC was so encouraged by the project that on January 1, 1927 a second network was inaugurated. The first NBC network was called the Red Network, and the second NBC network was called the Blue Network. On September 18, 1927, the CBS Radio Network began service to 16 affiliates. (Fig. 1-4.)

The government put pressure on NBC, and in 1943 the Blue Network was sold, becoming what is known today as the ABC Radio Network.

Fig. 1-4. A CBS radio sports crew broadcasting a football game. Cameras in background were shooting newsreels for later viewing in movie houses. (Courtesy National Association of Broadcasters.)

The Mutual Network began in 1934 with the linkup of WGN in Chicago, WLW in Cincinnati, WXYZ in Detroit, and WOR in New York. Mutual eventually became the largest interconnected network but often suffered economically because it served fewer metropolitan areas.

Immediately after the war radio boomed. In fact, the major networks used revenues from their radio networks to finance the development of television.

Television began to come into its own, and as this happened radio broadcasting underwent a very difficult period. The radio networks cut back on programing, some stations experienced financial troubles, and the disc jockey concept—one person talking between records rather than big staffs of announcers, producers, entertainers, and engineers—became the economic necessity of the slimmed-down radio industry.

A result of this very trying period was a new emphasis on news. The networks realized that the one service they could offer which would be popular was the hourly newscast. As stations changed their concepts, they began to find a market for locally originated news, and local stations gradually began to build news staffs to cover local events. (See Fig. 1-5.) The early attempts were often somewhat raw, with emphasis frequently placed on being first and fastest with spot events such as robberies and fires.

In some cases the growth of television helped radio stations to do a better job because the combined radio-television stations shared staffs and doubled up on duties. This permitted more stories to be covered.

In 1958 UP and INS merged to become United Press International (UPI). Transradio Press had long since faded into obscurity.

In the early 1960s a new concept in radio news was born. It was the "all-news" radio station. Texas broadcaster Gordon McLendon and a group of Mexican businessmen developed an all-news format for XTRA in Tijuana, Mexico. The border station covered Southern California with its signal. Later, in 1964, McLendon took his format to Chicago where he started an all-news operation at WNUS.

Westinghouse became interested in the format and changed several of its major market stations to all news. Later CBS entered the field and, after an initially slow start, enjoyed

Fig. 1-5. As soon as radio developed portable equipment, the microphone was seen everywhere in our nation. (Courtesy National Association of Broadcasters.)

considerable rating and revenue success using an all-news format.

The early all-news stations were run on slim budgets. The idea was to simply read wire copy over and over because, according to the experts, people would not listen for long periods of time.

The listener span assumption proved erroneous, however. As people began to get used to the all-news format, they listened for longer periods of time. The next broadcasters to try the all-news format went in spending big money and staffing their newsrooms with legions of writers, editors, and reporters.

While the first (rip-and-read) approach was not really satisfactory, the big spending approach was not financially wise. So after a while the all-news stations settled on a compromise format. Basically, most tend to select a group of stories (say the top 40) which they use for several hours at a time, updating them as necessary. Most all-news stations have limited outside staffs and rely heavily on aggressive telephone news gathering by writers and editors in the newsroom.

In addition, most all-news operations make heavy use of tape inserts from networks and audio services, and increasingly the all-news stations are heavily programed with features.

The advent of all-news stations has changed the nature of radio reporting. In earlier years a reporter working on the outside would worry about filing a story in time for the next hourly newscast. Now a reporter for an all-news station goes immediately to a telephone or a mobile unit and does a live report on a major story. Then the reporter files several supplemental stories on the same assignment. The main point is that today's radio reporter has to be able to go on the air live and make sense without the benefit of a formal script or a review by an editor.

Another development has been the emphasis on being able to go live quickly. The all-news station does not have to worry about "busting" in on other programing, so the equipment is designed for immediate live broadcasts. Mobile radio equipment plays an important role in these assignments.

As an example, if there is a major disaster, the reporters can go live from the mobile unit. They can roam the area with portable two-way radios and battery-operated tape recorders, bringing their material back to the mobile unit for live transmission.

Radio news is stronger and better than ever. It is no longer the little companion to television. There are highly professional, well-paid journalists working in radio, in contrast to earlier years when radio was simply a stepping stone to a career in television.

Over recent years the number and quality of news departments has grown steadily. It is now common to visit a small station in a rural area and find it staffed by two or more trained journalists, who may be backed up by other staff members having some news experience.

The radio networks are now primarily news networks. CBS operates one radio network. which programs news. sports. and features. NBC has a similar radio network and has begun a new service. which amounts to having a nationally oriented. all-news station. The network programs two big blocks of time each hour. and the local affiliate fills up the remaining time with local and regional news. The concept is designed to lower the cost of local news gathering. so that it would be possible to operate an all-news station in an area which might not be able to support an independent all-news station.

There are also specialized networks serving stations with primarily black or Hispanic formats. and there are regional news networks such as the Tobacco Network which programs news and farm features to portions of the southeast. United Press International. and the Associated Press offer news services which supply audio reports and actualities (voices of newsmakers). Both UPI and AP also provide hourly newscasts to their subscribers.

All in all. radio news is bustling and booming. More is being done better across the country. Radio as a medium has returned to economic health after losing its original programing to television in the 1950s.

Television traces its origins back to 1884. when a German scientist named Paul Nipkow invented a scanning disc which is essential to television theory. There were experiments with television in France in the early 1900s. and by the late 1920s television laboratories were well underway in the United States.

In 1923 an American. Vladimir Zworykin. patented the iconoscope. which was the grandfather of today's camera tube. Early experiments were conducted by RCA. CBS. and Dumont Laboratories. The first public demonstration of the new medium took place during the 1939 World's Fair in New York.

In 1940 the FCC ordered a halt to the expansion of television. pending completion of a study to determine the best technical system. Then along came World War Two. and television broadcasting had to wait.

After the war the FCC allocated twelve channels for television use. and by the start of 1947 there were six stations operating. Actually. the first application for a television station was filed in 1939 by the *Milwaukee Journal*.

By 1948 the Commission had 300 applications on file seeking permits for television stations, and almost a million television sets were sold in 1948. However, during the same period it became evident that serious interference problems were occurring in some areas.

In September 1948, with 36 stations on the air in 19 cities, the FCC froze all new television assignments. (However, during the freeze some 70 applicants who had permits were allowed to continue building.)

The Commission ended up taking four years to study both the allocation problem and to work out a single system for color transmissions. Even during the freeze, television grew rapidly. CBS and NBC made heavy investments in programing. ABC made somewhat less, and Allen B. Dumont Laboratories attempted to run a network until 1955, when the cost of programing and the lack of superior talent forced Dumont out of the race.

During the freeze the networks sustained losses because there were few opportunities for expansion. In many cities there was not a sufficient number of stations to promote healthy competition. In addition, the nationwide television link consisting of coaxial cable and microwave did not become available until 1951. Before that, film copies of programs had to be flown from coast to coast.

The freeze ended in July 1952 with 108 stations on the air in 63 cities. During the freeze period the number of television sets in use rose from 1 million to 17 million. Since then television has grown by leaps and bounds to the point where nearly every home in the country has at least one television set.

For a short while television news was "radio with pictures," but special technology soon was developed to take advantage of television's unique qualities. The earliest pictures were just photographs, often wirephotos taken off the newspaper wirephoto machine and pasted up on a board. The studio camera was then wheeled over to catch the picture.

Television executives realized very early that their newscasts would be more attractive to viewers if they could show film of events. So the early newsfilm was an adaptation of the movie theater newsreels.

In fact, in the very earliest days of television the news departments simply used Hollywood-style film equipment. They shot film with heavy 35 mm cameras on negative stock

Fig. 1-6. A photographer loading a sound camera into a mobile unit. Note that while the camera lens might be damaged by not being stored in a special container, most photographers travel with their cameras at complete readiness. (Courtesy WFMY-TV, Greensboro, N.C.)

and sent the film to commercial processing laboratories. All of this was slow and cumbersome. The techniques and equipment being used were designed for movie making, which is done at a more leisurely pace than news photography.

Gradually television news departments switched to using 16 mm film, which is less expensive, is less bulky, and requires less cumbersome equipment. A great deal of filming was done with small hand-held silent cameras which were spring wound. Sound film was shot with Hollywood-style cameras remodeled for television use. The sound recording left a great deal to be desired since the optical recording methods used were not well adapted to newsfilm conditions.

Stations began to use reversal (direct positive) film which allowed them to speed up the process of getting the film from the camera onto the air. Reversal film eliminated making a negative, one step in processing, and stations dissatisfied with being tied down to the operating schedules of outside processors began to buy their own processing equipment. (See Fig. 1-6.)

Then for a time television news settled into a routine, using adapted film techniques. However, in the mid-1960s color began to be more common after the networks started transmitting an increasing amount of programing in color.

The first use of color at the local station level was in the studio. News personnel and technicians learned how to paint sets and choose clothing which made best use of the characteristics of the early color cameras. Anchorpeople learned to appear calm and cool while working under intensely hot lights.

Then color slides were adopted. There was sufficient expertise around for many stations to begin to process their own color slides. Most had already trained their art departments to make color artwork.

The next hurdle was shooting color film. This was a big expense and many stations turned once again to commercial laboratories for processing. Of course, this limited their ability to air color film, so for a long time newscasts contained a mixture of color and black-and-white film: the late-breaking stories were shot in black and white and processed at the station.

Again, the film manufacturers and the equipment companies successfully overcame their problems and offered color processors within the financial reach of the stations themselves. At first many stations kept their black and white processors, but as soon as they became adept at using their color equipment, most stations went full color and got rid of the black and white equipment.

By the beginning of the 1970s the color conversion was almost complete in medium and large markets. The next move was to design film equipment exclusively for television. Cameras which were lighter, more reliable, and equipped with lenses adapted for television came onto the market. By this time the sound system had been changed to use the same type of audiotape as radio stations, and the advent of transistorized electronics brought improved sound quality, easier editing, and lighter sound equipment. Improvements in batteries to drive the cameras and new lighting equipment reduced the overall weight and size to the point that one person could, if necessary, operate sound and film equipment with complete portability—that is, the photographer could walk around and shoot sound film.

The reason we have talked so much about film is that until recent years the only way for most stations to record events or an interview was on film. Television cameras and the equipment needed to run them were so cumbersome that the only way to use them in the field was to fill a giant truck with equipment. Thus most outside television coverage was limited to network special event programs and sports events.

The local stations in most areas simply could not afford to maintain the equipment necessary for doing television outside the studio. In addition, for a long time there was no good way to record the television picture for later use. And when videotape came along to solve that problem, the machines were simply too big to transport conveniently.

Some very ingenious engineers kept working at the problem. First they developed relatively small, light videotape machines which would record black and white tape at standards which were only satisfactory for viewing at home by amateurs.

But persistence and the development of space age electronic parts made it possible to manufacture both cameras and tape recorders which were small and portable and produced pictures of adequate quality for broadcast.

At this writing the broadcast industry is in the midst of the ENG—electronic news gathering—revolution. Stations are buying all sorts of portable videotape recorders and attaching them to microwave equipment so that television pictures can be transmitted back to the station from anywhere in town for immediate live airing or for recording and editing to be used on the next newscast.

The development of portable television equipment for news coverage is important for two reasons. First, the picture quality more nearly matches the live studio quality (there is a difference between film and live television) which lends a desired "live" quality to the newscast. Second, there is the increased flexibility of being able to either record and transmit a picture back to the station immediately for editing while the reporter and technicians go on to another assignment (film always has to be transported back to the station and then processed) or to go on the air live if the story warrants it.

During the relatively short period in which television news has grown from "radio with pictures" to a medium of its own there have been many other developments. A whole breed of television journalists has arisen—people specially trained to know how to use pictures and television techniques to tell a story.

Writing for television has developed its own style. On-the-air presentation has become personal, relaxed, and informative. News departments have grown in size to the point that local television departments stand on their own and frequently do a better job of news coverage than the print media in their area. And with the advent of ENG, the story of television news is just beginning to be told.

2
The Broadcast Journalist

A journalist is an impartial observer of life who tells others what has been observed. If time were allowed to pass, the journalist would be an historian, but one of the unique qualities of journalism is immediacy. The journalist tells what is happening now.

There is more to being a journalist than just telling a story, because the journalist probes the ins and outs and the yeas and nays of an issue. He or she interprets what is happening. The journalist is an impartial ombudsman for the public.

Contrary to comic-book tradition, journalists do not leap out of phone booths in space suits to crush the forces of evil. They are people who work hard to dig out the facts of their stories while remaining impartial. Journalists try to be fair and thorough, even though they know there is no true infallibility in humans.

Broadcast journalists are a special breed. They must be able to do more than their counterparts in the written press. Broadcasting is based on technology: microphones, cameras, amplifiers, transmitters, and receivers.

The broadcast reporter takes notes like any other journalist. But these notes must be converted into a spoken performance, which will be supported by sounds and pictures. And all of this is done at top speed, with the fewest possible words and an artistic blending of the parts.

In other words, being a broadcast journalist requires not only good writing and reporting but a feeling for the product, which is directly affected by how the reporter visualizes the story.

The need to pay attention to production matters can frustrate the broadcast journalist. There are days when you ask yourself: Why can I not just go off in a corner and write a nice long story that glows with good prose and explains all the complexities?

Such moments are realized when you hear yourself describe the new municipal budget sensibly in 45 seconds or capture the sight and sound of a protest demonstration outside the school board meeting—and then you know that no other news medium can make what is happening so alive and so immediate.

ATTITUDE AND APPEARANCE

A journalist has to accept the fact that he or she is a public figure. You represent your employer, you represent a profession, and you represent the people. Broadcast journalists stand out—it is pretty hard to be overlooked when you have a microphone in your hand and a tape recorder hanging at your side or have a photographer trailing along behind you.

It is impossible to prescribe attire for today's reporters, but you must think about the prevailing standards in your community. Other factors are the image your station wishes to project and the surroundings in which you are doing your reporting.

During the Vietnam war reporters wore fatigues because the Brooks Brothers look would have been ridiculous. On the other hand it is unlikely that a network correspondent would show up at a State Department briefing in sweatshirt and jeans.

Frankly, being a reporter is an exercise in public relations. For the most part, being likable and nonabrasive gets you further than being surly. There are times to be abrasive, such as when you're conducting a tough interview or being blocked from getting your story, but courtesy and friendliness will usually do the job.

If you have pride in yourself and your profession and you do your homework, you will have the respect of the people with whom you deal. Even the people you "hardnose" with good questions will respect you.

News gathering is often hurly-burly in big cities where the press corps is large and the competition fierce. Unfortunately, this approach leads to breaches of taste and a public impression that journalists are a herd of boors.

Try to set yourself an ethical standard for your own conduct and stick to it. Remember that people genuinely appreciate friendliness and concern for their problems. Be cooperative, friendly, and helpful to your contacts. The Great Lakes could be paved with the good tips given reporters by behind-the-scenes people.

Being a journalist is a bit like living in a goldfish bowl, but it sure beats a lot of other jobs!

YOU AND YOUR COMMUNITY

You have noticed by now, no doubt, that I keep saying the journalist represents the people. To be an effective journalist you must know as much as you can about the people you serve and the places they live.

Broadcast journalists are usually generalists—they cover all kinds of stories. This means you have to keep up on international and national issues as well as those in your region, state, and community.

You must know the basic facts about such things as population, geography, forms of government, natural resources, and industry. You need to know something about history, economic trends, and social issues. Any and all of these can come to bear on an individual story.

Here is an example: You have been sent to cover a meeting of the city-county school board. The board is expected to make a final decision on where to build a new junior high school.

One way to cover the story is to go to the meeting, sit there until the deciding vote is taken, and then do an interview with the chairperson of the board and give the result of the vote.

That is a copout. Here are some facts that might apply: There are two proposed sites for the school—one inside the city limits and one just outside. What is the difference? Inside the city a strict municipal building and fire code applies, while outside the more liberal state codes can be used. So it would be cheaper to build outside the city limits. But the risks in case of a fire could be greater.

Another possibility: The law provides that the state will pay the cost of busing students to county schools but not to schools inside the city limits. So the superintendent of schools favors building the new school in the country. Then the state would pay the cost of busing from the state income tax rather than the board having to use local property taxes.

There is more. The question of busing also bears on the school system's racial balance plan. Some minority groups in the city feel the real reason the superintendent wants the school built outside the city limit is to appease parents in white suburban subdivisions. It is said they would not want their children transported into an urban slum.

Another faction says a better school can be built outside the city—after all, the minority children will benefit from the better facility and the suburban atmosphere. But, reply minority leaders, the urban children will spend all their time on buses and have no chance to share in sports and other social activities after school.

Then there is the matter of land. Two pieces of property are under consideration. One is on land the city has already cleared for urban renewal, using 90% federal money and only 10% local money.

The county site is old, worn-out farmland. And if you have taken the time to check records at the courthouse you know that the owner just happens to be the brother-in-law of a county commissioner. It seems he bought the property 14 months ago, after planning had started on the new school. Could something be amiss?

Would you still want to go to the school board meeting and report what takes place, or do you want to explain to your audience some of the background for the board's decision? If you're on the ball, you have already done some prior reports so that members of the community will know what's going on. They may even want to attend the school board meeting as a result of your reports.

This is just one illustration of why a journalist must know the community. No shred of knowledge is worthless, and almost everything that happens is intertwined with other facets of the community.

Newspaper reporters have an easier job reporting a complicated story such as the school board meeting we just described. They have more column inches to give details, and there is a tradition in newspaper work of doing advance stories on major issues. This is one idea that should be used more frequently by broadcast news departments.

You have to work harder because you need to know as much about your community and to say it in fewer words. For example, 1 minute of straight script runs about 150 words. In 10 inches of a newspaper column, a reporter could write at least 300 words on the same topic.

A good broadcast journalist gets *involved*. He or she learns all that is possible about the community and most likely participates in community activities.

One thought though: Broadcast journalists must exercise discretion about some activities—especially politics. Too active participation in partisan politics might compromise the reporter, or even force the station to take the reporter off the air to satisfy Federal Communications Commission regulations.

About the only way to get to know a community is to spend a lot of time educating yourself. You do this by reading: history books, public documents, magazines, newspapers, employee papers, and reports. You do it by talking: to the mail carrier, public officials, store clerks, secretaries, labor leaders, religious leaders, and everyone you can. And you do this by listening to and watching the competitive media.

The bigger the market, the more difficult it becomes to learn the community. But most metropolitan reporters who earned their stripes in smaller communities will tell you how the lessons they learned in those communities help them do their work much better.

ADVOCACY JOURNALISM

In recent years the literature of the journalism field has increasingly mentioned something called *advocacy journalism*. This differs from traditional journalism in that the reporter or the medium takes a viewpoint. The advocacy journalist prepares all of his or her reports from this often singular viewpoint.

The mainstream journalist remains the impartial observer, seeing and reporting all the facts, while the advocacy journalist is only a partial observer.

Ironically, advocacy journalism existed in the early days of our nation, when anyone who could get the use of a printing press could, and frequently did, turn out a newspaper. These papers were written from the editor's viewpoint and within the limits of his experience.

But American journalism has grown and matured, and today the standard of journalism is balance, a presentation of more than one side to an issue. Today, advocacy is reserved in newspapers for the editorial pages and in broadcast stations for the editorials, which are labeled commentary and are usually clearly separated from news coverage.

It is true that some advocacy journalists have revealed information that might not have been picked up by the mainstream media. This is a legitimate criticism of the mainstream: not being sufficiently curious or aggressive outside some of the traditional areas of news coverage. On the other hand, the Watergate affair was revealed by a team of journalists from the traditional media.

If you are serious about working in broadcast journalism, forget advocacy. The law and tradition of American broadcasting calls for balance in overall coverage of the news. This is based on the premise that broadcast frequencies are limited and the public deserves to hear or see news affecting all segments of the community.

Broadcasting is a mass medium, which means that broadcast journalists serve the *general* public, not a specific group or philosophy.

ETHICS

Most fields that stress professionalism also stress ethics. To professionals, ethical standards are a set of do's and don't's. Lawyers and doctors who subscribe to ethical standards do not advertise their services. It is unlikely that you have heard an attorney on the radio saying, "Let me represent you; I get more people off than eight out of ten criminal lawyers in the local bar society."

Some of the ethics of broadcast journalism are as follows:

We do not quote people without their permission (unless they have spoken in public), and we respect requests for anonymity from sources.

We do not accept payment or gifts specifically intended to pay us for doing a story.

We do not attack people just for the purpose of hurting them. In other words, the individual who is attacked should deserve it on the basis of evidence gathered through sound and impartial investigative reporting.

While editing of interviews and speeches is common, it is done for time purposes, not to distort the meaning of the speaker's words.

We seek to discover and tell the truth objectively and *without error*.

Codes that guide members of the two leading organizations to which broadcast journalists belong are included at the end of this book. The organizations are (1) The Society of Professional Journalists, Sigma Delta Chi, which is open to all qualified journalists, and (2) The Radio-Television News Directors Association, which is open to practicing broadcast journalists.

SELF-REGULATION

Broadcast journalists have participated in a number of self-regulatory efforts. Various news organizations have assisted such groups as hospitals and airlines in drawing up guidelines for their personnel and for news reporters.

An excellent booklet published by the Aviation/Space Writers Association not only gives solid hints on covering aviation accidents, but gives addresses and telephone numbers of key Federal Aviation Administration (FAA) offices and descriptions of widely used aircraft.

The booklet suggests that reporters be very careful in identifying the source of reports about an aircraft reported missing or down. Often these sources are state or local police who are not expert in aviation matters, especially the identification of types of planes, and the haste of an emergency situation can lead to reports that will later be corrected by FAA officials.

The booklet also admonishes reporters not to touch or move even the tiniest piece of debris, because it may be important in determining the cause of the crash. The purpose of the booklet is to aid journalists in covering air crashes while creating the least possible disruption of the rescue and investigation processes.

In North Carolina, the state hospital association combined forces with the medical society and the state's press association and association of broadcasters to draw up a news guide. The booklet describes cases of public record—for instance, persons under arrest or held under police surveillance—and prescribes the types of identifying information that can be given out. It also sets definitions to use in describing the condition of a patient and warns doctors and hospital personnel not to make statements that may be construed as "blame" for an accident.

These efforts at self-regulation are not censorship. They are designed to promote the open and orderly collection of news and to inform all parties involved of their legal obligations for disclosure. These codes help the journalist because they tell the reporter what information should be sought out and what may be properly withheld.

Once codes of this sort are set up. it is important that members of the profession not only police other journalists but make certain that the other signers of the guidelines stick to their word.

THE RESPONSIBILITY TO PROVIDE NEWS

The Communications Act of 1934 gives the Federal Communications Commission a peculiar sort of control over radio broadcasting. (The same precedent extends to television.)

The FCC decides who shall be permitted to use a radio frequency or television channel. and this decision is reevaluated every three years. The act prohibits the Commission from telling stations precisely what to program. but the FCC *is* allowed to determine if a station is operating in the public interest. convenience. and necessity.

As a result. the Commission has decided that this means a station should program news. The FCC's position is strengthened by its own "promise vs performance" philosophy. which holds that station license holders are liable to do most of what they promise when they fill out their original or renewal application forms.

Although most stations program some news. their performance varies from simple "rip 'n read" delivery of copy ripped off the wire service printer to newscasts prepared by adequate studio and field staffs.

In a sense. the broadcast station owner makes a contract with the Federal Communications Commission (FCC). The owner outlines a general plan describing the type of programing that will be carried and the approximate percentage each category of programing consumes of the total time the station is on the air each week. When that "contract" comes up for reconsideration. the Commission asks the station management to demonstrate that it has done what was promised.

News coverage has come to be thought of by the FCC as a necessary ingredient in any station's programing. There is no great conflict here. because the majority of station owners today feel that news is an essential part of their programing.

The only debate is over how much news there should be in relation to other program material. For instance, a station that specializes in music might prefer infrequent, very brief newscasts, while the Commission might feel this approach is insufficient to serve the community's needs.

A well programed station which enjoys popularity in its market seldom has any problem selling sponsorships within its newscasts. For radio stations, the most popular times to sponsor newscasts are during the morning "drive time" (6 to 9 a.m.) during the noon hour and during the afternoon "drive time" (4 to 7 p.m.). The early evening news on local television stations is frequently a significant source of revenue.

You may have noticed that I have not said a station's lineup of sponsors should "pay" the cost of news coverage. Sometimes this happens, but more often station managers weigh other factors when they evaluate the overall profit and loss involved in their news operations. One of those factors is the FCC's renewal powers; another is the station's image.

A station manager must consider the station's standing in the community. One objective is to attain popularity as defined by ratings, or measurements of the approximate number of people in homes viewing at any specific time. Ratings are derived from scientific sampling techniques. The more people the rating services report as listeners or viewers, the easier it is to obtain sponsors.

In addition, most station managers are concerned about a more subtle image: how the station is regarded by the community in general and by certain influential groups. For instance, a station that aims its programing toward mature adults wants to be thought of as a source of information as well as entertainment and will frequently invest a great deal of effort and money in its news operation.

Another station may feel that it should project an "on-the-ball" image, so it will want to be first and fastest to cover news stories, especially breaking events such as a fire or a bank holdup.

It may strike you that the rationale for doing news on a broadcast station is based on threat, on economic gain, and on a station's self-image. This is true, because a broadcast station differs significantly from a newspaper.

You buy a newspaper for news first and for certain supplemental information (such as features) second. A commercial broadcast station lives and dies by entertaining as well as by informing its audience. For the most part entertainment is the bigger part of most stations' programing, with the exception of a relatively small number of all-news stations.

What this means to the broadcast journalist is that she or he is part of a team. The team has a broader purpose than just presenting news, and most frequently the broadcast journalist must work within rather narrow time limits. This is why brevity is so important in writing for broadcast.

3
Writing for Broadcast

Writing news for a broadcast station is as easy as talking. Or is it? Good broadcast writing sounds like a narrative conversation. Unfortunately, you are taught in school and in many journalism courses to write to be read—silently.

You are about to be reeducated. I will start with writing for radio and move later to writing for television. (See Fig. 3-1.)

WRITING FOR RADIO

The problem in writing for radio is to make sure your audience listens. You wouldn't think that would be too hard to do, would you? After all, you'll just let those beautiful words roll off your well disciplined tongue, and you'll have them drooling all over the set.

Sorry! One of the problems with radio is that your listeners can do something else while they listen—if they do listen. For instance, they can sit in a traffic jam and honk their horns or they can tell at the kids or, heaven forbid, they can change stations.

The first step, then, is to say something interesting. Some time-proven methods include writing in a clear manner, choosing absorbing subjects, adding drama and excitement through the pace and color of your writing, and inserting audiotape in the newscast.

Begin with good writing. Write to be understood by the average person. True, there is no such thing as an average person, but you know that more people will understand you if you choose words with fewer syllables and keep your sentence structure simple.

There are scientific ways to break down sentences in a newscast by counting syllables, deriving a score, and then

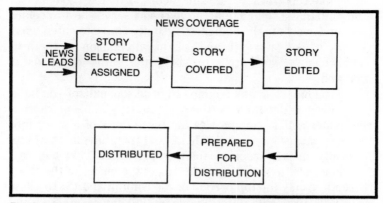

Fig. 3-1. This outlines the development of a radio or television news story. Distribution means putting the story on the air, no matter what form of transmission is used. (Courtesy CBS television stations.)

judging the effectiveness by the relative number of syllables. However, this is not very practical once you have to write against the gnawing progression of that clock on the newsroom wall.

The point to writing for broadcast is to use words that will be widely understood. Whenever fewer words or words of fewer syllables will express adequately what you wish to say, use them. Save the seven-syllable mindbenders for your thesis.

Think about how people talk. People who are easy to understand make direct statements. A child is frequently easy to understand because he or she expresses needs in simple declarative sentences such as. "Mommy, I'm hungry."

However, children tend to speak in bursts of ideas which may seem disjointed to adults. Their thoughts do not flow. Adults tie thoughts together; in fact, a great deal of conversation is narrative.

Here is an example: "Boy, was I surprised. Old man Jones called me in this morning and really dropped it on me. He said. 'Smith, I've been watching you.' Wow, for a minute I thought it was all over. Then he said, 'You work hard, keep your head up, and follow instructions. I think it's about time we gave you a little more responsibility.' Would you believe, he gave me a raise and put me in charge of two other people."

That little tale developed a story, pretty much in chronological order and with just a touch of drama. Basically the person writing broadcast news is headed in the same direction.

Unlike reporters in the print media, broadcast journalists often find that a straight narrative report serves best to relate facts and events to the audience. Listeners have to catch what you say when you say it, and it is usually easier for them to comprehend a story told in about the same order as it occurred.

If you have had any training in print journalism you have been introduced to the inverted pyramid style. This is where a newspaper article compresses the basic facts of a story into the first paragraph, called a lead, and then unveils the facts generally in the order of their importance. This has two functions: (1) to permit a reader to get the basics of the story by reading only the top portion of the column and (2) to allow the editor to delete some of the bottom paragraphs of the column if the page becomes too crowded.

If there is a narrative report, it may end up at the end of the story. The newscaster must tell it once, and that's it. So the radio news writer gives an idea of what is being told in the first sentence and often goes on to a logical presentation of the facts.

Here is a theoretical example: The mayor has announced a federal grant of $86,000 which will finance a one-year experimental program. People 18 to 20 years old will receive limited training in police duties so that they may perform some of the more routine duties now done by uniformed officers. If the plan works out the city will have a pool of applicants for police officer positions, which are open only to people 21 or over.

The newspaper writer might begin the story as follows.

SQUIRRELVILLE—Mayor Thomas A. Person in a city hall news conference Tuesday announced approval of an $86,000 federal grant for a pilot police cadet program. The federal funds, which come from the Law Enforcement Assistance Administration, will be used, the Mayor said, to train young people 18 to 20 years old in basic police skills. The trainees, to be known as police cadets, will be assigned some of the duties now performed inside headquarters by regular police officers, Mayor Person said.

That's enough to make my point. The basics are there, but if you read the story out loud, you will find it difficult to grasp quickly. The thoughts are interrupted by too many clauses, and the sentences are too long.

44

Now let's convert the same facts to a radio news item. First of all. the location can't be put in parentheses. so it must be included in the story.

> Mayor Thomas Person says Squirrelville has received an $86.000 dollar federal grant for an experimental police program. The money comes from the Law Enforcement Assistance Administration. It will be used to train 18 to 20 year-old youths as police cadets. The cadets will learn some jobs at headquarters now done by regular officers.

Let's try an item which involves facts happening in chronological order. Here's the situation: Three persons. believed to be two males and one female. wearing stocking masks held up a local branch bank earlier this afternoon. Someone tipped police that the robbery was in progress. and the first two police officers responding were involved in a gunfight with the robbers. who were just leaving the bank. The criminals were chased. and their car finally stopped. but two of the car's three occupants escaped on foot and are now being sought. The third suspect. a male. and one of the two police officers who first responded were severely wounded. The policeman is now on the operating table at a local hospital. as is the suspect.

Here's how you might write the story for radio:

> Surgeons at County General Hospital are trying to save the life of a Squirrelville police officer wounded earlier today during a bank holdup.
> The officer and his partner answered a report of a bank robbery in progress at the East Squirrelville Branch of the Last National Bank. Police say an anonymous caller gave the alarm about 2:20 this afternoon.
> The two police officers were in the first patrol car arriving at the scene and. according to Police Chief Thunder Jones. they apparently encountered the robbers leaving the bank.
> Police say shots were exchanged and one officer was wounded.
> Bank officials say the trio of robbers—believed to be two men and a woman—used stocking masks to disguise their faces.
> Chief Jones says the robbers fled in a late model sedan and were pursued by police. The getaway vehicle eventually collided with a stone wall near the Squirrelville city limits. Police say two suspects. believed to be a man and a woman. fled while the third suspect was found unconscious in the wrecked car.
> The injured suspect is now in an operating room at County General Hospital. a few feet down a corridor from the operating room where surgeons are working on the wounded officer.

The story has been told pretty much in the order that the events occurred. The item itself is a bit long. but length is relative. To listeners in Squirrelville, this is the big story. But a newscaster at a distant station would leave out a lot of details which would not interest people outside Squirrelville. For instance:

> Surgeons are working to save the life of a Squirrelville police officer who was shot earlier today during a bank robbery.
>
> Squirrelville police say the wounded officer and his partner were answering a report of a bank robbery in progress and became involved in a gunfight with the bandits.
>
> Police say the three suspects were chased by patrol cars until the getaway car was wrecked. A male suspect was found in the wreckage and a search continues for two other suspects. believed to be a man and a woman.

Besides your relative distance from the place where events are happening. you have to consider the amount of time allocated to the newscast and the station's policy on length of stories. Some stations plan newscasts that are long enough to take detailed stories; others feel all newscasts should be terse and have short items.

Regardless of the length of the story, the objectives are simplicity. clarity. accuracy. and interest.

SOME MECHANICAL RULES

Figure right from the start that you are going to type everything you write. If you don't already know how to type, you should put this book down for now and learn typing.

Broadcast scripts are typewritten, either double or triple spaced, so that they are easy to read and corrections can be made clearly and neatly between the lines of typing. The only exception would be a story you write by hand in your notebook while out on assignment.

Typing is necessary not only so you can read the copy but so others can read it. Most stations have a policy of doing carbons of all copy, either for filing purposes or so the stories will be available for later use or to rewrite. You should always put the date. the time, and your name or initials on each page of copy so that there will be no question when and by whom the copy was prepared.

Now for the bad news: You do have to know how to spell. While it's true that if you are the only person reading what you have written. spelling is not important; unless you work in a one-person news department. it isn't fair or professional to write copy that is sloppy and misspelled.

Okay, we've got our paper (and carbon paper) in the typewriter, and the space selector is set to double or triple space. What's next?

THE FACTS

The facts will come from a variety of sources: your reporter's notebook, reading earlier reports, or perhaps wire service copy. You must organize the basic facts in your mind and give them some sort of order according to importance.

The way to write a story is to say to yourself, "I've read everything I can about this story, and I've checked for additional facts. Now what is the story really about?" Then, lay aside your copy and write from memory, using your source materials only to insure accuracy. This system, once you have mastered it, will result in concise, clear copy.

Think of the central fact, the point of the story. Most of the time this will become the opening line or "lead." Sometimes, when you are writing a story updating earlier information, you may decide to pull out a different fact and focus on it for the sake of freshness. For instance, in the robbery story, you could have written a fresh item starting off with the police search for the bank robbers and then mentioning the wounded police officer.

Next try to lay out the facts in logical order, keeping in mind that the thoughts in one sentence should flow into the thoughts of the following sentence.

There are certain rules to keep in mind. One is to avoid sloppy language. In radio or television you write in the style of spoken language but you have to remember that what you say must be understood by everyone listening. Hence, use few contractions, avoid slang, and don't be flip or colloquial. Tell your story in plain language that anyone can understand.

ATTRIBUTION

Next you have to think about attribution. The facts don't come out of a clear, blue sky. You get them from someone or something, and you must tell your listeners the source of your facts so that they may judge their importance and truthfulness. For example, going back to the bank robbery, it was stated that some of the information came from the police ("police said") and some directly from Chief Jones.

In the case of important facts which might come into dispute, cite the source exactly. Let Chief Jones say the police officers engaged in a gunfight with the robbers and that this resulted in an officer being wounded. You never know, it might turn out that the officer shot himself accidentally or was wounded by his partner—so be specific in your attribution.

Less important facts, such as the flight of the suspects in a car and its subsequent crash, can be attributed to "police" since you probably got the information from one or more of the officers on the scene. Whatever you do, don't let yourself be the source of a fact: report facts as told to you or as recorded on documents. You don't pull facts out of your head.

The one exception is something you witness in person. Then report exactly what you saw or heard, and make no judgments on the broader meaning. For example, you can say you saw the building collapse after hearing a loud noise like an explosion, but don't say the collapse was the result of an explosion because you are not qualified to make this statement.

Sometimes you have to grant your sources anonymity. Then you have a problem. You must be absolutely certain that the information given is accurate as far as you can ascertain. This means checking with other sources. When experienced reporters use "informed sources" as their attribution, they know from experience and from cross checking that the information is highly reliable. Even then you may notice the reporter qualifies the source. For instance, a White House correspondent may say "a high source in the administration" because the close advisor to the President has declined to have his or her name tied to the report. But the correspondent knows from experience whether the comments of the advisor can be interpreted as representing the thinking of the President or whether they are just idle talk.

From day to day, though, be suspect of information given to you which cannot be attributed to someone or verified in a document or in some other source. Maybe it just isn't that important.

Here's an example of the type of situation you could run into: The City Council is thinking of raising the property tax. Generally the voting public does not take too kindly to any proposal for higher taxes, so one or more of the Council members may toss out hints to see if there is violent reaction from the public.

You may get the story in one of several ways. It may be that you sat in a closed meeting where the Council members tried out the tax increase proposal. They may have agreed that you could report the proposal, without labeling it as coming directly from members of the Council.

Since it is important to have public reaction to matters as important as taxes, you would go ahead and use the story, saying something such as "sources close to the City Council say ..."

Perhaps after some off-the-record discussion and an exchange of phone conversations the Council members tentatively conclude taxes should be raised. You may get wind of this from someone (the secretary of the Council, for instance), and a call to a Council member may confirm the story. But you can bet that the Council member does not want to be quoted by name until the tax question is discussed in a public meeting. Here again we end up with a "sources" attribution. But in each case the reporter knows who the sources are even though anonymity is granted for the time being.

Notice an important style rule: Put the attribution high in the story so your audience will not have to wait to figure out where the report comes from. And put the attribution at the head of the sentence rather than at the end as is done in newspapers.

You would say, "Squirrelville Police Chief Thunder Jones says ... " Your print counterparts usually tell us what the Chief said and then add a comma and write, "Chief Jones said." Unfortunately, a person listening to radio cannot go back over sentences that jump around, so we put the attribution up front.

In the example above we write "Chief Thunder Jones says" instead of "said." This is because radio news is attuned to reporting what is happening now. We try to be as current as possible. Of course, some critic is going to say, "Chief Jones said what he said once, so why not use the word 'said'?" True, he said it once, but in most cases he isn't about to change his factual statement and would stand by it if we were to ask him the same question some hours later.

However, while the use of the present tense is a stylistic peculiarity of broadcast writing, don't be afraid to be literally correct and use some form of the past tense when it is the best and most accurate way to write your story.

ORGANIZING THE FACTS

In the process of deciding what the most important elements of a story are, you will decide to discard some facts. Time is always limited, and there are some details that are just of too little consequence or are too technical to be important to a general audience. For example, you might report that the City Council approved a contract for 4000 feet of water pipe, but you would not bother to explain that it was 6-inch diameter cast iron pipe in 8-foot lengths unless there was some debate over the type of pipe itself.

Another example is that you would tell your listeners that police say a bank robber shot a police officer. But unless there were some special meaning to the fact, you would omit their conclusion that the robber used a .38 caliber revolver. Now this might become important later when police arrest a suspect who just happens to have such a weapon on his person. The weapon will assume even more importance during the suspect's eventual trial when there will be expert testimony as to whether or not the bullet taken from the police officer was fired from the gun in the possession of the suspect. But in an initial report of the robbery, the weapon is a fact which can be easily dropped.

There is no such thing as setting a proper length for a story or saying how many facts to use and how many to discard. You do have to think in terms of the nature of the newscast, how much time you have, and how many items you ideally would like to include.

By type of newscast I mean, is it a summary, just headlines, or an expanded report? Except in rare instances, newscasts are assigned a definite total length, and this is your absolute outside time in which to present even the most important story. Remember, too, that from the total length of any newscast you must subtract the standard open and close, commercials, and probably the weather.

You will find it an interesting exercise to listen to several different radio newscasts, network and local, and to count the number of stories. Also time the total newscast, the length of each story, and all the other materials like the commercials and the opening and closing. You will discover there is a definite pattern to how a newscast is put together, the number of items it contains, and their length.

As a rough measure, about 15 lines of typewritten double-spaced copy will take a minute to read. If you are going to be the person reading the copy, learn what your average reading speed is. This is done by reading a number of different items at different times for exactly one minute. Then figure out the average number of words you speak in a minute. You will probably find you type an average of about ten words to a line, which gives you a quick measure of how many lines you can read in a minute. If you are writing for someone else, find that person's reading speed.

NUMBERS

Numbers must be written to be read out loud. Generally the best idea is to write out numbers from one to eleven and then to use figures for numbers up through 999.

Larger numbers are better rounded off. If the public works director asks the city council for $13,958.13 for a new truck, say that he seeks nearly 14-thousand dollars for the new vehicle. An object 5,000 feet away is also "nearly a mile" away.

Numbers over 999 are usually written out until we get up into the millions. There are differences on this point. Some newsrooms write out "hundred", "thousand", "million" but use numerals in conjunction with the word. For example: 17-hundred, 33-thousand-500, seven million 800 thousand. The main thing is to be consistent, for yourself, and in the manner of your newsroom. This latter technique works well and is preferred by the author.

If you have two numbers close together yu may have to mix styles. For example: "...140 people were injured, thirteen were killed...."

Even though your your typewriter has fractions on the keys, write out all fractions—for example, one-third or three-fourths.

Numerals can be used for years, 1975; The same for time, 5 a.m. EDT; and for street addresses, 242 Eleventh Avenue.

Write out dates from one to eleven, then use digits: ninth of June, 13th of August.

Report votes as follows: "The Council voted 17 to 12 to approve the new tax." The "to" replaces a dash (-) and makes reading the sentence easier.

Never precede a number such as million with "a". Say "one-million" so it won't be confused with "eight-million." And if you have to begin a sentence with a number, write it out.

Newspapers often express multiples of millions in terms of points. One-point-five million (1.5 million). We would say, one-million-500-thousand dollars.

AGE

The style guidelines for numbers apply. Put the age before the person's name. Say "twenty-eight-year-old Janet Jones" instead of Janet Jones, 28. A good reporter tries to obtain accurate ages and use them where they are important. What ages are important? Ask yourself: "Would anyone be curious how old this person is?"

ABBREVIATIONS

Most abbreviations are taboo unless they can be instantly recognized. Broadcast writers use St. for Saint but would not write st. for street because this might be confused with St. Very common forms of address such as Mr., Mrs., Miss, Ms., and Dr. can be abbreviated since the person reading the script instinctively would say them correctly.

Be certain to spell out initials other than those which have become widely accepted acronyms. It is proper to write NATO for North Atlantic Treaty Organization, or U—S for United States, or U—N for United Nations.

Usually initials are handled this way. You spell out the first reference and then use the initials in subsequent references. Go back to the spelled-out version only if the story is long or complicated.

TITLES AND NAMES

It has become accepted practice to omit the first names of well known people after the first reference. Thus Secretary of State Jones is proper once you have given the secretary's first name earlier in the story. One exception observed by many news organizations applies to the President of the United States. In subsequent references you say, President Smith, or Mr. (Mrs., Miss, Ms.) Smith. This is the only instance when Mr. appears in broadcast news copy.

In recent years the custom of using Mrs. and Miss or even Ms. but not using Mr. has been modified. Now a woman's marital state is omitted unless it is pertinent to the story. Women are frequently labeled by last name only in the same manner as men. You should try to find out a woman's first name so that instead of referring to her as Mrs. Edward Brown you can call her Carol Brown, unless she has a strong preference for being known by her husband's name.

Along the same line, don't make reference to a woman's husband when he has nothing to do with the story. For instance, you would not say John Brown was elected to the state power commission and his wife is a psychologist. So why when psychologist Brown is elected president of the American Society of Psychologists would you say her husband is chairman of the state power commission?

A clergy member is *the* Reverend Jones, not Reverend Jones. There is still quite a debate on handling the names of cardinals of the Roman Catholic Church. They are usually called, in the church, Richard Cardinal Kelly. Some media organizations prefer to use the more familiar form, Cardinal Richard Kelly. I prefer to abide by the church's version, but you must be guided by the stylebook employed in your newsroom.

If a label is needed to explain who a person is, put the label before the name. Say Teamsters Union President James Jackson, not James Jackson, president of the Teamsters Union.

Middle initials are usually dropped in broadcast copy unless the person always uses the initial or there is a need to clarify which Paul Smith you are talking about. Even then, consider that you often tell Smith's age or address or occupation, which takes care of clarifying which Paul Smith we are talking about.

QUOTES

The direct quote is a difficult and generally confusing device to use in writing broadcast copy. The best way to get a direct quote in is to insert the person's voice on tape or film. But if you have to quote, set it up not with the awkward "quote" and "unquote" but with a lead in. If the quote is long, also lead out. Say: President Jones labeled the House Ways and Means Committee "vacillating and penurious" after the appropriations bill was tabled. The wording of your sentence plus the inflection of the reader's voice will take care of the quote marks.

If the quote is long, reinsert a word or two to indicate you are quoting, such as "and the President added."

When you write for radio or television, you must constantly think about how what you write is going to sound. It must read well. Sometimes this causes the written word to look a bit peculiar. You may find . . . (dots) or even — — — (dashes) in the middle of the sentence when you read an experienced newswriter's script. This type of punctuation, although unorthodox, does the job. It tells the person reading the copy to pause and treat the next clause with special emphasis.

A skilled writer can employ sentence fragments successfully, but this technique is not recommended for beginners. Others use phrasing which appears odd in print but works fine on the air. This approach is best left for newscasters who prepare their own copy since it only works effectively with a certain style of delivery.

The first rule in news writing is to play it straight. You can develop clever copy and an odd writing style later on if it's appropriate, but first you must master the basics of good, clean, smooth-flowing copy.

The acid test for a piece of copy—even if you are not an accomplished newscaster—is to read it out loud. When you finish reading the copy, if your reaction is "How can anybody read this trash?" then crumple the copy up in a ball and start over. If you have trouble reading your copy, most likely it isn't because you have trouble reading, it's because you have done a poor job of writing.

Inevitably, there must be a miscellaneous list of do's and don't's which apply to broadcast writing. They include the following examples.

Eliminate slang, colloquialisms, and dialect from your copy. In case it has not already occured to you, do *not* use profanity. You may occasionally find some of the mildest of profane words on some tape or in some copy (someone quoted President Harry Truman as being "mad as hell," and this was widely used), but those really nasty four-letter words do not belong in your copy.

To emphasize just what I mean, here is the text of Paragraph 1464, Appendix C, Title 18, of the United States Criminal Code:

> Whoever utters any obscene, indecent, or profane language by means of radio communication shall be fined not more than $10,000 or imprisoned not more than two years, or both. (June 25, 1948, Ch. 645, 62 Stat. 769.)

Be on the watch for words that sound like other words such as bear and bare.

Certain words carry connotations which have no place in broadcast copy. Avoid inflammatory words or words which have racial meanings. Use a person's race only when it is germane to the story. Do not label a situation a riot on your own judgment.

Watch out for words which mean nothing to your listeners. A listener thinks of "here" as where he or she is located, not where *you* are. You cannot say things like "the latter" in referring to a person, because your listener cannot turn back to the previous page of your newscast to pick up the reference.

If you want to destroy your newscast, fill it with all kinds of interesting statistics. All the statisticians in your audience will appreciate your effort. Everyone else will be listening to another newscast.

If you are paraphrasing a quote (which you should do whenever possible) be careful that your introductory word is neutral. Use "says" or "declares" but don't use "claims."

Don't bother with names of obscure localities, especially in foreign countries. It's better to describe an obscure location in terms of the nearest major city. Say: "The Shah of Iran hosted a traditional royal banquet beneath a tent set up outside a farming village 30 miles from Tehran."

Do not use nicknames unless the person is usually better known by the nickname. It's Senator Paul Miles, not Senator "Whirlwind" Miles.

PRONUNCIATIONS

Another peculiarity of broadcast copy is that it must contain phonetic pronunciations of difficult words. Any time you run across a word you think the person reading the copy does not know, insert a pronouncer in parentheses right after the word—for example, Chavez (SHAH-vez).

Various news organizations have their own systems for writing pronouncers. A safe rule of thumb is to write the pronunciation using words or word fragments which will be easily recognized. For instance, the Soviet city of Kiev would be (KEY-ev). Sometimes the syllable which takes the emphasis is capitalized, and the other syllables are typed in lower case. This highly readable method makes it possible for the person reading the script to pronounce the word correctly even if the copy has not been rehearsed.

More detailed suggestions are given in style books distributed by the Associated Press and United Press International. There are also books such as the NBC guide which can be used. A good dictionary will work in most cases. Use the first pronunciation, and after you have mastered the simple phonetic guide in the front of the dictionary, you shouldn't have any trouble making up pronouncers.

You should also begin right now to learn the correct pronunciation of difficult words by listening to skilled newscasters, especially those heard on major market stations or on network newscasts.

SPECIALIZED TOPICS

Some of the topics about which you will write are technical in nature. In these cases you will have to exercise special care to be accurate.

One difficult area is reporting legal matters. You must learn what the commonly accepted terms mean and then use them properly. There is a great difference between a person being indicted and a verdict of guilty. An indictment is a formal criminal charge which is drawn up after a grand jury has found "probable cause" for further action. The verdict comes only after the indictment is drawn and the person is tried for the alleged crime. The verdict is a finding of guilt or innocence.

During the peak days of America's space program the National Aeronautics and Space Administration distributed thick notebooks to reporters that gave very detailed information about the space flights. This type of reporting offers a great challenge to reporters who must accurately discuss very technical operations in language which will be understood by audiences who lack scientific training.

Volumes could be written on reporting these technical areas. Basically the rule is *study*. If you are going to write about zoning or courts or space travel, then learn as much about the procedures and terminology as you can.

Above all, if you are unclear about what you are writing, check with someone who knows. Never be afraid to ask a court official or a scientist or a politician to define clearly what is meant by a word or phrase.

As an example, say you are reporting a court case and after you get back to the newsroom you discover that you are not quite certain what the defense attorney meant by a certain term. Try calling the defense attorney. If the attorney cannot be reached. then call the judge's law secretary or someone in the prosecutor's office. But whatever you do, do not write about something that is not clear to you.

One important footnote in dealing with court matters: because the terms "guilty" and "not guilty" are easily confused by the ear. broadcast journalists usually write "guilty" and "innocent."

ADDING COLOR TO YOUR COPY

Up to now your aim has been to achieve factual accuracy and clarity in writing. But the key to outstanding broadcast writing is in the *use* of the language. English has some rather handy words called "adjectives" and "adverbs" which help us to describe what we see and hear. There is also something called "mood."

Thus. if you write about a trial. tell your audience more than just the facts such as the testimony, evidence, motions, and decision. Also describe the grimy, cigarette-strewn corridor where the defendant holds a whispered conference with his attorney during a recess.

If the verdict is rendered in a stifling hot courtroom, mention it. If the defendant collapses, perhaps you will want to say so. Every event has a mood; it is part of the drama of life, and it is important that a journalist describes that drama as well as the bare facts.

For example, it may be true that the Board of Aldermen voted to raise taxes. But it also is important to point out that there were only seven people in the room, including a snoring man, when the action was taken. After all, where were all those good citizens and taxpayers who are going to complain tomorrow about their taxes being raised?

You should point out that the Board action took place in a certain setting or atmosphere. It adds drama and color to your story. What sets off the outstanding reporters from the mediocre is their ability to translate into written and spoken words the mood and drama of an occasion.

As an exercise, watch or listen to a report by any of the better known network correspondents. Concentrate on the words that are being said rather than the pictures and sound which accompany the report. You will discover that some excellent writing goes into these reports. The report is a combination of fact-finding, sound and sight, and language.

Never feel that the words you write are any less important than the story. Too often reporters concentrate on their on-air performance or the quality of the audiotape, film, or videotape. They forget that it all starts with good writing.

In fact, if you have an opportunity, listen to some of the famous radio reports by the great war correspondents such as Edward R. Murrow. They converted information, mood, and emotion into words which painted pictures. That's all many of the early correspondents had—it was seldom possible to include sounds of people talking or battles being fought in their reports. The skill of Murrow, Charles Collingwood, and many others made the war come home to millions of worried Americans.

SOUND

Up to now I have concentrated mainly on putting words on paper. This is not much different from publishing a newspaper, except that I have stressed writing in a more conversational style. But people *listen* to radio. Radio is made up of sounds: people talking, music, and the cheering of sports fans. And radio news is made up of *sound*.

Basically, there are two kinds of sound: the voices of people and the background or "wild" sound. In the first case you get people to describe, explain, or complain. In the second, you try to capture the audio mood of the surroundings.

Audio reporting techniques will be taken up in a later chapter. For now I will concentrate on where tape comes from and how it is used.

First of all, you should begin to listen frequently to newscasts originating from the various radio networks. You will hear some of the writing techniques I have described as well as a great deal of audiotape.

You probably will note that the tape is fairly brief and has an introduction by the newscaster which moves you smoothly into the tape. There also may be some copy coming out of the tape. And after you have listened for a while you will notice that the tape is skillfully lacking in irrelevant matter.

We have suggested that you use the radio network newscasts and news programs as good examples because the quality and skill of local station tape editing varies considerably. The networks place a great deal of importance on tape, and they put highly skilled people to work obtaining and preparing their audiotape.

Audiotape comes from reports narrated in the field by the station's reporters or from interviews obtained by these reporters. (See Fig. 3-2.) It can be obtained by interviewing someone on the telephone. It may come from a network or from an audio service, or it may come from materials supplied to the station. It may be recorded off other sources, such as the public address system at City Hall or a television station co-owned by the same broadcasting company.

Field Reports

Your station's reporters should be prepared to narrate reports from the field, either (1) by recording them on their portable recorders and playing the reports by telephone to the station or bringing them in or (2) by calling the station and having their voices recorded at the newsroom.

Even more frequently reporters should be obtaining interviews with persons involved in current stories.

Fig. 3-2. A radio reporter for WMAL in Washington, D.C. holds a lightweight microphone during an interview. The strap of the battery-operated cassette tape recorder can be seen over the reporter's left shoulder. (Courtesy WMAL, Washington, D.C.)

Sometimes these interviews will be fed from the field alone; other times the reporter will narrate a "wrap" (introduction and closing). Another widely used technique is to call someone on the telephone and record an interview.

Tape for insertion in newscasts can come from regular or special network feeds. The radio networks usually permit some reuse of tape originally run on their newscasts. Even more likely, an excerpt could be taken from one of the network's daily closed-circuit feeds of reports and actualities (the voices of newsmakers).

Audio Services

There are also special audio services. Two of the largest are UPI Audio, a branch of United Press International; AP Radio, operated by the Associated Press.

Regional networks operate in some states, sometimes as a special service and other times through a mutual agreement among a number of stations.

Sometimes tape is sent to the station. One frequent source is the state's congressional delegation. Another source is public relations firms promoting products or causes.

While there are appropriate instances in which to use tapes from public relations sources, you must credit the source to remain within FCC regulations. The major danger to accepting free tape, either mailed in or provided on a telephone recording device, is that you have no control over its content beyond the most elementary editing. The source pre-selected the topic to be discussed and edited the content. You do not get the opportunity to question the person whose voice is on the tape.

Recording Off Sources

Many stations have arrangements to record certain public meetings—either on location or by installing a special telephone line back to the station. A frequent example: A station taps the public address system in the City Council chamber so that all the voices of the council members (and sometimes audience members) can be recorded. It takes concentration and patience to monitor a meeting, but the resulting tape can be far superior to doing face-to-face interviews with participants in the meeting after it has broken up. After the meeting the participants can tailor their answers to fit their own desires. But if you record what actually took place. then you are taking your audience to the meeting itself!

In the case of joint radio-television operations, the engineering department probably has equipment to allow radio to obtain tape from television. This can be done by taking an audiotape machine along on television film/tape assignments. The recorder is plugged into the television amplifier. Or. even better. the television reporter carries the audiotape machine separately and uses two microphones: one for radio and one for television.

Another technique is for radio to tape the sound track of film or videotape shot by the television side. This means that radio has to wait until the television crew returns to the studios. If possible. radio should get its copy (dub) of the audio track before the film or videotape is edited. since the radio editors may wish to edit it differently than the television editors. Also. waiting for television to edit the material means further delays for radio.

The final way for radio to get audiotape from television in a joint operation is to record the television newscast off the air. This solution would be regarded as totally unsatisfactory by any radio news director worth his or her salt.

Now we have some audio. What do we do with it?

Audio should be inserted in a newscast to act as a quotation—to advance the story by having someone say what you would have written. It adds drama and permits a reporter to give a first-hand. on-the-scene report on a current story.

Radio news directors generally feel that audio inserts in newscasts brighten the station's sound and add an element of drama to the newscast. The idea is to stimulate the listener's interest.

Before you write a piece of audio into a newscast you must be certain that it does tell its story accurately and in the least possible amount of time. This is a process known as editing.

Audiotape. which is made up of a magnetic oxide pressed between two layers of plastic. can be physically cut. Once the tape is cut. it can be rejoined by using a special adhesive tape called splicing tape. Audiotape moves through tape recorders at speeds slow enough for it to be relatively easy to find the separation between words and take out those you wish to drop. Audiotape editing is an easy skill to acquite. and any novice in the field should learn how it is done. The larger radio operations and the radio networks assign their editing to highly skilled technicians, usually under the combined demands of union regulations and a desire for a highly polished product.

In editing the same objective is sought as in writing: clarity. In dealing with editing, an important element is called *actuality*: the voice of someone involved in the news.

An actuality of 20 to 40 seconds is a good basic unit for most newscasts. So the trick is to determine one key statement and incorporate this into your story. You may find several sections of the tape you want to use, so the first time around pick out what you think is most important to someone who is hearing the story for the first time. On later newscasts you can use some of the other elements of the tape and rewrite your copy to fit them.

What do you listen for? Going back to the bank robbery example I used earlier: Your reporter arrives back at the bank after checking the scene of the first arrest (where the car was wrecked). The FBI spokesman is ready to give a factual statement on what has occurred. You would hear from the FBI in such a case because the Bureau investigates robberies involving a bank with a federal charter.

The agent will probably give a sort of narrative report, telling you the hard facts that can be released without complicating the arrest of suspects or damaging the chances of winning any future court cases.

Most people who give narrative reports tend to put things in chronological order. Listen to the tape. The first time you use something from it, you will probably want to take out something about the most recent events. So you go through the tape until you hear the FBI special agent say, "One suspect was found unconscious in the wrecked automobile and was removed to County General Hospital, where he is now listed in 'guarded' condition. Federal and local authorities are seeking two more suspects believed to be a man and a woman, probably in their twenties and Caucasian. The man is thought to be about 5 feet 7 inches, 140 pounds, and wearing a long brown raincoat, gray trousers, and black shoes. The woman has been described as being er, ah [cough]... pardon me ... blond, 5 feet 6 inches, about 115 pounds, wearing a yellow ski parka, brown slacks, and denim sneakers. They are believed to have left the scene of the auto crash on foot."

It's hard to say how long it would take the theoretical FBI spokesman to say that, but a good guess would be about 50 seconds, especially with the cough in the middle.

How do you shorten the statement? First, you can delete the opening sentence. The tape would then begin: "Federal ..." Then take out the "er, ah [cough] ... pardon me" to save another two or three seconds.

And you can delete the last sentence. The tape already says the suspects fled, and you really don't need to know whether they fled on foot.

Next, write an introduction (called an "intro") and follow the tape with any additional facts you wish to include. For example:

> Authorities are holding one suspect in the early afternoon robbery of an East Squirrelville branch bank. A police officer was shot during the robbery, and according to FBI special agent James Straightfellow, a search continues for other bandits:

[Tape—Straightfellow]
Open: "Federal and local authorities ...
Close: " ... and denim sneakers."
Time: 33 seconds

> Agent Straightfellow says the suspect in custody was found pinned inside a car which was wrecked following a police chase. Straightfellow says the suspect is listed in "guarded" condition at County General Hospital, where doctors are also working on a Squirrelville police officer who police say was shot as he and his partner approached the bank.

Then give a brief summary of the robbery and the shooting of the police officer.

Notice that the tape clearly indicates all pertinent information. It lists a name or key word, the opening words, the closing words, and the time. If there were more than one Straightfellow cut, you would give each cut a number and put the corresponding number on the script as well as the tape itself.

The *open* is needed to help in writing the script and, if a technician plays the tape, to help in confirming that the proper tape has been supplied. The end cue warns the newscaster (and the technician) that it is almost time for the mike to be turned on, and the time helps the newscaster to time the total broadcast.

This is standard operating procedure, whether the tape will be played by an operating technician, a disc jockey, or the newscaster. It also permits another member of the news staff to use the tape later without having to do more than auditioning it (listening to it). You should never air a tape you haven't listened to.

A really tough editor would have saved even more time by cutting into the opening sentence of the tape. The words "federal and local authorities are seeking two more suspects believed to be" would have been dropped, and the tape would start on "a man and a woman," providing the agent's voice had the right inflection on the "a."

I have described this particular tape insert as if you selected the actuality and then edited it and wrote it into the script. In many cases the reporter in the field feeds you a script (the "wrap") and a rough cut (the reporter plays a portion of the tape which relates to the wrap) of actuality. Here your responsibility is to make sure the wrap and actuality fit together smoothly and are editorially correct. Once these two things are done, you must write an introduction, known as a "lead-in."

You might write something like this:

> Police say they are searching for two of three persons who held up the East Squirrelville Branch of the Last National Bank. Reporter Ted Jones is at the bank:
>
> |Tape—Jones|
>
> "FBI special agent James Straightfellow stood in front of the bullet-scarred bank building and described the suspects:
>
> |Actuality| |Same as the first example|
>
> |Tape—Jones|
>
> "Agent Straightfellow says..."

It takes a great deal of care and coordination to make certain that what you write in the script does not repeat information in the actuality or conflict with what is said in the reporter's tape.

Perhaps you notice that the reporter started slightly in midstream by talking about the FBI agent standing in front of the bank. This is called a "second line lead," in which the reporter assumes you will write a lead for the tape that tells one or two primary facts—and so the reporter picks up the story in progress. If you had referred to the FBI agent by name in the lead, the reporter might have begun: "Straightfellow said ... " It takes practice to develop this technique so that it goes smoothly, but it adds a great deal of professionalism to a newscast and saves repeating information.

The reporter might do a straight voice report (voicer) describing the facts as known and what can be viewed at the scene. While this can be done without sound in the background, the report will have added impact if people are heard talking or sobbing or making some other related sound. The reporter must be careful in selecting background sound so that it does not overpower the narration. It's a good idea for either the reporter or the writer to refer to the source of the sound so that the listener won't be confused. For example, the reporter might start out saying: "Two bank clerks are sobbing as they tell police ... " Then the reporter would go on with the details.

Frequently the writer in the newsroom will have to edit a reporter's straight narration to shorten it. It simply may be too long, or it may have an opening line which needs to be chopped off in order for the tape to be integrated smoothly into the script. Perhaps the reporter has made a factual, grammatical, or pronunciation error.

Length is a common problem because a reporter, caught up in the drama of events or on the complexity of the subject, may want to say too much. You then have to decide what is important and try to judiciously edit the report without destroying it. Surprisingly, it is often easy to delete a phrase, sentence, or even a paragraph. Be especially careful to check for the agreement of facts. There are times when other sources contradict the reporter, and then you have to use judgment and consult with the reporter and other sources.

One example: A reporter sent to the scene of a bank robbery may not have the latest information from the hospital. Part of your job is to relay this type of information to the reporter for inclusion in the field report or to write your script in such a way that the latest information is worked in. Skilled reporters are careful to avoid being trapped by numbers that might change if there is any delay in airing the report.

The sound we insert in a radio newscast does not have to be of human voices. Sometimes a sound effect of something related does the job. Say, for example, police in your city discover an explosive device in a city building and decide to detonate it in a nearby vacant lot. You may well start your script something like this:

|Tape| (Policeman yells "let 'er go" ... pause ... BOOM ... fade remaining noise under)
:08 seconds

Newscaster: That was the sound of an explosive device being detonated by officers from the Mudville police bomb squad. They had just removed the device from City Hall. where it was discovered about 10 o'clock this morning. Maintenance man Clark Trembly says he opened a service closet about 20 feet down the hall from the Mayor's office and found a suspicious package ...

Imagination is important in radio news. Tell your story the way it best conveys not only the facts but the atmosphere of the event. This applies just as well to events you would not ordinarily think of as having drama.

For instance. a reasonably skilled writer would tell listeners the mayor and an alderman got into a shouting match. A more skilled writer would try to get a tape of the shouting match. even if the voices were not close to microphones. Then the writer would script the report so that sound of the shouting would be in the background while the altercation is being described in the script.

I have gone into writing for radio at some length. There really is no shortcut to becoming a good broadcast news writer. You have to practice. practice. practice! Try to get a supply of raw wire copy (check your school radio station and newspaper office. the local wire service office, local broadcast stations or. local newspapers. What you want. ideally. is the newspaper-style copy the wire services transmit. It is long and detailed and provides a challenge to you because you can't copy someone else's broadcast news style.

If you can't get wire copy. buy newspapers, especially some of the big metropolitan dailies which run detailed stories. Then follow these steps: study the copy. decide what the important facts are. and write your own brief version of those facts in your best broadcast style. Then read your copy out loud. Read it to yourself. and then read it to someone else who can at least tell you if it sounds fluid or choppy and if the point you are trying to make is understandable.

Then. of course. try to get an experienced broadcast journalist to critique some of your best copy. Anyone who is serious about a vocation in broadcast news and who plans to write—that is. be a writer or producer or network correspondent—should try to get into a newsroom where a great deal of writing is done from wire copy. Another good way to get the needed experience is to get a job in a wire service bureau. You will learn the good habits of brevity and accuracy, how to write and report under pressure, and how to do broadcast-type rewriting. The wire service broadcast desks turn out tight, workmanlike—if sometimes mundane—copy. You can learn how to make your copy sparkle after you have mastered the basics.

Most major broadcast news organizations put considerable stock in a wire service background, providing the applicant hasn't stayed with the wire too long and become inflexible.

WRITING FOR TELEVISION

In some newsrooms the radio writers call television "radio with pictures." It's far from an accurate description, but it's true that all the elements that go into being a good radio writer can be applied to television.

I'm not going to bore you by repeating a lot of information about how to write and style and the like. Instead, I'm going to talk about the basic differences. Television is a visual medium. The best thing you can do on television is show someone pictures—live or recorded—of real events and real people.

Everything you write for television is done to go with a picture. The picture may be the torso of the anchorperson sitting at a desk, a still picture in the background, or a motion picture showing a sequence of events or people doing things.

You can't stick the anchorperson with a long, complicated paragraph, because he or she must maintain eye contact with the viewer. Otherwise, the newscast might as well be on radio.

A television script is prepared differently from a radio script. In radio you can type the full width of the paper if you want, setting off the tape inserts by spacing, or you can leave a little space on the left margin for tape instructions.

But in television, you must leave nearly half the left side of the page blank so that the visual instructions which accompany the script can be inserted. Everything you write has video, whether it's a live shot of the anchorperson, a slide, the rear screen behind the newscaster, or a film or videotape. These instructions must be on your script, located opposite the copy that matches the pictures.

Here's a brief sample of a television news script:

Newscaster	The first section of Modern City's rapid transit system opened today.

Freeze frame of train pulling into station on rear screen behind newscaster	The innaugural ceremonies at the Glenville avenue station began on an unusual note as ...
Take sound-on-film arrival	[*Audio* ... background sound only on track.] the Mayor and City Council arrived on the first official run of the Glenville Avenue Express Train. The Dignitaries got out of their computer-controlled. air-conditioned subway train as the South High School Band played "Workin' on the Railroad."
[Pictures match action described]	[*Audio* ... bring up band :06 seconds and under]

Superimpose names:
  Glib Handshake
  Rapid Token
	The ribbon-cutting ceremony itself was pretty traditional ... with Mayor Glib Handshake and Transit Authority Chairman Rapid Token trying to cut the little ribbon with a giant pair of shears...

	[*Audio* ... track up :15 seconds] [Out on cue: " ... mighty proud."]
Silent film	The pretty young lady wearing the big sash was Karen Lovely ... "Miss Modern City Transit of 1975."
Newscaster	Today's light-hearted ceremony marks the beginning of service on the city's first rapid transit line. The Glenville route is two and eight-tenths miles long. It runs from City Hall Plaza northeast to Green Acres Park. Eventually the transit system will have six lines and 35 miles of track.

If you wish, you can, indicate precisely where in the script you want visual material inserted. At many television stations this sort of instruction is penciled in by the director on the director's script.

This sample script was relatively simple. The newscaster introduced and closed the piece. A single shot was taken from the film of the event to project behind the newscaster, and then the film was started at the same point where the frame was taken out so that a smooth transition took place. Most of the film had only background sound. The only sound of voices heard other than that of the newscaster occurred when the ribbon-cutting ceremony was shown. Just as the mayor and the chairman appeared on the screen, their names were superimposed (supered) on the lower part of the screen to make it easier for the viewer to identify each participant.

When you write for television, remember that the viewer is apt to pay minimal attention to the sound, so choose clear and easily recognizable sound. The sample script used the background noise of a train arriving and people murmuring plus a few bars of some recognizable band music.

Next chance you get, watch a local station's early or late evening newscast, paying special attention to the duration of the on-camera appearances. You will probably find that they aren't very long—probably 15 to 40 seconds. One theory is that viewers would really rather watch pictures—especially moving pictures—than talking heads in the studio.

In reality the reason for brief stories is a combination of television news being a summary of what has happened up to that point in the day and the relatively small amount of actual time in a television newscast. By the time you subtract the open and close and commercials, the "news hole" in a half or full-hour newscast isn't as great as you would think.

Brevity is very important. Tell the story, but don't embellish it with insignificant details. Your style must be easy and conversational with simple sentence construction. But you must not use "slang."

One reason for simplicity of language is that the anchorperson has to be able to read your copy while attempting to maintain eye contact with the viewer. This means "memorizing" a sentence and glancing up from the paper. Some stations make this process easier by using a TelePrompTer or some other device which positions the script in front of the camera so that the anchorperson can look directly into the lens while reading the news.

The anchorperson must look relaxed, which means the copy must read smoothly, just as you would expect someone to sound who sits down over coffee to tell you what happened today. (See Fig. 3-3.)

Television today is no longer stilted and pompous. It's people talking to people. When you are writing for the anchorperson, think about the pictures that might accompany the story. Facilities vary greatly from station to station, but in general a picture can be put on the air in one or more of the following ways:

1. *Pictures*: Photos, wire service pictures, and the like can be pasted up on a wall or backboard, and then a studio camera can take a picture of them. (The best

Fig. 3-3. A television newscast being done from an actual newsroom. The anchorperson at (right) is reading a script from a special projection device attached to the camera (left). (Courtesy CBS television stations.)

picture is in a ratio of approximately four units of height to five units of width.) This is a crude technique and is fast disappearing as even the smallest stations buy more sophisticated equipment.

2. *Slides*: Positive transparencies (the same kind of slides you show at home) can be projected full screen by using the same equipment normally employed to show commercial, station identification, and program slides. Sometimes individual frames clipped from motion picture film can be projected this way. Slides are frequently shot in advance so that the station can have a library of local scenes and personalities. There also are services which provide regular shipments of news slides. And some stations have equipment to make slides rapidly using a camera which develops its own film. Most stations employ at least one artist to help the news department with visuals.

The files of "stock" slides are frequently augmented by slides sent to the station. For example, a major industrial firm may provide some stock shots of its local plant, or a political candidate may send along a slide or two for file purposes. As a writer, remember that there is a tendency to pull the same slide of Senator Jones out of the file. Try to vary the slides you use, if possible, and don't be afraid to suggest that more or different slides be obtained.

3. *Rear Screen*: Another technique that enjoys particular favor with television producers is the rear screen. There are a variety of ways to accomplish this effect. The viewer at home sees the anchorperson usually to one side and toward a lower corner of the screen. One system is to project a slide or visual on a screen behind the anchorperson. Today the projection of rear screen pictures is rapidly being replaced by the electronic mixing of the picture of the anchorperson and the visual the producer wishes to use.

If you watch the screen very closely you may notice a slight line around the image of the anchorperson. Actually two pictures, one of the anchorperson and the other of the visual, are combined electronically. You might say the image of the anchorperson is inserted into the picture of the visual. It's sort of a "cut-out."

A smooth, modern newscast on a well-equipped station is an almost continuous sequence of visuals. Watching the director or technical director on such a show is quite an experience. There is a lot of fast-moving action and quick reflexes involved in setting up shots, making decisions, and executing those decisions.

When you sit down to write a story to be read by the anchorperson, make a list of the visuals. I have talked about slides, photos, and rear-projection (or electronic inserts). You may need a chart or map or even some lettering.

For instance, say that the Senate Majority Leader today revealed the tax package which the Democratic majority in the Senate would like to see passed. You might write your story in this manner:

Anchor on camera	Senate Democrats have issued a tax proposal designed to counter a plan announced by the White House last week.
Rear screen: pix majority leader	Senate Majority Leader Horatio Hardfellow says the Democratic proposal includes four major tax measures ...

Zoom past anchor to rear view visual with 4 key words:
  rebate
  tax cut
  corporate tax
  import tax
	The Democratic plan includes immediate income tax rebates ranging from 100 to 300 dollars per taxpayer.
	They also propose lowering the withholding percentages on this year's earnings, giving taxpayers more take-home money.

Pull out to anchor (and next item)	Two other possibilities are imposition of higher taxes on corporate profits and levies on imported goods.

In this example the information was organized to take advantage of an available visual—a stock shot of the majority leader—and then a piece of artwork was prepared to drive home the four major parts of the tax proposal. Note that this story did not elaborate further or describe when this legislation would go to committee.

Another point about writing for television: Unless you are working in a very small news department, you must deal with other people. Before writing an item such as the preceding example, you should talk over the visuals with the person producing the show. Then, if the suggestions meet the producer's approval, check the file for the shot of the majority leader and make out the paperwork to order the artwork from the station art department.

The writer should deal directly with the artist, since the writer is most knowledgeable about the story being illustrated, and the artist, about how to do the illustrating.

It's important that the writer take responsibility for helping the producer keep track of visuals that aren't already in stock. If artwork will be delivered later in the day or a slide is being made, the writer should keep track of items due and remind the sources and the producer as air time approaches.

All through the process of putting together a television newscast, you will discover that concern for the visual element will affect what is written. For example, most television reports follow a logical sequence or chronological order. This is because it is very hard for the viewer to jump around: you can't tell the station to stop the newscast and back up. The writer must organize the story in an order which tells the facts logically and makes best use of the visuals. This differs a bit from a radio story since you may not put quite as much value on the lead when writing a television script.

Going back to the bank robbery example used earlier, the film for that story could be chronological, beginning with scenes of the bank, police officers milling about, and an ambulance leaving the scene and then moving to the site of the wrecked getaway car and finally going to police conducting a search for the escaped suspects. It would be possible to open on the search and then go to the bank, but this tends to distract the viewer, who may not be able to jump back in time.

A great deal of the writing done in television newsrooms consists of introductions and closes for film and tape reports and, narration scripts for silent film or tape. Again, the film or tape may come from the station's own crews, may be part of a network feed, or may come from a news service such as a wired syndicator of television news reports.

In many cases the audio is already part of the film or tape, having been provided by the field crew or the network or syndicator. So your job is to write an up-to-date lead-in that puts the viewer smoothly into the visual piece. This means that if at all possible you must screen the piece, so that you know what will be seen and heard. Again, if possible, it is good to use the "second line lead" so that the on-camera anchorperson can give one or two key facts and then have the reporter in the packaged piece pick right up and go on. An example follows:

Anchor	Bulldozers moved into the South Street urban renewal area this afternoon—to begin work on a new civic center. Channel Ten reporter Pervasive Eise was there ...
Videotape	''Most of the dozing and digging was symbolic. The serious work ... ''

Writing lead-ins is not very exciting. But it is necessary that they be well written or the newscast will look and sound choppy and disorganized.

Before going on to talk about writing voice-over scripts, I will pause to talk a little bit about film and videotape.

Film

Most television stations shoot what is known as "reversal" film. Traditionally film is exposed to create a negative and then, through another process, a positive "print" is made. This would take too long for a television station, so a special film was invented to "reverse" the negative images to positive all in one continuous process. This means a film can be shot, brought back to the station, run through the station's own processing equipment, edited, and then projected directly onto the air.

There are two ways to shoot film—silent and sound. Silent film can be shot with a lighter, smaller camera because there is no need for an amplifier, recording head, or sound mixer as part of the camera. However, today less strictly silent film is being shot. Sound equipment and videotape are changing the techniques for covering stories because they are becoming lighter and more portable. Today background sound is recorded simultaneously with the picture in a great many cases, even if the film does not have narration or an interview on the soundtrack.

The silent camera is popular with stations that have some or all of their film shot by reporters. Since the reporter is doubling in brass, it is necessary to use simpler, lighter equipment. In fact, there are silent cameras which are virtually automatic in that they self-adjust for light levels and usually come equipped with only one variable-focus lens. This leaves the reporter with very little to do except stop and start the camera and load and unload the film.

Many stations load sound film into their silent cameras. The sound film (in the vast majority of cases) is of the "magnetic stripe" variety. This film has a narrow band of audiotape pressed onto each edge of the film. One side is used to record the sound, and the opposite side is used for what is called a "control track." Even if silent film is shot, it is possible to record sound on the track later. By using this type of film for all cameras, a station has maximum flexibility, and there's no risk of silent film being loaded into a sound camera.

A few stations which have not updated their equipment use optical film in which the sound is recorded by varying the amount of light reflected on a narrow strip along the edge of the film. This type of sound is common to motion picture film, but it is a very poor system for television news, in terms of the cumbersome and sometimes unreliable equipment and the poor quality sound usually resulting under newsfilm conditions.

A great number of stations are now shooting mainly sound film, even if it is only background sound. Generally this type of cinematography is done by a photographer, since it takes greater skill. A reporter trying to do extensive sound filming would be burdened with too much equipment and too many technical details. Some stations use more than one person for filming, hence, the term "crew." Local stations often have a photographer and a sound technician to make up a three-member crew.

I am not attempting to teach you cinematography. But it is necessary to acquaint you with some of the basics of film so that you will know how to use film as a writer or reporter.

Videotape

In recent years television news departments have been moving rapidly toward using portable videotape recorders. Videotape is similar to audiotape, but it is more sophisticated, since it is capable of recording and playing back color pictures as well as sound.

It is now possible to go on location with videotape equipment which is no more cumbersome than comparable film equipment. This is a recent breakthrough made possible by the fantastic miniaturization of electronic components.

There are portable videotape units which weigh as little as 22 pounds, which is competitive with sound film equipment. For a long time portable videotape received little acceptance because the quality of the picture was not satisfactory. And

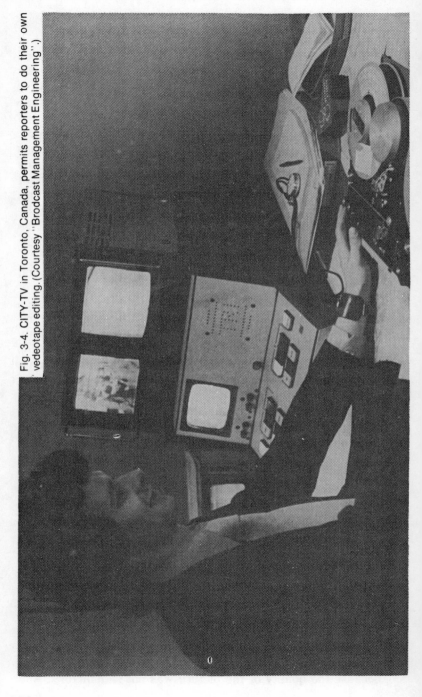

Fig. 3-4. CITY-TV in Toronto, Canada, permits reporters to do their own vedeotape editing. (Courtesy "Brodcast Management Engineering".)

Fig. 3-5. A camera operator using a new lightweight, portable, color television camera. This model weighs less than 15 pounds and can be hand held or mounted on a tripod. (Courtesy CBS television stations.)

videotape was difficult to edit. However, technological breakthroughs have made it possible to electronically edit videotape. (See Fig. 3-4.)

In many cases the portable camera and related equipment used in portable videotaping also can be used to transmit the picture and sound back to the television studio for recording or for airing live. The necessary backup equipment fits tightly into a station wagon or conveniently into a small van truck. The signal is transmitted by microwave to the station.

This technique is being used extensively in some of the larger markets, especially if a picture-worthy event is taking place which should be inserted live into the newscast or aired as a bulletin or special report. (See Fig. 3-5.)

The network news departments have made significant innovations and spent large amounts of money on portable electronic equipment. The new technology, sometimes called Electronic News Gathering (ENG) is spreading rapidly, and once some conflicts between film and electronic unions are resolved, the electronic camera will become very common as the basic tool of news-gathering crews.

While portability and the "live" appearance of the television picture are important reasons for using electronic cameras to cover television news stories, there is another big reason: cost. The initial amount of money spent to buy the electronic equipment is quite high, but the day-to-day cost may be lower. Film can only be used once; hence, television stations buy from hundreds to thousands of feet of film each month. Videotape can be used over and over before it wears out, which cuts the cost of raw materials considerably.

THE TELEVISION REPORT

A news report prepared for television may be similar to one done for radio. The reporter may "wrap" a piece of film or tape of someone the reporter has interviewed. Both the reporter and the cameraperson have to worry about picture quality and background. As the writer, you must be concerned about the picture, too. Never be afraid to question pictures that don't make sense.

For this type of report, your job will be to check the editorial content of the piece, make sure it fits within time

Fig. 3-6. Electronic news coordinator's console in foreground with decision booths (for editing) in background. (Courtesy CBS television stations.)

limits, and then write a lead-in and maybe a lead-out for the anchorperson. Your skill will be put to the test when the photographer brings in film or tape for you to script. This is called a voice-over and usually is read by the anchorperson. If the reporter is going to read the voice-over, the reporter would write the script because it should be based on personal observations.

When you set out to write a voice-over script, collect all the information you need to write the story and even jot down what you think might be an outline of the story. Do this while the film is being processed or the tape dubbed—before you worry about the visuals.

Then view the film or tape. There is no magic formula on how to construct the visual part of a story. Often a more or less chronological order will be best, but there can be reasons to break this cycle. The one reason chronological order is good is that it takes the viewer through the story in about the same order as if he or she had been there. (See Fig. 3-6.)

In order to talk about using visuals, I have to make a few observations about editing film or tape without attempting to teach you the skill.

Film can be assembled in any manner you please, since it is almost always shot in scenes or takes with a selection of shots: close, meduim, and distant. Editing is the art of putting the film together. If the events being filmed tend to be sequential, an experienced photographer can shoot the story "in the camera," that is, in an order which results in a coherent story which could be aired with a minimum of editing.

For example, if the story is something simple, such as a house fire, the cameraperson would probably open on a wide shot as soon as he or she arrived to give the viewer an idea of what was taking place. Then the photographer might get a medium shot of firemen rushing to get their equipment into place. A variety of close and medium shots then would show the fire and the firefighting efforts, followed by shots of the cleanup and damage.

An experienced photographer shoots so-called "cutaway" shots. These are shots of relevant activity (such as the faces of bystanders). The film editor can then insert one of these shots as a bridge between two scenes that don't connect logically. Some other cutaways might be a family dog wandering around looking confused, a street sign, or a broken doll left on the lawn as the children were taken to safety.

When you view the film, tell the editor the scenes you want to use. Then decide the order in which they will appear and approximately how many seconds you think each scene should last. The scenes should relate to the script, which is why it is a good idea to outline what you plan to do if you haven't already written a rough script.

Once you have given the editor your instructions, you can go write a polished script. After you are finished, go back to the editing room and check the timing of your script with the film by running the film through a timer or by showing it on a projector. If the anchorperson has time, you might have the script timed to the anchorperson's actual reading pace.

Final editing of the script and film then takes place. Then there is a last check by projecting the film and reading the script. Then it is aired.

The process with videotape is similar. However, the sophistication of the editing done with tape at various stations can differ greatly. Some stations try to "shoot" their tape so that the story is nearly in usable order. Others shoot by scenes and use multiple playback machines plus a computer to reconstruct the scenes into a finished story.

This is how a script might look in finished form:

Longshot fire; anchor reads over	Five members of a Squirrelville family had a narrow brush with death before dawn today when their house caught fire.
Medium shot firemen laying hose	Firefighters were called to the James Madison home on Harbor Road when a police officer spotted flames on the roof of the Madison residence.
Closeup police officer talking to family	Officer Harvey Right gave the alarm by radio, and then awakened the family and led the two younger children to safety while Mr. and Mrs. Madison and their eldest daughter stumbled through heavy smoke to the safety of the front lawn.

Medium shot firemen with hose	The first fire units on the scene discovered that the rear of the two-story home was engulfed in flames.
Closeup exhausted firemen taking off air pack	It took nearly two hours for the firefighters to extinguish the blaze.
Medium shot damage	Later, Fire Inspector Victor Sylvester said the fire apparently started in an attached garage ... perhaps from lawnmower fuel which ignited.
Closeup dog wandering	All five members of the Madison Family and their dog were unhurt.
Medium shot fireman with family	But the house was so badly damaged that city building inspectors have condemned the structure. The Madisons have been relocated to homes of relatives.

The fire story serves as a simple example of how pictures and a writer's script are combined. Unfortunately, modern television newscasts are not that simple. In the first place, television news departments today are shooting fewer simple stories such as fires, meetings, and auto accidents, and instead are doing investigative reports and complex visual stories. This means reporters and writers have a variety of raw material to combine into their visual and aural package.

Many stations now shoot sound film or sound videotape for almost all assignments. This means that there is background sound available, even if the film does not contain an interview or other foreground audio.

Sound in television can be handled two ways: It can be recorded right on the film or videotape (single-system) or it can be recorded separately (double-system). In either case, your handling of the story changes. For example, if sound had been used with the fire story used previously, there would have been fewer separate shots. Instead of shooting a series of short scenes in sequence, the cameraperson would probably have used a zoom (variable focus) lens which allows changes to be made from long to medium to close shots without having to stop and change lenses.

The result would be that the sound would have been consistent throughout the picture story. This is not to say that the sound track cannot be edited, but you must consider both the picture and the sound when planning the final "piece." For these reasons you will occasionally hear some pretty terrible soundtracks on television—when a decision needs to be made between getting a good picture sequence and a good sound sequence, sound loses out.

One way to overcome the complexities of using sound and pictures, other than the simple interview situation, is to edit the film or tape on two or three separate reels. The separate rolls can be combined by playing them on more than one projector or videotape machine and adding what is known as a "mix."

A simple version of this which is done frequently in newscasts is to run a sound interview on one channel and run silent film or tape (which could have a little sound in the background) simultaneously. The director then decides when to show the face of the person being interviewed and when to switch to related scenes on the other channel. This way the person being interviewed can be talking about something, such as a new building, while the viewer sees pictures of the building.

The average film story usually comes on one roll, with silent film at the beginning and end and a sound interview in the middle. Videotape stories sometimes can be a little more complicated if the station has more than one playback machine in the editing room.

There are many interesting ways to tell a story on film. One popular way is to let the participants tell their own story. I once told the story of a college student protest entirely with a sound film of the protestors, college administrators, and various observers without any narration over the film. All that was added was an introduction and closing by the anchorperson.

The newcomer to broadcast writing will have to work a while before he or she gets a chance to use the more complicated television pieces. While you are learning, you should observe closely the newscasts of local stations and the networks. Try to analyze how each piece was put together.

Then observe the writers. reporters. producers. photographers. engineers and editors in your station or a station you can visit. Pretty soon you will be able to figure out how most of the stories were prepared.

If you are already working in a television station, try to read the script so you can compare it with the finished piece shown on the air. You will learn a great deal about what works and what does not. And you will be able to ask intelligent questions.

If you can, take film courses, especially ones which require you to go out and shoot film and then edit it into final form. There are enough similarities in principle that you can adapt anything you learn about film to videotape. This sort of education will help you to be a better writer and to work well with the skilled personnel who shoot and edit the pictures.

4
Reporting

The reporter is an impartial observer. The press serves as the eyes and ears of the public. As a reporter, you are acting as an observer for the public, making sure tax dollars are properly spent, courts are fair, and legislators are honest. The evolution of the American press has carried this role into many other fields. Reporters cover the activities of business, science, medicine, law, and many other specialties.

Your job is to observe all that transpires, ask questions, read public documents, and find out all that you can about your subject. You must give the public the facts, not interpret them.

WHAT YOU MUST LEARN TO DO THE JOB

There is more to being a reporter than simply being an impartial observer. A reporter must seek to achieve balance. If city Alderman X fires a verbal blast at Alderman Z's proposal for a new municipal swimming pool, you must seek out Alderman Z to get the rebuttal. Furthermore, a good reporter goes to the municipal department responsible for swimming pools and checks whether the city has a place to build the pool, whether there is a need for the pool where it is proposed to be built, and whether the city has the money to pay for building it. A superior reporter would check around to see if either alderman or any of their associates would benefit from a decision to build or not build the pool.

The process we have just described illustrated what should be done. Too often broadcast newscasts contain only the statement of Alderman X without at least a mention of Z's retort or any of the background necessary to do a complete story.

Since the reporter is an observer of life, it is important to learn as much about life as possible. There are certain areas that are particularly important to reporters.

Government

A reporter must learn as much as possible about the federal, state, and local governments. Their structure, how legislation is passed, how government is financed, and the services government provides all are important. Some of this is theoretical knowledge which comes from college courses and reading. But much of it is practical. You acquire it by reading the daily newspapers closely and by the face-to-face study of government operation. This means attending meetings—even long, dull ones; it means talking with every official you can; and it means sitting in on seminars for journalists. A good reporter, even a general assignment reporter, must have as complete a knowledge of state and local government as possible. You also need a working knowledge of the federal government, because its influence increases all the time.

Politics

A reporter must have familiarity with politics at all levels and know who is who in each office and the relationships of the major parties in each jurisdiction.

Here's a practical example: Suppose you are hanging up your coat one morning when the assignment editor says, "I've got a job for you. The Treasury Secretary is speaking at the Chamber of Commerce this noon, and afterward she's going to hold a news conference."

Your first reaction is going to be, "My gosh, what do I ask the Treasury Secretary? After all, what do I know about federal monetary policy?"

Well, think for a minute. What kinds of questions would an average citizen in your community ask? What worries people in your town? Is it taxes or inflation or unemployment? Also scour the wires and the newspapers to check on what types of controversies the Secretary is presently involved in and how she stands on current issues.

Check the newsroom morgue (the file of clippings and copies of scripts). What is the political opposition saying? After all, the Treasury Secretary usually belongs to the party that controls the White House.

Get to the meeting early, and be certain to hear the speech and observe the types of questions Chamber of Commerce members ask. They represent at least a cross section of the business and economic life of your community. Remember, while you can't stump the Secretary (after all, you're not an expert), you can ask intelligent questions which will interest people in your area.

But no amount of last-minute cramming is going to make up for a basic understanding of economics, federal government finances, and the current issues in Washington.

The Courts

General assignment reporters frequently have to cover trials. It is important to have some basic understanding of the Judicial process. You should know how a person is first charged, what the prosecutor and the grand jury do, what happens in a trial, and what happens after the trial.

This means you have to read up on the basic legal system. Then you should observe the courts in action and ask as many questions as you can of clerks, lawyers, judges, police officers, and anyone else who knows the courts.

If you are going to cover a trial, you should learn as much about the case as you can. Read the material in the morgue. Ask to see the indictment (formal legal charge) when you're at the courthouse.

Talk with the arresting or investigating officers, the defense attorney, the prosecutor, and any other people concerned.

As a general assignment reporter you could be assigned to a beauty pageant, a demonstration, the opening of a new section of the botanical garden, or almost anything. The only way to cope with these diverse assignments is to educate yourself as widely as possible so that you will have at least some basic understanding of the subject.

KNOWING THE ISSUES

Reporters deal with issues—conflicts of ideas. These occur at every level. It is important for a good reporter to keep up with the major issues being discussed. Federal issues are important as you will have one or more members of Congress serving your coverage area.

State issues are even more important because you will undoubtedly be asking questions of state government officials and state-level politicians who deal with these issues, such as taxes, prison reform, and highways.

And since your most important area of coverage is the territory reached by your station's broadcast signal, you must have an excellent working knowledge of local issues and the people who represent the major opinions.

Some examples of issues on which you must be informed are the following:

Federal tax legislation
Federal health legislation
Federal education policies and legislation
Major congressional investigations of
    government operations
Any federal issue which has a local angle,
    such as school integration

State taxation
Statewide transportation policy
Statewide energy policy
Banking and public utility issues
Mental health policy

Local taxes
Local educational policy
Local attitudes on abortion and sex education
Local attitudes and policy regarding welfare
    and senior citizens
Local planning and zoning activities

You need to be familiar enough with these matters to interview someone about them on a moment's notice. It might be that the congressional representative from your district is about to catch a plane back to Washington just as a major congressional committee takes some important action. The local member of congress will be asked to vote on the legislation in a few days, and obviously you are going to try to find out just how your local representative stands on the issue. Or suppose your local school board suddenly approves a school busing plan. You would want to promptly interview people who represent major viewpoints on the issue of school busing.

This is why you must know how public officials stand on important issues and why you must understand the issues. It isn't good enough to ask the leader of a minority group, "What do you think of the School Board's action?" It would be better to know that the person you are talking to has threatened to go to court to block the School Board's proposed busing plan. Then you would ask, "Will you now take the Board to court over this plan?"

You follow up by asking the minority group representative to tell you just what steps will be taken and when. The answer might surprise you. It may be something like, "I'm on my way to meet our attorney, we're going to file suit this afternoon."

Then you rush back to the School Board chairperson or school superintendent to find out how the minority group's action will affect the busing plan. You might be told that the plan will not be implemented until the suit is settled, if indeed a suit is filed.

By the time the next major newscast rolls around, you'll have one heck of a story. For television it would be a major "take-out" covering the whole package; for radio it would be a series of reports as each part of the story broke, followed by several major wrapups for the major newscasts.

INSIDE THE COMMUNITY

All communities have similarities. They have streets, houses, stores, factories, municipal buildings, and courtrooms. But the people who occupy the buildings—and how they conduct their activities—are part of what makes one community different from another.

Why is it that some cities are clean and attractive while others are dirty and depressing? Why is it that employment is high here and low there? Why do farms in one area look neat and prosperous while farms in an adjoining area are rundown?

A reporter must learn who and what makes a community run and, how the community in general reacts to new ideas (conservative, moderate, and liberal). Where does the economic power lie, and where is the center of political power?

A reporter needs to know a little about the racial and ethnic mix and the types and proportions of religions present. But perhaps the most important thing is to understand what is called the "power structure." Who really decides how the community is run?

Sometimes the people who appear to give the orders really do not. The mayor may be elected by the populace, but certain wealthy residents or big business leaders may influence the major decisions. They may simply point out that a certain step would be good or bad for the city—that is, good or bad for their interests.

This is not meant to imply corruption. It is part of how the political structure operates in any community. Similarly, the person who speaks the loudest may not always be the most powerful. You have to know how much power and influence a community leader really wields in order to evaluate that leader's statements.

This kind of information is usually gained by talking to as many people as you can, often off the record (not for quotation) and then cross-checking when you converse with others who may be well informed. Some progressive government administrators and politicians even welcome informal conversations with reporters, knowing that the reporter does a better job simply through being better informed.

Try to engage as many people as you can in conversations. You never know when a little shred of information you get from a nurse at the hospital or a drafting technician in the planning director's office will be useful. One reporter recalls that his best source to tap the City Hall rumor mill was a clerk in the purchasing office whose duty was to sell used and surplus city property. The job was obscure, but the individual was well informed and talkative.

A good understanding of who is who in your community will help you when you need to seek out reaction to one of your stories. You will be able to go to someone who represents some solid body of opinion rather than someone who likes to talk just to hear his or her own voice.

WORKING A BEAT

Most news departments have "beats." These are points of contact which are touched at regular intervals. In the case of a small radio station it may consist of a list of phone calls to be made two or three times a day. In a larger station reporters may actually go out and visit certain key locations.

The telephone beat is almost universal. Usually this involves calls at regular intervals to nearby police agencies, hospitals, and fire departments. The list may be expanded to include certain public offices if the officials will give out pertinent information on the phone.

For the most part the telephone beat is a way to check on major auto accidents, fires, and perhaps routine legal filings such as civil suits. This is an important routine because you often deal with these contacts only by telephone, and their attitude toward you may be based solely on the way you conduct yourself during telephone conversations. If they like you, your telephone contacts will be more cooperative in doing what for them is an added task. In smaller communities, smart reporters make an occasional personal visit to shake hands with and say hello to their telephone contacts.

The telephone beat is an efficient way to take care of certain routine stories without much effort as well as to get leads on stories which will require more intensive pursuit.

The outside beat is the real test of a good reporter. You have the opportunity to interact with people and to compete directly with other reporters. As a rule, even the smallest station will attempt to have a reporter make short daily visits to some of the major government offices. These might include the mayor, the city manager, the city clerk, the police department, and the court clerks.

One of your objectives is to find out what these offices are doing of public interest. The mayor is apt to have something he wants you to know in hopes you will disseminate it. And you may have questions you want to ask. The same is true for the city manager. The city clerk and the court clerks are the keepers of public records. There are certain records you will learn to check daily, including indictments for criminal offenses and filings of civil suits. It never hurts to see if someone very prominent is being married or divorced, sued or suing.

The kinds of records kept in these offices are often difficult to understand, so the smart reporter is friendly and polite to the clerks, who frequently respond by taking the time to explain what is really meant by their documents.

Frequently, information you pick up in one office leads to your asking questions in another. You might discover a land sale in the city clerk's office which would lead you to ask questions of the city manager. Then perhaps you would get in touch with a local real estate executive.

Working a beat is fun. You meet people, and there is a bit of detective work since you seldom get the whole story at any one stop on your tour. Another way to use your time effectively when working a beat is to check on upcoming matters. If the Board of Aldermen is due to meet in the evening, see if you can pick up the agenda in the morning. If nothing else, you will have a good advance story on the meeting, and you may well find that an important story is likely to break during the meeting.

Your assignment editor or news director will probably be very interested in any advance information you pick up which can be used to help figure out the amount and type of news coverage needed.

SOCIAL CONTACTS PAY OFF

A good many stories and lots of valuable information comes from social contacts. A dedicated reporter never stops being a reporter. Just because you are having dinner with friends, don't forget your job. You may meet someone who will be a good news source or may hear a rumor which bears checking out for its authenticity.

Experienced reporters will tell you that their spouses, friends, or relatives often come up with the most amazing information. In fact, this process starts right at your station; most news directors keep after other staff members to tip the newsroom when they think they know something newsworthy. It's like having dozens of extra sets of eyes and ears.

Social contacts frequently give you advance notice when politicians are about to make a major move or some important official is about to resign or due to be fired. And the people you meet under the relaxed atmosphere of a social meeting will feel more at ease with you when you have to deal with them in their official capacities. Sometimes it amounts to nothing more than recognizing you. Public officials are especially ill at ease when strangers walk up and start asking questions.

THE INTERVIEW

Interviewing is a basic skill in broadcast reporting. While you may conduct informal interviews, where you take notes during a conversation, the important interview is the one you do with your tape recorder, camera, or videotape machine. This is because one of the basic objectives of broadcast news coverage is to present the newsmakers telling the story themselves.

Usually the reporter tries to make the interviewee comfortable. If your subject is relaxed, you usually get more meaningful, candid, and lively responses. However, techniques vary with reporters and according to whom they are interviewing. Sometimes you have to be hard and abrasive, while other times you can be very relaxed. You may go along being quite relaxed, spring a tough question, and then follow up on it tenaciously.

The most important thing in conducting an interview is to ask a few intelligent questions in logical order. Your subject is much more likely to give good answers if your questions are well thought out and clearly phrased.

The interviewee's ego is complimented when you ask questions which show that you understand what you are discussing and are seeking new and important information rather than rehashing some generalities the subject has discussed dozens of times before. However, one cardinal rule: the interviewee is not interested—and the audience is not interested—in your opinions. So don't bore the subject by trying to show how smart and opinionated you are.

No interview ever seems long enough to a good reporter who is talking with an interesting subject. But there are practical limitations. First, your subject probably has a limited amount of time to give you. Second, what you commit to tape or film has to be listened to and watched by yourself or someone else. There just is not enough time to look at or listen to a lot of irrelevant material.

Irrelevant can be defined as material with low potential for use on the air. For example, you should not ask a background question with tape or film running when you already know the background or could just take notes for future reference. Also, most interviews have a topic or central point, and you should stick to this central point unless you have a special reason for asking other questions. You might have been told, for instance, to ask a couple of questions for inclusion in a documentary your station is working on.

You also have to remember that audiotape recorders, videotape recorders, and film cameras have limited capacities and must be stopped for reel changes. In addition, if you are filming an interview, the film costs money, and film can't be reused.

You may have to guide your subject. If the interviewee begins to ramble or go into a long, complicated explanation, cut in—try to politely but firmly keep the subject on the track.

THE NEWS CONFERENCE

Nowadays, a weekday seldom goes by in major cities without one or more news conferences. Some are important, but many trivial; all require skill if they are to yield journalistically worthwhile material.

News conferences are called for two reasons: convenience and control. If an important announcement is to be made or there is great pressure from the press to talk with a public official, then the news conference gives the press a chance to query the individuals involved in a highly competitive but basically fair situation.

But the news conference permits control. The person or group sponsoring the news conference can avoid answering questions simply by not recognizing a reporter, and frequently the person giving the news conference selects the topic to be discussed. If the questions get too tough, the subject can either evade by not answering fully and then avoiding followup questions, or by terminating the news conference.

Who gives news conferences? First and foremost—politicians. Politicians talk for a living, and most politicians realize that frequent media exposure is good for their reelection effort. As a rule, they are sophisticated individuals who can fend off sticky questions while putting their best foot forward.

News conferences are sometimes called simply to get a body of information into the public record at one time. For instance, following a major crime, a high-ranking police official may hold a news conference so that the official version of what happened can be explained once, rather than having a number of different individuals giving out sometimes conflicting information.

Business organizations give news conferences. They usually want to announce something, and because most business organizations today are counseled by skilled public relations advisors, the news conference is used to get maximum coverage by timing the session for the best selection of newspaper and broadcast deadlines. Sometimes business organizations even schedule news conferences to take into consideration the deadlines of weekly publications which play important roles in the business and financial communities. Of course, any organization which feels it has something to say in public will call a news conference. Protest organizations, charities, and chambers of commerce all use news conferences.

The news conference is a frequently criticized device. Some journalistic leaders say the news conference leads to lazy news coverage. especially on the part of broadcast stations. Some stations will attend a news conference in preference to seeking out an in-depth presentation of the story or cross-checking with other sources, looking over records, and seeking face-to-face interviews with involved individuals.

Another criticism of the news conference from a journalistic point of view is that it generally puts the group or person giving the news conference at an advantage. This is because the "giver" controls the content, and the news conference dilutes the effectiveness of individual reporters by spreading out the questions and answers.

But news conferences will take place, and they will be covered. The best we can hope for is tough journalistic decisions from news directors and editors who have to display the strength to ignore an irrelevant news conference even if every other station in town is going to be there. This technique, while likely to give ulcers to the newsroom's management, sometimes leads to getting rid of the less important news conferences. And those who give such news conferences are still willing to grant personal interviews if that is the only way they are going to get exposure.

When you cover a news conference, plan on getting to the site early. This allows time to set up equipment before the room gets too full. Also, most news conferences are backed up by printed material, which you should read over before the conference begins.

The tough decision you have to make is what to record. For radio, this may not be difficult because your tape recorder may accommodate up to an hour of tape, depending on the machine and type of tape used. All that is necessary in this case is to keep a good record (using the machine's counter if it has one) of what goes on so that you can easily locate the portions of the tape you wish to use.

If you are using videotape, you have to be more cautious because you do not have quite as much playing time available. And if you are shooting film, you must be very selective unless you want to spend a fortune in film stock and have your film running through the processor for most of the rest of the day.

It is not unusual for a news conference to begin with a formal statement, which is frequently accompanied by a transcript so you can read through and mark the parts you wish to record. When you get to a question and answer format you will have to make some very quick decisions to stop and start your equipment if you are recording for television. This is where your advance work plus a knowledge of what is going on in your community pays off.

Listen carefully. In addition to posing the questions you want to have answered, note what other reporters are asking and how the interviewee answers. Not only will you want to record the newsworthy questions and answers, but someone else's question may bring up a point that you wish to pursue.

In addition, you may uncover something which needs to be developed further. For example, if the nature of the news conference yields charges against a person or group, then you are going to want to try to get a statement from those attacked.

You may want to go to a location, either just to look it over or to tape or film something there. Say, for example, that a business firm announces plans to build a new plant near the edge of town. It behooves you to see if anyone objects—the neighbors or perhaps the alderman from that area. And you should make inquiries from public officials to see if the firm will have any zoning problems. Or perhaps the company is asking for changes in the street system, or needs a special agreement regarding water and sewer facilities. Any one of these topics could develop a whole new set of considerations for the city administration. And frankly, not every new plant that has been announced has been built. Sometimes the announcement is part of a plan to force certain concessions from the local government or to crush public objections.

What if you were to talk to the public works director and found that the new factory plan had been announced before the environmental impact study for the site had been approved. This would trigger you to talk immediately to local, state, and federal environmental officials. It could mean that the whole project will go down the drain.

Keep detailed notes. Often glowing predictions and promises are made during news conferences which do not reach fulfillment. After a time you may want to check up on the content of the news conference and see if those predictions and promises have been accomplished. You might come across a very interesting story if events have not taken place in the manner originally described.

As the news conference breaks up, stay on your toes. Sometimes it is possible to get a face-to-face interview with a participant to further develop some aspect of the questioning. This is easy for radio reporters but a bit more cumbersome for television reporters. And you may overhear a comment to an aide or to another reporter which will give you an idea for some further road to explore.

Also, you may be able to isolate other people who have significant information. Usually the top person in an organization takes the questions at a news conference, but this sort of person is often accompanied by staff members who have valuable detailed technical information which you may wish to include in your report.

MEETINGS

Meetings are not universally popular with reporters. They usually involve sitting for quite a while as people debate matters which do not produce a story. But meetings are important. They are an essential mechanism for the conduct of government. Our elected leaders are expected to conduct the majority of their business in public, giving the population of the area a chance to confront them. Unfortunately, most of the public seldom attends these meetings. Thus you become the ears for the community, reporting what has taken place, impartially.

Meetings are used effectively by skilled reporters. For one thing, they are frequently sources of story ideas. A discussion at the city council may not yield a decision, but it may give you an idea for a story about some problem bothering residents of one area of the city. Meetings also are part of the education of a reporter. You learn who is speaking for whom, and get a chance to listen to the viewpoints of a number of people on topics of local interest.

The ground rules for reporting meetings differ. Sometimes it is possible to audiotape or film in the meeting room. Usually a determining factor is having equipment which does not interfere with the meeting. For television, this frequently can mean shooting without lights. Fortunately, an increasing number of communities are remodeling their major meeting rooms and making provisions for broadcast equipment.

More often than not, you have to either write a story or catch the participants in the hallway in order to get an interview. The radio reporter does not find meeting coverage much of a problem. The reporter can slip out of the meeting, pick up a telephone, and phone a report to the newsroom. But the television reporter has cumbersome equipment and sometimes ends up either narrating over silent video or doing a standup—reading a script into the film or videotape camera on location. Both techniques are being disavowed by some news directors, who feel that if you can't advance or illustrate the story with sound or pictures, then just go on camera live back at the studio and tell what happened. Meeting video can be particularly boring when it is made up of general (cover) shots which tend to look the same everytime you show pictures of a meeting.

Most broadcast stations have been or are presently engaged in battles with government officials to insure (through law and policy) open meetings and the right to bring broadcast equipment into the meeting room.

Covering meetings is time consuming and ties up manpower and equipment. For this reason some stations ignore all but the most significant sessions. Others realize that good reporting takes time and encourage their beat reporters to attend important sessions.

EVENTS

Events are scheduled happenings that do not recur at short intervals. They might include a parade, Fourth of July ceremonies, or a university graduation. The reporter often functions more as a producer than strictly as a reporter in covering these occasions. Because events tend to have definite schedules and rigid arrangements, you must know what will happen. You must then think how you will get the proper equipment in place and how you should cover the story. Since this sort of coverage relies largely on mood, sound, and pictures, a great deal of effort is put into being in the right places to capture the mood.

SPOT NEWS

A reporter is a great deal like a firefighter or police officer. You spend a lot of time in the newsroom (the firehouse) or covering your beat (patrolling), but every so often your world explodes. You must always be ready to cover the major fire, the fatality auto accident, a drowning, or a plane crash.

How can you be ready? Part of your preparedness is knowing your community and your contacts. You need to have a good working relationship with the police departments, the fire departments, the local hospitals, the state police, and officials at the airport and weather bureau. Being able to tap these resources for information and interviews while they are under stress will make or break your coverage of a spot news event.

The other part of preparedness consists of having whatever equipment you carry as a reporter ready at all times. This starts with having a writing implement and a notebook or paper on you at all times. If your station equips you with a tape recorder, the batteries should be fresh and the tape clean, and somewhere close by you should have fresh batteries, and extra tape. You should also have your equipment for telephone feeds with your tape recorder.

If your station equips you with a silent camera, then it should be loaded with fresh film and have a light meter. Of course, you will have spare film and takeup reels with you.

Reporters who drive their own or company cars are wise to keep certain basic equipment on hand. This would include spare tape, film, batteries, writing implements, notebooks, a flashlight, foul weather gear and, depending on the climate, bad weather equipment for the car. In addition, it isn't a bad idea to carry some basic emergency equipment, such as an old blanket and flares (which state and local police frequently will supply). Reporters who have police/fire monitors or two-way radios sometimes get to the scene of a disaster or accident before the emergency equipment.

While you should leave rescue and emergency work to the experts, you can put out flares or light an endangered area or help temporarily with traffic. Most of all, you should know how to cover your story without interfering—which means putting your car out of the way of ambulances and not blocking emergency workers.

What does a reporter do when a spot news event takes place? If possible, he or she will be sent directly to the scene, with a supporting crew if necessary. Whether or not a field reporter is available, someone gets on the telephone and starts checking every possible source for information on what is going on.

Let's use an example: You and another reporter are working in the newsroom when both the police and fire monitors come alive. A light aircraft apparently has crashed into a residence, which is on fire. You both listen for the location and then one of you moves out quickly, heading for the scene. Check to be sure you have your press identification, because the police will shut off the affected area as soon as possible.

The other reporter will immediately call the police, the fire department, and the Federal Aviation Agency or the airport manager. This is to confirm the report, because legally you are not permitted to rebroadcast information you hear over police, FAA, and fire monitors without confirmation. Get additional details so you have some facts for early news bulletins and in case you need to call in other news personnel. Using the information you hear on the emergency radios, you can ask the authorities intelligent questions and start to clarify what has happened.

After the reporter in the newsroom gets some basic facts together (and on the air), he or she will call you on the car radio and fill you in. Then the inside reporter will try calling people who live in the affected area or who have businesses nearby to attempt to get some preliminary eyewitness reports. For radio, these will be taped and aired. For television, the inside reporter will call you and suggest you contact these people.

In the meantime you will have arrived at the scene. The first thing you do is look around. Don't panic and rush up to a police officer. Get as close as you can to the action and look. You should be able to determine some obvious but necessary facts such as the type of structure hit by the airplane, what part of it was struck, how much of the building is on fire, how the fire spread, where the wreckage is of the aircraft, and a general description of the plane (you don't have to be an expert to tell a light aircraft from a DC-9).

Count the number of emergency units and note what type they are. Later you may want to illustrate how serious the situation was by saying that 18 fire engines and seven ambqlances were there. Now before you look for someone to talk to, radio back to the newsroom and tell them what you have seen. You will be giving the staff back there a way to visualize and describe the situation.

Now find the person in charge—in this case, probably the fire chief—and get as many preliminary facts as you can. Try to find out if there were any fatalities and injuries and where the injured were taken. It will help in the case of television if you get some idea of locations: where the plane hit or where the worst of the fire is. If you are not shooting the video, tell your crew.

Be careful during the height of an emergency situation to check reports of casualties. They may be inaccurate. Tell the newsroom what you have learned, and they will check the hospitals in an attempt to corroborate the number of persons injured and their conditions.

After you have gotten a preliminary outline of what happened from official sources, start looking for eyewitnesses or survivors. Talk to them; they will probably give you graphic descriptions of what happened. Talk to other eyewitnesses, and be sure to talk with enough people so you can compare notes. Sometimes eyewitnesses provide graphic details of events they have not seen, just so they will be heard and seen. Sometimes people's impression of a sudden happening will be distorted by the very suddenness of the event. The descriptions of eyewitnesses are important, but it is of paramount importance that you get an "official" version of events from someone in authority who is trained to look at this type of situation logically and dispassionately.

If you are a radio reporter, you will be constantly feeding reports, information and audiotape back to your station. If you are working for a combined radio-television department or a television newsroom, you will be working with your camera operators to make certain you have good visuals to go with your interviews. Then you must doggedly track down the facts and figures, exact number of casualties, type of aircraft, where the casualties came from (house, street, or aircraft), injuries to emergency workers, and damage to the house.

Telling someone how to report spot news is pretty much like telling someone what to do when a boat capsizes. What you will actually do will be the result of how well you have trained yourself and the amount of experience you have dealing with situations. But you can prepare, and preparedness is essential to doing a good job on a spot story.

REPORTING GOVERNMENT AFFAIRS

We have already talked a bit about covering government, running your beat, and attending meetings. There are some generalizations which can be made about government. Basically, the federal, state, and local governments all follow the same formula. There are three branches: executive, legislative, and judicial. Usually there is some system of checks and balances so that one branch can prevent excesses by another branch.

The executive branch is usually made up of an elected head and a group of political appointees who fill key positions. Municipal government may be more "professionalized," employing a city manager and allowing the manager to hire specialists to run the departments. Either form will have a staff of civil servants, who change less frequently than their elected or hired bosses. It is to this group that you look for an understanding of the continuity in government and an explanation of the technical operations of government. For example, you do not realize how much there is to collecting and disposing of garbage until you ask the head of the sanitation department about the job.

The legislative branch lays down the policy guidelines. This group is elected and in a general sort of way represents the wishes of the population of the political unit. The legislative branch has several strong weapons, including the right to hire and fire top professional managers and control over budget allocations.

The judicial branch has many duties, but it is the arbiter when there are disputes over legislation or the actions of the administrative branch.

A good reporter talks to as many people in government as possible. At the very least, learn the basic duties and operations of the three branches—especially in your local government. And try to converse with enough different people to understand the political relationships and the duties of various departments.

One important fact about government: A significant proportion of government records are open for public inspection. The exact records differ by jurisdiction. There is federal legislation which defines the records open for public inspection. On the state level, the laws differ from state to state, and generally local governments are covered by state laws.

The meetings of government are generally open to the public and the press. And there are specific laws in some states which govern open meetings. However, some legislative bodies will go into executive session to, they say, consider personnel or real estate matters. The closed executive session may be appropriate to discuss a personnel matter in which the person might be held up to public redicule or to protect the value of land under consideration for a government project. But reporters must be vigilant to ascertain that the private business conducted is limited to the items claimed by the government body.

Another trick is for a government board to have a public meeting but to have decided what actions will be taken either by telephone earlier in the day or in an earlier closed meeting. If you learn such meetings are being held, demand the right to attend. Just because meetings are supposed to be public, it doesn't mean they are. You as a reporter may have to force certain groups to let you attend.

A thorough reporter does some homework. Whenever you are going to cover the meeting of a public body, try to obtain an agenda in advance and then check up on any interesting items. This way you will have some idea of what is going to be discussed.

It's a good idea to occasionally check certain public records that are seldom viewed by the public. This reminds government officials that you know you have the right to inspect. and prepares the way for you to make a thorough inspection when you need to dig into the files.

THE COURTS

We have already made some generalizations about courts, and no effort will be made here to do more than give you an outline of how courts work.

For the sake of simplicity, let's talk about state courts, which handle the serious matters with which you would be concerned. For the most part you will have little to do with municipal courts, which usually handle minor crimes, small suits, and traffic violations. Only occasionally will you cover a federal court.

The courts operate in two distinct areas. One is civil law, and the other is criminal law. Reporters tend to get more involved in the criminal aspects of the courts. The civil courts handle damage suits. and legal maneuverings that surround union activities. and other matters which don't involve criminal offenses. Usually the civil court is concerned with negligence, damages, and arbitrating disputes or interpreting laws passed by the legislative branch.

Much of the activity of civil courts can be covered by checking actions filed with the clerk of court and by talking with the judges' secretaries or assistants. In large cities, reporters spend some time in civil court because groups in dispute, such as the labor unions and the city, will file various writs to counteract each other's moves.

Criminal matters are quite different. Generally the sequence in a criminal matter goes like this: The police arrest a suspect. A record of the arrest is made, which is usually called "booking" the suspect. Then the matter goes to the prosecutor's office, where a prompt arraignment is held. This is a proceeding in which a judge determines if there is sufficient evidence to charge the person and, if so, whether the suspect should be held with or without bail or released in his or her own recognizance.

If the judge orders the person held for a grand jury, then a group of citizens is convened to hear the prosecutor's evidence and charge. If the grand jury feels that a case exists, an indictment will be handed up. Then a trial will be ordered to be held either before a judge or a jury, depending on the defendant's choice. Sometimes the defendant and the prosecution work out an agreement in which the defendant pleads guilty to only certain charges and, if the judge concurs, a plea is entered. This is "plea bargaining" and it is common in big city courts today. Otherwise the case goes to trial, and eventually a decision (verdict) is reached. If the defendant is found guilty, an appeal can be filed to higher courts.

There are a number of activities that take place within the criminal justice system. I have mentioned the prosecutor, who speaks for the state. There is also the judge and the court, where trials and hearings take place.

There is a jail, where some people are kept awaiting trial and where a few with minor sentences are held after trial. There may be a probation department to investigate persons who are convicted before they are sentenced and to supervise persons who are allowed to remain outside jail.

A reporter can learn a great deal by simply observing trials and by talking to key people in each of the offices we have mentioned. The rest comes with experience gained by covering trials.

The records which you may inspect at a courthouse are pretty well defined and depend on the law of your state.

The police department keeps a public record of people they "book." Reporters routinely check these records to get clues on major arrests. Sometimes the records are augmented by reports filed by arresting and investigating officers. Simple investigations such as auto accidents are usually adequately covered in this type of report, but you often need to talk in person or on the phone with the investigators in major criminal cases.

Similar records are usually available in the prosecutor's office or are on file with the court clerks. The formal charge against an individual is most often a public record. However, grand juries sometimes hand up sealed indictments which may not be made public immediately. An actual trial is public, and most courts have provisions for reporters so that the press can see and hear well. However, reporting courtroom activities presents a large problem for the broadcast journalist. Very few courts permit recording or filming equipment.

The broadcast reporter sits in the courtroom and takes notes the same way the written press covers the trial. Sometimes an artist is allowed to sit in the courtroom, and the broadcast reporter can at least narrate over the artist's sketches.

As a general rule the prohibition on recording equipment is extended to the hallways outside the courtroom and often to part or all of the court building. This means that as far as getting interviews on tape or film are concerned, you are limited to talking to those individuals who are willing to be interviewed outside the court building. This explains some of the mob scenes you have seen on television.

Remember, too, that the comments of the prosecutors, defense attorneys, and defendants have their own biases. If you must interview the participants, realize that you are being manipulated to affect the trial or appeal. Some stations will interview members of a jury once its verdict has been delivered. This practice is not universally condoned in the profession.

Jails vary considerably as to access by the press. Security problems and the constant movement of prisoners in city jails makes press access difficult. The federal prisons do permit press visits to inspect the facilities. As far as communicating with prisoners, the inmates may write to the press and their mail will not be censored. You can write to a prisoner. However, phone calls are less likely to go through just because it is difficult to bring an inmate to the phone. Sometimes, especially in minimum security institutions, prisoners are allowed to return telephone calls. Generally, visits to prisoners require fairly complex approvals. It is difficult to generalize about state prisons, but they tend to be less accessible than federal correctional institutions.

The press ground rules for probation and parole departments are fairly stringent. A great many of the duties of these departments are confidential. Reporters find more to cover from the viewpoint of the system than individuals when they study probation and parole.

TAKING THE LID OFF

The Watergate scandal has done one thing for the American press: it has put solid investigative reporting in the forefront. At times there have been overreactions, but Watergate has pointed out the necessity for the press to be inquisitive and to look behind the obvious facts of a story. Investigative reporting is really a matter of doing your work well: it means continuing to ask questions until (1) there are no more questions and (2) there are some answers.

The broadcast media have turned in a particularly spotty performance in the investigative area, crying poverty and lack of time when sometimes the problem has been lack of commitment. Fortunately, this is changing. Better reporting is being encouraged, staffs are growing, and solid journalism is being accepted by an increasing number of broadcast managements, with a healthy push from the Federal Communications Commission, which has some good ideas about serving the public interest.

THE VALUE OF DOCUMENTS

Read the success stories of investigative reporters. Time and again you will discover that a great part of their work was doing what no one else wanted to do—reading through tons of dull files, reports, and literature, and cross-checking these against other material until the facts, dates, amounts, and relationships of people began to establish meaningful patterns.

This is why a good reporter learns what files are where. Even routine checks of files can produce some interesting stories. Checking property records will sometimes reveal corporate slight of hand by certain organizations. Careful checking and a bit of memory may reveal a pattern of land acquisition which will point out a plan for some future construction project. And of course if there is discussion about building a major new highway, it would be interesting to discover a pattern of land-buying along the right-of-way just as the state begins to acquire the roadway.

CROSS-CHECKING AND FOLLOWUP

Usually what you get from reading files and musty records is hints of other sources of information. Reporting is really detective work. You get leads and clues, and you follow them to the next set of leads or clues until you finally put together enough information to have a story. In investigative reporting the process is more tedious than a routine followup.

Even after you have done a story, you have to go back and see what has happened. It is fine that you gather together facts enough to force some public body to begin an investigation. But then you have to keep after the investigators until a report is made, and if the report calls for action, you have to see that the action takes place.

All reporters should be skeptics, but not cynics. The world is not evil as a matter of course, but neither is it as rosy as most public and many private figures would like us to think. Question everything you see or hear until you are satisfied that you have explored the story fully.

THE SPECIALISTS AMONG US

Increasingly broadcast reporters are following on the heels of their print counterparts and developing specialties. If you have a specialty, a hobby, a technical education, or whatever, don't hesitate to exploit it. You may well carve a very satisfying nitch for yourself. A few years ago you would have had difficulty convincing people at a network news organization that they should have business or economic specialists, or legal correspondents. Today these specialties are relatively common.

Superb reporters are born. They have innate curiosity, an effective style in dealing with people, and an instinct for the newsworthy, but excellent reporters are made through a solid education and hard work.

5
The Radio Reporter

A radio reporter must translate the body of information which is gathered to sound. This means writing in a conversational manner, exploiting every opportunity to add sound to a report, and being able (in many cases) to speak well enough to do on-scene reports and deliver newscasts.

TOOLS OF THE TRADE

To a radio reporter, the newsroom is a home away from home. Most stations attempt to have the news department occupy at least one room set aside for news. The area should be relatively isolated from other parts of the office because a considerable amount of noise can be generated in the average newsroom.

The newsroom typewriter most likely is a vintage model manual. Typing is a mandatory skill for today's broadcast reporter. Most stations require you to make one or more carbon copies of your script so that it can be reread or rewritten and used by another newscaster. If you don't already type, spend the money and invest in a typing class.

You will need a working pencil and a notebook. While it is said that radio journalists substitute the microphone for the reporter's pen and pad, this isn't entirely true. You need to take quick, accurate notes both of the content of the event and to keep track of material you are taping.

A good reporter never goes anywhere without a writing implement and paper. A great deal of written note-taking is still done. One reason is that radio reporters frequently file voice reports on what they have covered, which means taking notes and writing a script while out in the field. You must learn to take fast and accurate notes and to listen for usable quotes.

Many stations and the network news organizations want their reporters to file a voice report (which is the radio equivalent of a written story) immediately after the event they are covering is concluded (or in the case of a running story, as soon as sufficient facts are gathered). Then, when the reporter has a few moments, he or she can work up a report using tape.

The telephone is one of the most potent tools in radio news. Given enough gumption and guts, a reporter can reach the most extraordinary people. Most stations have a device connected to their telephone line so that conversations may be recorded. While it is no longer required that a sound "beeper" be on the line to alert the party on the other end that you are recording, you *must* establish clearly that the person is willing to be tape recorded.

Here is an example of just how effective the telephone is: a radio network newsroom in New York can be in direct voice contact with an overseas bureau simply by picking up a telephone and either direct dialing the overseas number or giving it to an operator. Except for the underdeveloped countries, the call will probably go through almost immediately, and once the connection is made, the reporter can file a story by either speaking directly into the telephone or by hooking a tape recorder to the mouthpiece. In some countries a correspondent can file directly from a telephone booth or a hotel room. In others, he or she must go to a specially designated international telephone—probably at a post office. The networks have nearly given up ordering special overseas radio circuits because the combination of telephones, the new space communication satellites, and tape recorders have made it possible to file good audio quality from around the globe.

You can use the telephone in many ways. Radio reporters make routine canvasses several times a day of major spot news sources. In a smaller community the news department may be able to use the telephone to cover a great deal of what is happening.

Perhaps this point and some others can be best illustrated with excerpts from a description of a small town Iowa station, KOEL in Oelwein, written by news director Dick Petrick. I have taken the liberty of rearranging the order of Petrick's thoughts slightly and of omitting names of staff members.

Petrik says: "KOEL operates full time on 5,000 watts on the AM and 100,000 watts on the FM. Although we are located in a small town, we are the dominant station in Northeast Iowa. This is despite competition which includes 23 radio and 3 television stations in our coverage area.

"KOEL news operates with three men, each works 48 hours, and I work at least a 70-hour week. The only real beat coverage we do is attendance at the local school board, city council, and other meetings in town. Our main coverage is done through our phone system, which is used to cover 14 area counties in our listening area—consisting of over 150 cities—all but two being smaller than Oelwein, which has a population of 8,000. We gather an average of 60 local stories daily and make about 200 long-distance calls daily.

"We use both an in-watts and out-watts system, as we try to keep in constant touch with our family of communities. Besides making calls to all law enforcement agencies for spot news, we keep in contact with many hospitals, city councils, school boards, county clerks, chambers of commerce, and other agencies. We cover the happenings of the council and school board meetings of about 100 communities by phone. KOEL runs up a phone bill of $2,000 a month, but we feel it is worth it.

"We use a lot of actualities during our newscasts but try to make sure they add something to the story and don't use them for the sake of adding extra voices. Most of our recordings are done by phone on either our ampex or spotmaster, which we operate from the newsroom, although we do some with our portable recorders or from our news studio which is hooked up with the newsroom. I would say we have increased our tape coverage by 25% during the past 5 years."

How do you do a telephone interview? You call the interviewee, explain who you are and why you have called, and immediately get the subject's permission to have the conversation taped for possible broadcast. The subject may state that there should be some discussion of the topic before the questioning begins, so make certain you know what remarks are for background and what are for recording.

It's always a good idea with a telephone interview to jot down a few questions before you start. Getting someone prominent to answer the telephone is sometimes difficult, and you don't want to stutter and stumble when the party finally picks up the receiver. Keep your questions simple, direct, and easy to understand. Be polite; do not make flip comments.

Sometimes, when the subject has been called by many news reporters, a few words of sympathy about the bother may yield a better response.

Many newsroom telephones have push-to-talk switches on their handles or on the wall nearby. Be sure you know the switches which accompany the telephone. It will save you lost tape and occasionally an experience with feedback (a shrill sound made by electronic equipment which is recycling its own signal).

The telephone is a handy instrument to use in tracing down newsmakers. Say you are covering your beat at City Hall and you pick up some tape of the mayor blasting a City Council member from the opposite party. Well, a quick phone call to the newsroom allows you to file your story and at the same time ask the reporter in the newsroom to call the Council member.

In emergencies the telephone works well. You should routinely phone the area around the scene of any accident or disaster seeking an eyewitness. Some newsrooms purchase a special telephone book which is set up by street addresses so that they can phone adjacent locations when an emergency arises.

A field reporter can use the telephone in two ways. The reporter can narrate the story through the telephone mouthpiece if the quality of the connection is good. Or a tape recorder can be attached to the telephone, allowing the reporter to use the tape recorder's microphone and amplifier to improve the signal. Depending on the construction of the machine, it is sometimes possible to feed a narration "wrap" and an actuality insert in proper order by attaching the tape recorder to the line. The telephone is invaluable for feeding tape to the newsroom, whether or not it can be intermixed with the narration.

We need to talk about how a tape recorder is used to send tape back to the studio. There are two methods. One is to simply hold the telephone next to the recorder's speaker and play the tape into the telephone. As you might guess, this is a poor choice and is reserved for emergencies, because the microphone inside the telephone receiver isn't very good. Also, you might pick up noise in the background outside the telephone booth.

The better choice is a direct connection into the inner workings of the telephone. This is a good technique, and it can be approached in at least three ways. There is a simple device which can be made up by any technically inclined person. It's a set of "alligator clips." The device consists of two clips with saw-toothed jaws on one end of a pair of wires and a small plug on the other end. In the middle there are a few electrical parts which make up what the technicians call a "pad" used to match the signals.

What you do is to unscrew the mouthpiece of the telephone. Inside, once you lift out the disc which is located inside the mouthpiece, you find two flat metal terminals. Clip an alligator clip to each of these terminals and plug the other end of your device into your tape recorder's output terminal. It's a good idea to get your connection with the newsroom first and then take the phone apart.

Another device which serves much the same purpose is called the "doughnut" by some people in the field. One end of the device is plugged into the tape recorder's output, and a ring on the other end is laid on the telephone receiver. You don't have to unscrew the telephone, but some reporters feel the doughnut is less efficient than other methods. The telephone company provides "acoustic couplers," but they also have quality losses.

One firm markets a device which looks like the mouthpiece of a telephone. You remove the outer casing of the telephone and screw this device on instead. It has it's own high-quality microphone, plus an input for a tape recorder and a switch which permits voice, straight tape, or mixed report. This device can be used at a remote location to adapt a telephone line as an instant "line" for a remote broadcast.

The telephone company frowns on having its permanently sealed telephones taken apart. In some cities it has applied epoxy glue to outside and booth telephones due to vandalism.

You have probably surmised that the telephone really takes on its effectiveness because of the tape recorder. Audiotape recorders have been so miniaturized that there is really no reason for a reporter not carrying one everywhere he or she goes. The advent of cassettes has been a boon. They are self-contained rolls of audio recording tape which are easy to handle. They just slip in and out of the recorder. Cassettes vary in length, but the typical cassette will record 30 minutes of material on each of its two sides. Some tape recorders have built-in microphones, which reporters should steer away from because of their sometimes poor quality. It also looks bad to have to thrust the whole tape recorder in someone's face.

The lightweight, portable, battery-operated cassette tape recorder has freed radio news from many of its constraints. Now it is possible to move quickly to the site of a news event and to talk directly with the people involved. At least one network and several stations have done complex documentaries with nothing more sophisticated than portable, battery-operated cassette recorders.

Cassette tape is flexible, because if you want you can air the output of the tape recorder directly, or you can dub the cassette to quarter-inch tape (on reels) for editing. Cassettes, because of their shape and the small size of the tape, are impractical to edit.

Sometimes radio stations use heavier equipment for recording. There are fine battery and electric-powered recorders which are used where quality is desired or where it is necessary to add a mixer to handle multiple sources of audio. These machines tend to be used for specialized work: documentaries, music, and recording speeches for rebroadcast. They are too heavy to be conveniently handled by a reporter.

Here are some good rules when using a portable battery-operated cassette recorder: (1) replace the microphone that comes with the unit with a high-quality, heavy-duty one equipped with a windscreen for outdoor work, (2) carry the microphone you replaced as a spare, (3) buy good quality cassettes, (they run better and give you clearer recordings with a lower signal to noise ratio), and (4) use good quality, long-life batteries in the machine to insure consistent speed and to lessen the possibility of battery leaks.

Most of the portable audiotape recorders are elementary to operate. The typical machines have automatic level control, which means the reporter does not have to watch a volume meter while recording, except to check occassionally to make sure the machine is working. However, this device has one built-in problem. It is designed to emphasize the sound closest to the microphone, so if you pause too long while talking, the background noise will be emphasized.

This is important if you are doing an interview in a noisy area or are preparing material for a documentary. If you are preparing a documentary, record some room noise or background sound (without any talking in the foreground) while you are interviewing. This may help you when it comes time to edit, since you may want to add some background recording.

For interviews, all you have to remember is to say a couple of words before you start. This sets the automatic volume and prevents distortion at the very beginning of the tape. If you are recording a report, just do a countdown: "five, four, three, two, one (pause)," and start your script. Ironically this little difficulty is also an advantage, because the tape recorders equipped with automatic level control will permit you to do interviews in some noisy places where you wouldn't normally think of interviewing. If you need to record sound effects or background sound for a documentary, you might consider using a tape recorder with manual volume control to get best results.

Some of the better models are set up so that by pressing the record switch only you can use the microphone to talk through the machine into the telephone line. This permits you to improve the quality of your feed by using a good amplifier and microphone. Also, you talk with the party on the other end without reassembling the telephone (you listen in the telephone earpiece).

Reporters often feed wraps by doing just what has been described: pressing only the record button, doing the narration live and, at the appropriate point, canceling record and pressing the play button to play the actuality tape insert—then reversing the procedure and recording the closing. Then all the personnel in the newsroom have to do is to make two very quick edits to tighten the bridge between narration and actuality. You can also do live broadcasts using this technique.

One peculiarity of cassette recorders: the cassettes use plastic gears, which sometimes make noise, so place the recorder on something soft or as far away from you as practical to prevent the squeeky noise from ending up on your tape.

Electronic journalism utilzes the two-way radio. It uses electronics to report sounds and images and to make them available to the public as soon as possible. Two-way radio equipment has been around for a long time. But in recent years two-way radios have become commonplace in newsrooms.

Both radio and television stations use two-way equipment to keep in contact with their reporters and crews. While the equipment is a little expensive initially, it is invaluable as a time-saver in giving instructions to personnel in the field or in alerting and moving personnel when a story breaks.

Many two-way systems are good enough to permit reporters to go on the air live from the mobile unit. Some of these systems have been adapted so that a tape recorder can be played through them, thus eliminating the necessity of finding a telephone.

Some of the equipment is very sophisticated. It is possible to take a walkie-talkie radio to the scene of a story, and if its signal won't reach the station, then sometimes the signal can be relayed through the mobile unit's radio. If a radio reporter is carrying a walkie-talkie radio he or she can be in constant touch with the newsroom and can quickly file reports when a news story breaks.

A note about two-way radios: they are regulated by the Federal Communications Commission. You must find out from the station engineer just what FCC rules apply to the equipment you are using. Usually you are required to possess one of the classes of radio-telephone operator's licenses in order to use mobile radio equipment.

One of the standard items in the newsroom are emergency service monitors. At the barest minimum, a station will listen to the local police frequency. Most stations monitor other frequencies, including the fire department, sheriff's department, state police, and aviation frequency.

Monitoring these frequencies is a bit of an art. You must understand the language or "code" used. Most functions are abbreviated to speed up communications and to lessen the effect of eavesdropping. Here is a portion of a police code used in one city:

10-7 — out of service (or out of the vehicle)	10-14 — report of prowler
	10-28 — vehicle registration information
10-8 — in service	10-29 — check records for wanted
10-9 — repeat	10-30 — illegal use of radio
10-10 — fight in progress	10-31 — crime in progress
10-11 — dog case	10-32 — man with gun
10-12 — stand by	10-33 — emergency

A police officer who stops a suspicious automobile would report that "Unit 9 is 10-7 on the Dullsville ramp northbound at Interstate 57." Then the officer would ask for "a 10-28 on

Nevada registration WXY-5692J, white over blue Chevrolet, 1973, two-door sedan, with four male occupants." The officer would also ask for a 10-29 to see if the vehicle is stolen. If there appeared to be some question about the identities or activities of the vehicle's occupants, he might ask for a similar records check of the driver's license or some other identification. If the officer's suspicions were heightened there might be a 10-26 call, meaning that suspects are being detained. Any police department worth its salt would then immediately send one or more additional units to provide backup help. Any officer who is running that thorough a check on a car with four male occupants who says a suspect is being detained has a potentially dangerous situation at hand.

If you are in the newsroom or a mobile unit and hear a conversation like the one just described, you will instinctively follow the action. If the radio suddenly crackles with someone yelling "10-33," you scramble fast, because that police officer has big trouble.

Police and fire monitors act as initial tipoffs that certain types of activity are taking place. How you react depends partly on the area in which you live and the station's approach to news. In a small community, almost any personal injury automobile accident, store break-in, or house fire gets a few lines on a newscast. Often the final information on these situations is collected by telephone, but the original tip comes from the emergency service monitors.

A skilled newsperson will learn a great deal more from these monitors. In certain parts of the country you can tell when some major action is being taken against manufacturers of illegal liquor (moonshine). This is because you will hear state (or perhaps federal) agents carrying on certain types of conversation. If you have good sources available by phone, you may get the first lead on a big story about breaking up an illegal still.

It is an art to monitor more than one frequency while going about your business. After a while you get so that only the important material penetrates your consciousness.

Monitoring is not limited to emergency radio. Someone in the newsroom should be listening to the competition and any other news outlets nearby so that you don't miss any important stories. You listen as a check on your own coverage, and if the competition has something you should have, go out and hustle and catch up.

A mobile unit sounds like a pretty fancy name for an automobile, doesn't it? Today many radio station mobile units are nothing more than radio-equipped automobiles, but in the early days, when equipment was heavier and radio was the only means of broadcasting, stations would send out van trucks full of equipment to do news or remote broadcasts.

A mobile unit need not be just an automobile. Many stations use helicopters, light aircraft, boats, skimobiles, and overland vehicles. The type of equipment depends on the terrain to be covered.

But the simplest mobile unit is an automobile, either the reporter's personal car or a station-owned vehicle. Generally the minimum equipment includes a two-way radio or radio-telephone and one or more police monitors. But some stations add special AC/DC converters so additional tape recorders can be used; some have remote amplifiers so that more than one microphone can be used at one time, and some are set up so that the two-way radio can be locked "on" and the reporter can rove nearby using a walkie-talkie.

Mobile units also serve as a public relations device for some stations, which display their call letters and frequency prominently on the vehicle. However, in large cities during the riots of the 1960s the well-marked mobile units became targets for various missiles and gunfire. As a result, many major market stations use unmarked sedans.

The Teletype printer is a standard piece of equipment in newsrooms. Typically, a station will subscribe to the broadcast wire of either the Associated Press or United Press International. Both are written in broadcast style so that you can tear off the copy and read it directly as a script. Whether your station does this will be a function of size and policy. The broadcast wires are written at a central national location, and allowances are made for "splitting" the wire to allow nearby wire service bureaus to file local and regional stories.

The broadcast wires are rewrite wires. That is, the wire service broadcast departments cull the various newspaper wires operated by the service and rewrite the information into broadcast form. In principle this is a good system, since the broadcast writers have considerable background material to use in preparing their summaries.

The fallacy is that the newspaper wires that make up the main activity of the wire service are written by newspaper reporters for newspaper consumers. The wire services do a spectacular job of providing fast coverage of some breaking events, especially in Washington. But the bulk of their copy moves through a cumbersome process in which a newspaper reporter calls a nearby wire service bureau (after he or she has written the local version of the story), and a wire service reporter rewrites the local reporter's story. The story is written and edited wire service style, and then it is usually transmitted to a central national office, where it goes through another editing process. Finally, it is put on the newspaper wire, from which a broadcast report is written. This process on an interesting but routine story can take hours.

In radio we make an effort to be as up to the minute as possible. Many stories written for radio are not static—they move, new developments take place, and people comment on actions taken earlier. The wire service tends to freeze a story in time, updating it hours later for the next cycle of newspapers, unless there are particularly significant changes which must be made.

Ironically, you may find that wire service coverage of state and regional news is somewhat more up to the moment. There are two reasons: (1) it is easier for station news directors to put pressure on the nearby wire service bureau and (2) many of the broadcast writers in regional bureaus are experienced broadcasters who understand your needs.

As a radio newsperson, you must be aware of how your wire service performs. Be very careful in using wire service copy, especially if you are going to read it as written. Often it is written and edited by people who have no experience reading copy aloud. You may have to edit, update, or rephrase the copy to give it the proper style, freshness, and time frame. One problem with wire services is that they seldom realize that in addition to telling you what has happened, and sometimes what is happening, they need to tell you what is going to happen.

Future stories—those which tell us about upcoming events—are an important mainstay in radio. Radio's most important listener time is the morning, when the news available deals with what happened late yesterday. So a good reporter checks to see what important events will be taking place today. You would naturally tell your listeners what is on today's city council agenda. They need to know in case they want to attend. And your wire service should tell you what the state legislature and the Congress plan to take up today.

Some of the larger broadcast stations use the same writing system used by the wire services and networks. The stations subscribe to one or more newspaper wires and write all their stories from raw newspaper copy. This is an excellent method since each newscast is tailored to the station's own audience, the time of day, and the availability of local news.

You should read over any broadcast wire copy you plan to use, after all, anyone can make an error. Your newsroom may have another type of Teletype machine. Many stations subscribe to a weather wire which carries the official United States government weather forecasts. These are very helpful, especially in areas where severe weather strikes unexpectedly. Also, you have the opportunity of selecting the specific area forecast which best serves your audience. In addition, since the wire services get their weather forecasts from the same wire, you have the weather forecast sooner than you would otherwise.

A word of caution: meteorologists are not journalists. You have to edit or rewrite weather wire copy or you will be speaking gobbledygook as far as your listeners are concerned.

Weather news is important. Almost everyone wants to know about the weather, especially if a storm threatens. Business people, aviators, farmers, and schoolteachers are all affected by the weather. You should remember to include any unusual or noteworthy weather information as part of your newscast. You will be doing an important service for your listeners.

All newsrooms have procedures about "clearing" the wires, which means ripping off the current copy and distributing it to staff members or hanging it on pins for later use. Each staff member in a newsroom is expected to keep an eye on the paper supply for the wire machines and make sure they have fresh ribbons.

Today's radio reporter may encounter a number of other devices in the newsroom. Some areas of the country have weather bureau radio stations which may be monitored by the news department. These can be particularly useful during severe weather, when the weather bureau replaces its tape-recorded forecasts with live reports. A few newsrooms have weather radar to help pinpoint approaching storm systems.

Many stations subscribe to a paging service. These services provide a little monitor or "beeper" which can be put in a pocket or worn on a belt. When the device "beeps," the reporter calls a designated number to receive a message. Combining this device with two-way radio gives the radio newsperson great flexibility in responding to new or emergency situations.

Many radio newsrooms are equipped for recording and tape editing. This is largely determined by whether a station has a technician's union and, if so, what functions the union reserves in its contract. Assuming your station has no union, you will probably work with various tape recorders, cartridge machines, and editing equipment.

The ultimate tape recorder is a heavy-duty machine which plays quarter-inch-wide reel tape. It will offer high fidelity response and precise editing capability. Few newsrooms get into this sort of equipment unless they produce documentaries. Most newsrooms have somewhat smaller reel tape machines which can be used for editing, recording telephone conversations, and dubbing off cassettes.

Stations usually play back news tapes on reel tape or cartridges. Cartridges are plastic containers which have an endless spool of quarter-inch audiotape inside. When something is recorded on a cartridge, the cartridge machine automatically puts a signal on the tape, which causes the endless tape to stop when it returns to the beginning. This is called recuing.

Cartridges are very convenient because they are easily labeled and can be inserted into a playback machine in a couple of seconds and will start precisely on cue. Since news tapes are frequently played by the control board operator (who may be either a technician or a disc jockey), this is a convenient system. The mechanical operation is smooth and efficient with cartridges. Reel tapes take longer to cue up since they must be threaded on a tape recorder and then rewound for removal.

Editing means physically cutting the tape and joining up the proper pieces. One popular device is the editing block, which is a rectangular piece of metal with a slot running its length and an angle-wise groove. The block is used with a single-edge razor blade, which is pulled across the diagonal slot at precisely the point the cut is to be made. There are other devices which generally have built-in blades and some type of clamp to hold the tape in place.

Tape recorder maintenance is generally a technical job, but you should keep the machine and the area around it clean. It is also a good idea to keep a little container of alcohol handy along with some cotton swabs, which are used to clean off the tape recorder's heads. A little film of magnetic oxide rubs off the tape and impairs the effectiveness of the heads. The alcohol-soaked swab removes this film and other dirt.

Editing is easy unless you need some very precise work done, and this takes experience. But radio production is complicated. If you hope to do documentaries or your station wants very sophisticated reports involving background sounds and the like, you will have to become acquainted with control boards, mixers, and the use of multiple tape recorders. If you have the opportunity, take a course in radio production. It will prove useful.

HOW THE NEWSROOM FUNCTIONS

In the majority of cases your newsroom will have a supervisory person responsible to management. The title may be news director, news editor, managing editor, news manager, or news supervisor. This person will play a major role in determining who does what in the department and will have a say in hiring personnel and evolving a budget for the news operation.

You must take into consideration the fact that the news department is only one of many functions of a broadcast station. Unless you are working in an all-news or news-and-talk operation the larger part of the broadcast day will be taken up by other types of programing, probably music. In addition, every station has sales personnel, engineers, publicity specialists, operations specialists, and accounting specialists. The relative importance of the news department within the station's organization varies with the attitude of management and the quantity of news programing done.

In the broadcast journalism field, the objective is to have a news director who reports directly to the top management—probably to the general manager. In some stations the news department is under the overall supervision of the program department, but the specialized interests of the news department often lead to a rather unhappy union.

Under the ideal situation, news personnel would do only news, but this standard varies according to the size of the station. But for the sake of this discussion, it is assumed that the news department has equal status with other departments and that its personnel do only news.

The news director in a radio station also may deliver one or more of the major newscasts. Most radio stations cannot afford the luxury of having a news director who only administers.

From day to day one of the most important management activities which takes place in the newsroom is assigning story coverage. Depending again on the size of the station, this may be done by the news director or by an assignment editor.

The assignment editor's job is to keep track of everything that's going on and to be alert for breaking stories. The assignment editor allocates coverage according to personnel available. Good record keeping is important. The editor will have a filing system for newspaper clippings, carbons of news scripts, press releases, letters, notes, and the like which are used to plan upcoming events. In addition there are certain routine events which may require coverage. The City Council and School Board will have set meeting days and times. The assignment editor will determine if coverage is necessary by talking with the beat reporter and by studying the agenda.

The assignment editor (along with the news director) also thinks up assignments. It is important to take an overview of what is going on and to see if there is a story that needs to be told. Perhaps the assignment editor will read in a magazine somewhere that garbage dumps can develop pockets of highly volatile methane gas. So a reporter is put to work finding out how garbage is handled in your town, and it is discovered that this dangerous condition could exist at the local dump. This is thinking journalism.

The reporter is an important link in the assignment process. Be certain to keep notes on upcoming events you come across in your travels. Examples include meetings that are announced during other meetings. The planning director might tell the City Council that a particular zoning problem will be discussed later in the week by the Planning Board. You would give the assignment editor a note about the meeting including when it will be held, why, and any background you can gather. You are your editor's eyes and ears in the community. Any time you come across a news source, get your station on the source's mailing list so you will be notified of important developments.

And as a reporter you have to jog the assignment editor about dates. For example, suppose you covered a murder trial three weeks ago in which the defendant was found guilty. It's up to you to find out when the judge will pronounce sentence, and then you must tell the assignment editor.

You also should be looking for stories to cover. Perhaps you are driving through town and discover that construction equipment is being moved onto a piece of vacant land. Stop and talk with the construction people, and then contact the assignment editor. It may be worth a story if the new building plays some important role in the community.

Some news departments have copy editors. A copy editor reads every piece of news copy that is going to be read on the air. Corrections are made, rewrites are ordered, tape inserts are planned, and generally high standards of quality are preserved. In stations which have this system the copy editor has the final word—if the editor says no to a piece of copy, it does not go on the air.

News departments in larger cities often have writers who prepare the newscasts and take in tape reports from field reporters. They also interview newsmakers on the telephone. The writers often direct the cutting of tape material recorded by the news department. For example, if the Secretary of Defense is speaking at a local hotel, the station might order a direct line to the room where the speech is being given. A technician sets up microphones and a remote unit, and a writer listens as the speech is being recorded back at the station. The writer then selects appropriate cuts (excerpts) and writes the script to introduce them.

Very large news departments may have a secretary or news assistants who take care of routine duties, such as answering phones and clearing wire machines. It's difficult to generalize about news department organization. While small stations usually have only one, two, or three news staffers, you occasionally come across a small-town station with a much larger staff.

A typical arrangement is for a station to have combination reporter-newscasters who write their own copy. Each reporter may be responsible for a certain number of broadcasts plus some field reporting. In smaller markets, as we noted in talking about Oelwein, Iowa, the newspersons work long hours. Sometimes each reporter is given responsibility for covering certain routine events, such as City Council meetings. If the Council meets twice a month, then the reporter assigned goes, regardless of regular working hours.

Here's how the staffing of a theoretical news department in a small city might work:

5 a.m. — News director visits city police and state police and then returns to station to make phone calls and prepare and deliver early newscasts.

8 a.m. — Next newscaster arrives to start with 9 a.m. broadcast and do newscasts through 1 p.m. News director then takes care of administrative matters and checks the day's assignments. News director may stay at the station acting as a backup reporter or may run a regular beat. In addition, there are meetings to attend and studio interviews and public affairs programs to record. News director also may prepare a special news analysis or write the editorials.

10 a.m. — Next reporter arrives to work outside during the morning and reads newscasts in the afternoon. The 8 a.m. newscaster works outside in the afternoon.

5 p.m. — Evening newscaster arrives. This is strictly an inside job. Night assignments are handled by the reporters who cover specific meetings with support from part-timers and the news director.

Most stations employ part-time newscasters who do the weekend newscasts, and sometimes during low listenership hours they may be supplemented by staff announcers reading the news. Many stations manage to train one or two part-time reporters, frequently bright college students getting their first professional exerience.

What we have described is a bare bones radio news department with everyone doing a number of jobs and working very hard. Obviously, a great deal of news gathering is done by telephone.

SOURCES OF NEWS

Some of the sources have already been discussed. They include wire services, emergency service monitors, phone beats, and the assignment file.

The newsroom will get the local newspapers. Generally, well-run aggressive news departments don't need to copy anything from the newspapers. They serve as sources of assignments and provide background clippings for stories. Also, since the newspapers can afford to have more reporters on the street, they may cover news sources not normally contacted by a broadcast station.

In this instance, the best that can be done is to pick up the story at the point it appears in the paper, confirm the facts, and then try to advance it or elaborate by making phone calls and interviewing the people involved.

For example, say the Sanitation Department might be bypassed by a busy radio reporter, but the local newspaper's City Hall reporter has more time and will occasionally visit the Sanitation Department. Good radio reporters seldom get caught this way, because they will plan to make one extra call a day to the less frequently contacted sources so that, hopefully, they will be contacted when something important comes up.

If the station is affiliated with a radio network, it not only gets hourly newscasts and a selection of features but will get a limited number of separate audio reports for insertion in local newscasts. Some affiliation contracts also permit stations to lift news reports from the network newscasts and reuse them. Some all-news operations do this, but music and news stations seldom need the extra audio.

You should check the billboards of the closed-circuit tape feeds provided by the network. They may include stories not only of national interest but of specific interest to your community. Say your city has a major automobile assembly plant. Then an actuality cut of the president of the United Auto Workers union might fit into your local newscast. Some stations use the national and international stories provided on network closed-circuit feeds on their major newsblocks when it is desirable to repeat the world and national news, even though it has been covered earlier by the network. This is particularly true of stations which program half-hour and hour blocks of news and information during morning and evening drive times.

The major networks are ABC (four separate networks), CBS, Mutual, and NBC. In addition, there are specialized national networks providing news of particular interest to black and Hispanic audiences.

Recently NBC added another network, called the News and Information Service, which operates like a nationwide all-news radio station, providing large blocks of world and national news each hour with breaks for the local station to do community and regional news. The end result is a continuous news service, except that unlike the original all-news stations which did most of their news locally, a majority of the news on the NBC affiliated stations comes from the network.

There are a number of audio services available to radio stations. The two largest are those of United Press International (UPI Audio) and Associated Press (AP Radio). They operate round the clock, providing reports and actualities.

Usually the companion wire service carries a list of upcoming material on its radio wire. Many stations have automatic equipment which starts at the beginning of each audio feed. Thus, the news personnel can check the billboard and then quickly run the tape back to the particular actuality or spot they want.

The audio service is a big help to an independent nonnetwork station because it increases the station's ability to cover national and international news with the voices of the newsmakers and reporters. It makes for a much more interesting newscast.

The two major services, AP and UPI, also provide hourly newscasts to their subscribers. They have positions for local commercials and also internal cutaway cues so that various lengths of newscasts can be carried. Small stations find this service very useful in off-peak hours when there may be no local newscaster on duty. It also allows the staff of a local station to spend more time on regional and local stories.

There are many more services. For example, the Westinghouse stations have their own private news exchange. There are specialized services for ethnic stations, and in some parts of the country there are regional networks. Some of these provide only news reports and actuality; others provide full-fledged network wervices including newscasts and features. Frequently these regional networks concentrate on state capitol news.

In some areas the wire services also participate in a news exchange. A station which has a piece of tape of statewide interest will call the wire service bureau and ask that a short note be put on the broadcast wire. Other stations can then call the contributor to record the feed.

Another type of audio service is offered by private industry and the government. This is a prerecorded statement or actuality that is obtained by calling a number which actuates an automatic tape recorder playback unit. There is one inherent problem with these services. The material is prerecorded by the source, so you cannot talk to an individual to get more details or expand on a point. You will be lucky if you can even edit the tape effectively. What you get is a report purposely designed to put forward certain ideas. The better run news organizations steer away from these services. Also, there are legal requirements about entering the source of the material or announcing it in the newscast copy.

There is one major exception. The national weather service in a number of localities has set up a recorded weather forecast for broadcast stations. This is a matter of convenience for the service, and the weather reports are designed specifically for use on broadcast stations.

One major source available to any station is its corps of "stringers." *Stringers* are people who provide tips or news stories for a small per-story fee. Stringers can come from almost any background. In rural areas one good source of stringers is the weekly newspapers. The reporters for these small papers may need quite a bit of guidance as to what to supply promptly, but they usually have an intimate knowledge of their community and can provide unique coverage.

Sometimes stringers are retired news people or ex-reporters working in some other field. The stringer does not have to be a trained reporter, because the most important thing the stringer does for you is to give the initial information. You should be able to follow up in person or on the telephone once you have the tip.

There is another type of stringer called the *freelancer*. The freelancer usually makes news gathering a fulltime occupation but has no definite affiliation with one station. This type of relationship is useful for coverage of the state capitol or some large nearby city which is not in the station's primary coverage area. In one large Eastern city a radio freelancer provides actuality audio coverage for a number of local stations. He feeds them raw tape of certain events, and they cut it to fit their needs. It saves the stations from all having to go and record certain static events, such as news conferences.

The stringer process works in reverse, too. The wire services, radio networks, audio services, and regional services rely on stringers for their stories and leads. Many news departments permit their employees to supply stories to these outlets. It provides a small supplement to their salaries, plus exposure and contacts which are helpful to the young and ambitious newsperson.

Sometimes radio stations work out exchange agreements with other stations. Usually these situations occur where the station feels a need to cover stories which take place in some other locality not in its primary service area. Usually the stations involved are basically noncompetitive and exchange the stories on a no-cost basis.

Many radio news departments have a regular system of encouraging tips on news stories. It used to be a popular idea to pay a small amount to members of the public who called with news tips. This sort of approach is less common today as radio stations have somewhat reduced coverage of crimes, auto accidents, and fires. Some stations do have another type of tip system. For example, the station might agree with the chief of the county fire station that if the dispatchers had a major fire working they would call and tell the station about it. In turn, the station would make a contribution to the firemen's welfare fund or the like. This works very well in areas which have volunteer fire departments. Usually a charity is donated to so that no individuals can be accused of having a conflict of interest.

There are also unsolicited tips. Some people will call and tip their favorite station gratis. Sometimes they do this because they know the reporter and other times because they just want to be involved in the news process in some manner. Tips of this sort have to be checked thoroughly. And don't turn away the irate or complaining caller. He or she may have a point and may end up revealing a whole new angle to your story.

A small but very necessary part of a reporter's time is consumed by record keeping. Most stations keep records of general phone calls, stringer calls, and tapes. In addition, careful filing of newscasts as read is mandatory.

Whatever the system, do your part to keep it functioning. Systems in newsrooms usually are there for a good reason, primarily to keep a record of what went on in case a question is asked later, and to make sure that stringers and the like receive their accurate pay.

ALL-NEWS RADIO

The most exciting development in radio news in recent years has been the growth of all-news radio. Radio went into a period of depression in the 1950s when television became popular. In the 1960s the emphasis was on music, but as FM stations began to move into the music market, AM stations began to look around for a new formula. Two trends developed. In the mid-1960s a few large stations in major markets converted to doing only news for the greater part of the day. Other stations experimented with talk radio, in which a moderator held telephone conversations with members of the public. Both formats enjoyed gradual success and have led many industry observers to say that the future of AM radio is in talk and FM in music. Interestingly enough, the competition among music formats is so stiff on FM that experiments are underway doing all-news on FM.

All news formats gained early acceptance in New York, Philadelphia, Chicago, Los Angeles, and Washington, D.C. Gradually stations in other markets experimented with various forms of extended news formats, news, and talk, with big blocks of news in drive time.

An all-news station is very different from a music and news station. Even a very large music station is not likely to have more than a dozen employees in the radio newsroom. But an all-news station may have a very large staff. There are anchor reporters who must be changed relatively frequently to lessen monotony. There are editors, producers, writers, and assistants. There are also specialists in public affairs programs who produce features and minidocumentaries. And there are sports reporters, weather reporters, business reporters, consumer reporters, and other specialists. This type of operation also requires a large engineering staff.

In some ways an all-news radio station is a continuous newspaper. It differs in that there is no need to stop the presses and deliver an edition to the street. So the basic budget of key stories often remains the same for some time, but instant updates are done as a story unfolds. The all-news station still suffers from a lack of depth because the concept is not built around taking 5 or 10 minutes to explain one story.

However, some all-news stations are now putting newsmakers on the air live and interviewing them for several minutes at a time. The way a more complicated topic is handled is to take 20 minutes of material and split it into five 5-minute features, which can run on following days or following hours, depending on how you want to space them.

All-news radio is a format designed to permit the listener to tune in for a short time to be brought up to date on the major news at that hour. Ironically, although the all-news stations started out with the idea that people would tune in for short periods, they have now found that many people listen for extended periods. As a result many all-news operations are paying more attention to the personality of their anchor reporters and to more interesting features to break up the monotony.

I asked Morry Alter, news director of all-news KSDO in San Diego, California, to describe an all-news operation. KSDO has drawn a great deal of attention for attempting the all-news format in a medium-sized market which receives signals from two all-news stations in Los Angeles.

Alter described KSDO this way: "KSDO has a staff of 20 full- and part-time newspeople. About 12 of them are editorial employees. They are not on the air; they do everything from rewriting local community newspapers to carting audio feeds to telephone beat checks. We have seven and one-half on-the-air people; one is a sports director. Included in the 20 are 4 editors who man the desk for 4-to-5-hour periods and a managing editor. The managing editor is generally in charge of the editorial people and does some street reporting. I am your basic news director, but I also am your basic business news editor doing on-the-air reports in morning drive, and I also anchor a few hours of the midday.

"Coverage: The above set-up allows us, by having each anchor doing 4- or 5-hour stretches, to put 2 or 3 on-the-air people on the street during the day. It even allows some street coverage in the early evening. We stress live reportage of whatever it is we are covering. So if the City Council sneezes, we do a live report "from where it's happening." For instance, we have our own booth and line at City Hall, three radio-equipped mobile units, etc. There is also one other live aspect of KSDO. Within the context of our all-news format, we do live interviews. In morning drive they are rare, short, and

99% of them would be of a hard news nature, i.e., Cranston in Washington on a bill just signed. In midday a live interview might consume most of a 6- or 7-minute news package and be as soft as an author interview. We find these live interviews generate considerable material for the rest of the day."

KSDO is a network affiliate and so has the benefit of an hourly network newscast and roughly one feature an hour from the network plus special coverage of major events. The advent of the all-news station has raised radio news journalism to a much higher status. The number of opportunities for topnotch radio journalists has increased a great deal.

The principles the individual radio journalist applies to all-news radio differ little from any other news operation. The most important element to consider is that an all-news operation can at any time update a story or develop, while traditional music and news formats have less flexibility. All-news reporters must work faster, be quicker getting their reports in, and be prepared to do live reports from notes and memory.

The all-news stations have a format. It usually involves headlines or a full-fledged network newscast on the hour, followed by quarter-hour summaries. The sports, weather, traffic reports, and certain features all have their predetermined positions.

The exact mixture of features and hard news differs with the time of day. The commuter hours are heavy with headlines, weather, traffic reports, and the like. Features which might be of greater interest to homebound people are scheduled for midmorning to midafternoon. And in the late afternoon, there is usually a heavy diet of business news. On weekends the all-news operations often have frequent sports capsules.

When an important story breaks, the all-news station is one step ahead of the game. There is no hassle over interrupting or preempting a music program. The news budget is simply expanded and changed to account for the developing situation. A good all-news station can do an outstanding job with a rapidly breaking story.

Some all-news stations put great emphasis on the personalities of the anchorpersons, often using a dual anchor arrangement in drive times. Other all-news stations believe the anchorperson is incidental to the news itself and tend to choose a less recognizable anchorperson.

Some all-news stations in smaller markets have survived by having more than one network affiliation, thus cutting down on the amount of local time that has to be filled. This is the essential idea to NBCs News and Information Service—to provide world and national news for the greater part of the hour and let the local station fill a shorter period.

Another outgrowth of all-news radio is a major push to utilize electronics in news gathering. An all-news reporter can be carrying a tape recorder, a paging device, and a portable police monitor. And the car or mobile unit is probably parked nearby with two-way radio equipment, police monitors, and possibly a portable telephone to be plugged into telephone outlets installed in key locations around the city.

The all-news reporter not only has to get the initial report and its format on the air quickly, he or she must be thinking of a way to write the story for use overnight, when there aren't any new stories breaking. And some all-news reporters also find themselves being asked to file stories for networks or other stations owned by the same company.

Inside writers and reporters at all-news stations do a great deal of their work on the telephone, following up stories to get interviews and to quickly gather facts and actuality on breaking stories.

The anchor reporters have particularly challenging jobs because they must give the station a good air sound, deal with updates while broadcasting, handle live interviews or short notice switches to reporters and, in most cases, read commercials. As a result, salaries in some markets for all-news anchor reporters compare favorably with salaries of big-city television reporters.

One odd thing about radio: All-news and talk stations are taking over the role of providing the live human voice for the listener. Music stations have moved so heavily into automation to reduce operating costs that they have nearly eliminated the humanity of the announcer who occasionally makes an error or gets a cough.

The advent of all-news stations has also created challenging opportunities for radio journalists. Not only are writers, editors, and reporters needed, but all news radio has moved heavily into features and documentaries.

6
The Television Reporter

Television news gathering is going through an electronic revolution. Until recently television news provided a summary of the day's events up to a certain hour. in much the same manner as is done by a newspaper. But recent developments in electronic news gathering. or ENG. have moved television news gathering more nearly into the same frame of reference as radio. (See Fig. 6-1.) It is now possible for a television station with the proper equipment to put a news story on live at any time during the day as well as inserting new material into a scheduled newscast with little or no delay.

The reason the newscast on television used to be similar to publishing a newspaper was that like a paper. there came a point when news gathering had to stop. The last two hours before the newscast were largely devoted to getting materials ready. Similarly. newspaper gets its type "locked up" and then has to wait a while for the paper to be printed. folded. bundled. and delivered.

The television station used to have to figure on having enough time to develop and edit film or to edit tape. This meant that only a bare minimum of new material could be added at the last minute. In most cases. late-breaking stories had to be covered by writing a fresh script for the anchorperson or by using a live or recorded reporter's voice with a slide or film taken from the files.

The development of lightweight video equipment and high-quality. battery-operated videotape recording equipment has changed the whole pace of television news. (See Fig. 6-2.) Videotape eliminates the time lost in processing film.

Add new portable microwave equipment to relay the on-scene sound and picture back to the studio. and you

Fig. 6-1. A new lightweight electronic camera in use at Chicago fire. (Courtesy CBS television stations.)

Fig. 6-2. A lightweight camera and portable videotape in use. Note that the camera operator is using a motion-picture camera tripod for stable support. (Courtesy WFMY-TV, Greensboro, N.C.)

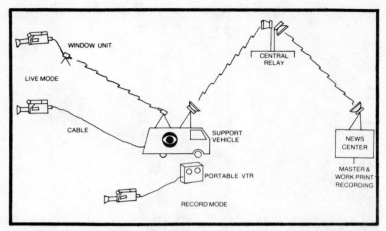

Fig. 6-3. This illustrates the various ways in which electronic news gathering (ENG) equipment can be used. In the **upper left** the camera output is transmitted from a window of a building to the truck on the street. In the **lower left** the camera unit is connected by cable to the equipment in the truck. In the **center** the camera is connected to a portable tape recorder. The truck can send the sound and picture back to the newsroom using a microwave transmitter, whose output is aimed at a fixed relay station called the central relay. The central relay retransmits mobile unit pictures from several locations back to the newsroom. (Courtesy CBS television stations.)

eliminate the time it takes to transport the story materials back to the station. (See Fig. 6-3.)

Poof! There goes the 2-hour barrier. Now. it is possible to broadcast live from the scene of a news story using highly portable equipment. Today. doing a live remote no longer means moving a vehicle approximately the size of an intercity bus into position. and then making extensive arrangements with the telephone company for transmission lines. All that is needed is a station wagon or panel truck and two crew members to accompany the reporter.

In fact. for small stations the package is smaller. providing you do not want to broadcast live. All that is needed is a portable videotape unit weighing as little as 22 pounds—very competitive in weight with a film camera. (See Fig. 6-4.) A reporter and camera operator. or even a reporter alone. can go out. shoot a story with sound. partially edit the tape in the portable machine. and return to the newsroom with a story ready for airing.

The other developments which have transformed television news gathering have to do with editing. Years ago

Fig. 6-4. A lightweight, portable videotape recording unit. This three-piece unit is popular because of its convenient size and relatively low cost. (Courtesy "Broadcast Management Engineering".)

videotape had to be physically cut, like audiotape. Then, electronic editing came along. Now you can select scenes from a raw videotape and instruct a computer to assemble the finished story.

Television news has now completed its breakthrough into the electronic age. The resulting challenges will create a new breed of television reporters.

THE TELEVISION NEWSROOM

There are similarities between radio and television newsrooms: they both have typewriters and desks, police monitors, and wire service machines. But in many television newsrooms, the electronic revolution has brought about a total change in the appearance and operation of the newsroom.

Until recently a television newsroom resembled its radio counterpart except that nearby there were film editing, processing, and viewing facilities. But today there's a touch of the science-fiction spaceship in newsrooms which have been redesigned specifically to accommodate electronic news-gathering equipment and techniques. (See Fig. 6-5.)

A common approach is to have the newsroom dominated by a big console. The assignment editor—sometimes called the news coordinator—sits at the console. Several television

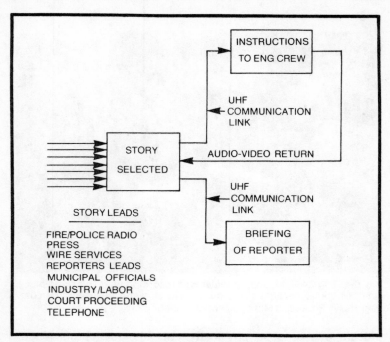

Fig. 6-5. An outline of electronic news gathering. Story leads are gathered by the electronic news coordinator, who assigns reporters and crews, giving separate instructions to the ENG crew and the reporter. They keep in touch by UHF radio, and all parties share in their ability to look at the picture and listen to the sound on the audio-video return. Using the UHF radio, they compare notes about the editorial and technical aspects of the story. (Courtesy CBS television stations.)

monitors (closed-circuit television receivers) are built into the console. The news coordinator can watch the pictures being transmitted to the station by the mobile units. Using two-way radio equipment also built into the console. the news coordinator gives instructions to the field crew. Often the coordinator and producers in the newsroom have a better idea how the picture looks than does the reporter on the scene. If a change needs to be made. the coordinator can use the radio link to tell the reporter or crew what needs to be done. This two-way radio system also permits the coordinator to make suggestions about the manner in which the story is covered and even to suggest questions to the reporter. (See Fig. 6-6.)

The coordinator can watch the station's on-air signal. which is important during newscasts and when live coverage

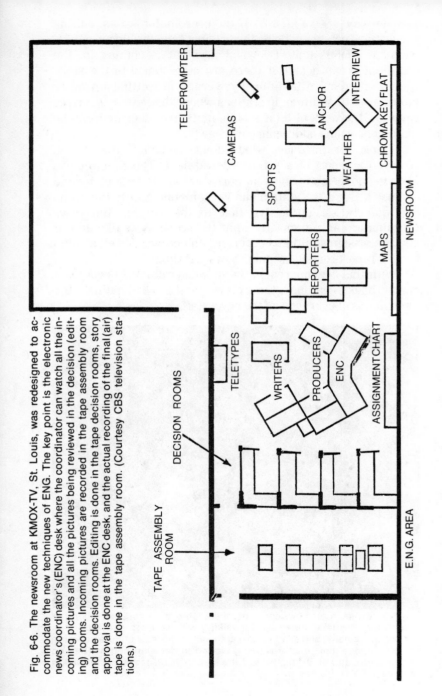

Fig. 6-6. The newsroom at KMOX-TV, St. Louis, was redesigned to accommodate the new techniques of ENG. The key point is the electronic news coordinator's (ENC) desk where the coordinator can watch all the incoming pictures and all the pictures being reviewed in the decision (editing) rooms. Incoming pictures are recorded in the tape assembly room and the decision rooms. Editing is done in the tape decision rooms, story approval is done at the ENC desk, and the actual recording of the final (air) tape is done in the tape assembly room. (Courtesy CBS television stations.)

is underway. (See Fig. 6-7.) If the coordinator wants, editing suggestions can be made as the original tape is being received from the mobile unit. By watching what is coming in, the coordinator can decide if there are other parts to the story which will require additional coverage or setting up other interviews. In addition, in stations where the news executives can view the work of their mobile units live, decisions can be made concerning additional coverage.

Think, for instance, what might happen if the station received a report of a subway derailment. The first reports from the police and transit authority are apt to be sketchy and confused. But if the station can get a mobile unit to the scene and quickly set up a live link to the station, the news coordinator can see exactly what the scene looks like and, if need be, assign additional reporters and crews as well as plan for live reports outside regular newscast times.

With this new approach, the news coordinator becomes a quarterback, calling the plays and coordinating the movements of everyone on the news staff.

Fig. 6-7. An electronic news coordinator standing at his console, talking to a reporter. The telephones are for talking with sources and reporters. Television screens (at his left elbow) are used to monitor pictures coming in from mobile units, pictures being viewed in decision booths (behind coordinator), and on-air pictures of the station. (Courtesy CBS television stations.)

Fig. 6-8. An assignment editor at work. Here an electronic news coordinator at KMOX-TV in St. Louis checks pins on his map to locate the best microwave transmission point for an ENG van. (Courtesy CBS television stations.)

Regarding structure. most television newsrooms have a more formal organization than radio newsrooms. This is because there are apt to be more people on the staff and because television requires more of a team approach.

In addition to the reporters and the film or tape crews which accompany them, there are behind-the-scenes people who play important roles in the production of the newscasts. The anchorpersons and reporters are the people publicly identified with presenting the news, but they are only part of a bigger team.

The chief executive of a news department is usually called the news director. The news director, depending on station policy. also may appear on the air. In larger stations news directors usually concern themselves with long-term planning, policy. budgets, and the administrative direction of their team.

The key job in the newsroom usually belongs to the assignment editor or news coordinator. (See Fig. 6-8.) This person must keep track of assignments, juggle personnel to get the assignments covered. research stories. and coordinate the logistics of the station's news coverage.

In larger stations a producer (sometimes called an executive producer) is assigned to each newscast. It is the producer who is really responsible for the appearance and content of an individual newscast. The news director will set the format and policy. but it is the producer—working closely with the assignment editor (or news coordinator)—who really builds the newscast.

Some stations employ news writers to write the on-camera scripts and lead-ins and lead-outs for film or videotape reports. In addition. writers frequently prepare stories for the air. while the reporters move on to other assignments. This is particularly true in newsrooms which have converted to electronic news gathering. If the station has a microwave link the writer can watch the incoming picture (see Fig. 6-9) and begin picking out key parts for the story. Even if the tape has to be transported back to the station. the writer can view it and begin constructing the finished story. Usually the news coordinator and the producer watch the initial showing of the tape and make suggestions on how they would like to see the story handled. Frequently the reporter joins in the conference. by radio. so that the views of all key participants in the final preparation of the story can be heard.

The writers also take care of certain routine duties. such as viewing the stories fed on the network closed-circuit transmission and writing lead-ins for the pieces that will be used on the early or late news. Sometimes a writer will watch a network feed or a sporting event and write a script to go with excerpts of the videotape of the event which the writer has asked the engineering department to pull out.

Some news departments have associate or assistant producers. They are usually responsible only for part of a newscast. An associate producer may be asked to prepare several stories and to see that all the parts are coordinated and additional coverage ordered if necessary. It's like producing a miniprogram. The associate producer is responsible for one or more segments of perhaps 2 to 4 minutes each.

Most news departments have positions that utilize young people just out of school. They may be called interns or desk assistants. Depending on union rules. these young people may do little more than answer telephones. tear copy off wire

Fig. 6-9. A writer viewing tape from an ENG remote in a decision booth. High-quality copy of the incoming tape was recorded in the tape assembly room (through the window) while the editing copy is simultaneously recorded on a machine at the writer's left. She watches the bottom of the screen for key numbers, writes down scenes she wishes to use, and makes out an editing form which is then used by engineers in the tape assembly room to program a computer to make up an actual air tape. (Courtesy CBS television stations.)

machines. and run errands. But in some stations the bright and capable assistants are given increasingly more important tasks to do. and if there are no other rules preventing upward mobility. they may become writers, assistant producers, or even reporters.

There's another side to a television newsroom. The reporting efforts of the newstaff must be backed up by technicians. There will be camera operators (whether the station uses motion picture film or videotape) plus additional crew members for the field crew. In a small station a camera operator may work alone, but in a larger station a videotape crew will consist of at least two persons, and a film crew can be made up of from two to four persons (including the camera operator, the sound operator, the lighting specialist, and the stagehand or "grip").

In film operations there will be one or more technicians who specialize in processing the film, and in electronic operations there will be technicians (see Fig. 6-10) who record the incoming tapes and the final assembly of the finished stories.

In some stations that use film there are specialists known as editors who edit the film once it has been processed. In other stations, the editing is done by the camera operators.

ASSIGNMENTS

The assignment process is more formal in television. Usually when an assignment editor thinks up an assignment a

Fig. 6-10. A tape assembly room. The incoming picture and sound are recorded on a tape recorder in front of the engineer. A computer (not shown) is given instructions, and it does the final assembly. Engineers in the tape assembly room have communications links with engineers in the mobile units. (Courtesy CBS television stations.)

form is filled out. It gives pertinent information about the location and objective of the piece, who will be interviewed, and some guidelines regarding technical needs. The assignment sheet will include information about meeting the reporter, special equipment or types of film which will be needed, and an estimate of the amount of film or tape which should be used. When the crew comes back from a film assignment, they will note the amount of film actually used. This is less important with tape because videotape can be erased and used again.

The reporter and the assignment editor usually do some preliminary work on the assignment. They call and gather background, discuss any special arrangements which need to be made, check the background files and, if time permits, do some actual research on the assignment.

If a group of people and a car or truck full of equipment are going to be sent out, it is best to have the clearest possible idea of what they are being asked to do.

FIELD REPORTING

A television reporter is more than a note-taker and interviewer. The reporter must be aware of production techniques and problems and also must be constantly thinking about appearance and performance. This can lead to a case of schizophrenia for the novice reporter, but this multilevel approach to duties is soon gotten used to.

Let's dream up an assignment: suppose that you have to interview a City Council member who takes serious exception to a proposed exit ramp off the interstate highway. The first thing you do is to make an appointment with the Council member. Say it's set for 11 a.m. at the member's office. The time is now 9:20 a.m. You type up an assignment sheet for the specific task and check it with the assignment editor. The editor then assigns you a crew.

The crew checks out the mobile unit and equipment. Batteries must be fresh, and there must be fresh supplies of videotape put aboard to replace what was used yesterday. Before you go downtown you decide to drive by the site of the proposed exit ramp. The crew shoots tape of the site, both from a stationary position and as you drive up and down the ramps.

After you have finished shooting the interchange area, you park the mobile unit, and the electronic technician on the crew lines up the microwave antenna with a fixed relay point the station has established on a downtown building. The signal goes to the relay, which then retransmits it to the television station. The engineering department makes a high-quality copy of your feed, while a "work copy" is recorded for use by the newsroom. During the transmission the assignment editor or news coordinator watches the incoming picture and makes notes on what has been transmitted. One of the writers also watches, so that he or she can start thinking about the visual approach to your story.

This procedure out of the way, you continue on to the Council member's office. (See Fig. 6-11.) While you and the Council member are discussing the proposed ramp, the camera operator sets up the lightweight camera on an equally lightweight tripod and then runs the camera cable to a small, shoebox-size portable microwave transmitter, which is set up on the window-sill. The shoebox transmitter is aimed down at the mobile unit, which is parked below on the street. (See Fig. 6-11.) (If you had been in a windowless area, you would have simply videotaped the interview and then transmitted it to the station when you returned to the mobile unit.)

Fig. 6-11. A miniature microwave transmitter (left foreground) is transmitting pictures from an ENG camera out the window to a mobile van parked below on the street (lower right). (Courtesy CBS television stations.)

Fig. 6-12. A electronic news-gathering van. The truck has microwave equipment (the engineer atop the truck is adjusting the microwave "dish"); a lightweight, portable, color television camera; a portable videotape recorder; and a two-way communications equipment. (Courtesy CBS television stations.)

The electronic technician in the mobile unit (see Fig. 6-12) makes sure you have a clean signal coming into the videotape machine and then lines up a microwave relay to retransmit your signal directly to the station. When all the links are established. the news coordinator will be able to talk with you and with the crew during the interview. Because the television camera is so sensitive. it isn't necessary to set up any lights, even though the office is not brightly lighted.

You ask your questions and then. at the suggestion of the news coordinator. go back over one point with the Council member. The news coordinator who was watching and listening to the interview noticed that one response would not seem clear to someone in the audience who was not familiar with the topic. Sometimes a reporter. who has studied up on a topic. does not notice that the answer is a little technical or difficult to understand, and this is where having the live link with the newsroom helps. This way a question and answer which might have to be scrapped otherwise can be salvaged by rephrasing the question.

The whole procedure of setting up and doing the interview takes only 20 minutes, and before a half-hour has elapsed you are back in the mobile unit, the equipment is stowed, and you are ready to roll.

Then the news coordinator calls you on the radio and tells you that a 1:30 p.m. interview has been set up with a city Transportation Department official who favors the new ramp. Since all of your material has already been transmitted back to the studio, you may do one of two things. If you have a bit of spare time before lunch you may get on the radio and confer with the news coordinator and the writer about how the story should be edited. In fact, the writer may go ahead and edit the first interview once everyone agrees on how it should be done.

The editing process consists of looking at the videotape and writing down key times or numbers which are projected on the screen at the same time as the picture. These in-and-out times for scenes will be given to the engineering department for assembly of the final piece, either manually by cuing up the appropriate sections of the tape or, more likely, automatically by a computer which will store all the key numbers and then assemble the finished tape.

This amounts to a major time saving, since now all that has to be done is the editing of your second interview and the insertion of the pictures of the traffic using the highway. Roughly half of the work has been done, and it's not yet noon. Ordinarily, it would be one to two hours more in a film operation before any work was done on the morning film.

The second possibility is that you may be sent to another assignment. The news coordinator may call you and say that there is a small protest demonstration underway at City Hall Plaza, just a couple of blocks from your present location.

You drive over, set up the camera, and establish a live linkup with the station. This takes 5 to 8 minutes at the most. The protest is over a decision to shorten the number of hours children attend school each day, and the news coordinator wants this part of the story included in the noontime news.

You are told to prepare for a live cut-in. Fortunately, you already know enough about the general reasons for the new

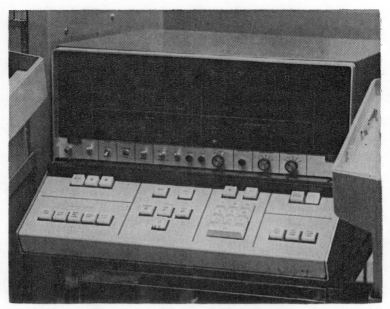

Fig. 6-13. A computer in the tape assembly room. Editing instructions from writers are fed into this computer, and it produces final, assembled air tape. The edited version is then transferred to standard (2-inch) videotape and is ready for broadcast. (Courtesy CBS television stations.)

school hours and why some groups oppose them. In addition, the coordinator has filled you in by radio on details of this particular protest and given you the name of the leader.

You walk up to the group's leader, discuss possible interview questions, and arrange to have her standing by when you get the signal to go on live. In a couple of minutes, the signal comes. You open looking into the camera as the pickets march behind you; then the camera operator widens the shot, and you walk over to join the protest leader. You do a quick interview and close the piece. Right after you get the signal that you are off the air, you record another interview for possible use on tonight's 6 p.m. news. Then for some lunch, and on to your next assignment.

The routine for the 1:30 p.m. interview with the city transportation official is much the same. When you get back outside the building, you tape a short "standupper" consisting of an opening to the topic and first interview, a bridge to go between the interviews, and a closing to go after the second interview. You should try to memorize these short pieces of script so that you can do a smooth on-camera presentation. By 2:15 all of your materials are on file at the station, and the viewing and editing process is well underway.

By the time you return to the newsroom, your piece will be ready for your review and then will be fed to the computer (see Fig. 6-13) for automatic assembly. The editing process is so flexible with electronic news-gathering equipment that if the producer of the 11 p.m. news decides your story should be included in the late news, a whole new piece can be created at the same time the 6 p.m. piece is being assembled by giving the computer a second set of instructions. This is much more efficient than using film, in which it is often necessary to take the film used on the 6 p.m. news, disassemble the reel, and reedit the film for 11 o'clock. Among other advantages, it allows the producer of the late news to get important work done when the newsroom is at full staff rather than trying to edit a new piece with a skeleton crew.

Chances are that your finished piece will be transferred to a videotape cassette. This is similar to an audiotape cassette—a self-contained reel of videotape which can be made to return automatically to its starting point. If your station has a videotape machine which plays cassettes, the producer of the news has maximum flexibility to move your piece around within the show's sequence to meet last-minute changes in the format. Many stations do not yet have this sort of equipment, they simply dub each piece onto a master videotape reel in the order it will be used on the air, much the same as film is handled. As each report is finished, a technician runs the tape forward to the next piece and cues it up to wait for the director's start signal.

Since you have wound up your highway story and it's only 2:15 you and the crew will most likely be sent on at least one more story. This illustrates why a broadcast reporter has to be well-informed and flexible. Unfortunately, the economics of broadcast news are such that in order to have adequate coverage, you have to be prepared to report on from two to four different topics in the same day.

ELECTRONIC NEWS GATHERING

As you have noticed, in constructing our example of a typical reporter's day, I have assumed that your station is fully committed to electronic news gathering. ENG is growing so rapidly that in a short time the industry norm will be completely changed from film news gathering to electronic news gathering. The reasons are twofold. First, there have been significant breakthroughs in equipment and, second, the cost figures are impressive.

A key link in the development of electronic news gathering was the construction of a sturdy, lightweight, battery-operated videotape recorder. Currently, it is possible to get high-quality color pictures on a machine which weighs only about 25 pounds. Most machines use 3_4 in. wide tape, but some experts say it won't be long before the industry will adopt as standard a 1_2 in. wide tape which will run at only 3 in. per second. This will make the equipment even lighter and will increase the amount of recording time available on each reel of videotape.

Another important development is a small television camera capable of operating under extremely low light levels. One network news department demands that any equipment it buys must give a perfectly acceptable hard news picture with only 3 footcandles of illumination. By comparison, an office with only average fluorescent lighting might have 15 footcandles of illumination. This means that a television crew can shoot in a dimly lit office which is paneled in dark wood or out under bright streetlights. A film crew would have to pack up and leave under these conditions or spend quite some time setting up lights.

Developments are moving rapidly in the ENG field, but the equipment has already proved to be so flexible and reliable that it has become standard procedure to use only electronic equipment on both domestic and overseas presidential trips. On the overseas trips, the output of the tape recorders can be hooked directly to the equipment at a satellite ground station, allowing instantaneous live or tape relay of events as they are happening. In fact, the network news departments are rapidly converting their foreign bureaus to electronic equipment. By doing this they automatically eliminate the problem of time lost due to film processing. If a satellite station is readily available, they can eliminate the tortuously slow transportation of their film back to the United States or to major overseas relay points.

After two attempts on the life of President Gerald Ford in 1975, the three television networks switched to all-ENG coverage, because if spot news warrants, they can get on the air very quickly with pictures—again without waiting for film processing.

However, even the best-laid plans can fall apart. In the case of an attempt on the life of President Ford in San Francisco. CBS News found itself falling back on film shot by an affiliated station. The network ENG unit had been turned off to conserve its batteries just before President Ford left a hotel. Even though it takes only ten seconds to get the unit up to power, that was enough to prevent taping the first important seconds after police and a bystander deflected a shot from a would-be assassin's weapon.

Today the majority of ENG-equipped stations are going with the basic package. This consists of a camera and portable videotape recorder and matching editing equipment back at the station. The use of microwave links is developing more slowly because it is costly.

One expert says stations are switching to ENG for three reasons: immediacy, productivity, and economy. Immediacy is important in two ways: (1) If the news warrants doing so, you can go on the air live (with a microwave-equipped unit) either within a regularly-scheduled newscast or by interrupting regular programing. (2) You can eliminate the dead period before a newscast when no new filming is done.

The latter is very significant because many important news events take place in the late afternoon, within two hours of the early evening news. Major boards wind up their deliberations, mayors announce policy, and political hopefuls announce their candidacy.

Another application of ENG which points up immediacy has been tried in St. Louis and other markets. If some controversial public figure has made a statement, you can locate someone with an opposing view (or simply a member of the general public), go to that person's home, and set up the camera. The person is shown watching your report on the news, and then you can switch live to the person in his home for an immediate reaction. This gives the news a genuine feeling of immediacy.

In New York City a major station has on occasion set up its ENG equipment at two widely distant points, invited a panel of experts into the studio, and then let members of the public question the experts live on the air on important questions of general concern.

Productivity is important to a station's management and news director. First. it means being able to cover more stories without enlarging staff. which is crucial with personnel costs in a news operation so high. Second. since the station can cover more stories. the news director and the producers can be suddenly put into a position of having a *choice* of what stories to use rather than using everything that's done. as is the case in most markets. This also means that the 11 p.m. news can have different stories from the 6 p.m. news rather than just reediting some of the stories used earlier.

The increase in productivity (said by one expert to be a 50% increase in number of stories gathered by one crew in a day) also means that on a day when there is a deluge of good stories. the news director does not have to worry about finding staff and crews to cover everything that's happening.

Cost savings is another major reason for switching to ENG. Although the capital investment needed to buy ENG equipment is far greater than to buy equivalent amount of film equipment. the long-run cost of an ENG operation is less.

Recently some comparisons were devised between film and electronic news-gathering costs for three crews operating in a major market. In making the comparison. it was assumed that the station did not use microwave to relay its materials to the station—thus the transportation time and cost would be equal for either a film crew or an ENG crew. Both crews consisted of two operating persons.

In this comparison the equipment needed to take film, process it. edit it. and transport it would cost $87,000. Comparable electronic news-gathering equipment would cost $200.400. (See Fig. 6-14.) Obviously the savings in ENG are not in the initial cost of the equipment.

So let's turn to the cost of labor. The same study showed that film labor costs for one year for three two-member crews would be $234.804. This includes broadcasting. editing and assembling of stories. film processing. and gathering news in the field. The labor costs for comparable ENG crews would amount to $181.054 for the year. So our theoretical television station would have saved almost $54.000 in labor costs during one year. (See Fig. 6-15.)

Turning to operating costs. the study found that the theoretical film operation would spend $114.754 in one year. The ENG crews would cost $32.936 in the same year. The study

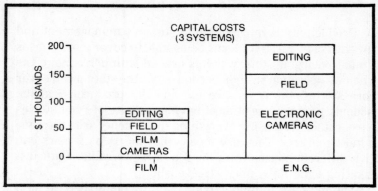

Fig. 6-14. A capital cost comparison for equipping three film and three electronic news-gathering crews. (Courtesy CBS television stations.)

took into consideration space rental. mechanical maintenance, gas and oil. spare parts. electronic and processor maintenance. stock (film or tape). and other factors. Ironically. the maintenance and spare parts costs for ENG are higher. but the big saving comes in the absence of processing chemicals and the reusability of videotape. compared to film. which can be used only once. The difference here favors ENG by $81.800. (See Fig. 6-16.)

The study cited looked at total operating costs based on depreciation. expense. and labor and came up with a total cost for a typical film operation of $366.958 compared to a cost of

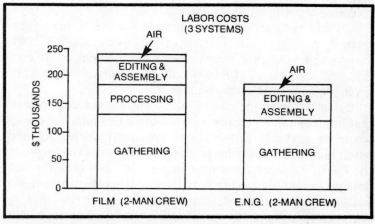

Fig. 6-15. An annual comparison of labor costs for three field crews of two persons each. (Courtesy CBS television stations.)

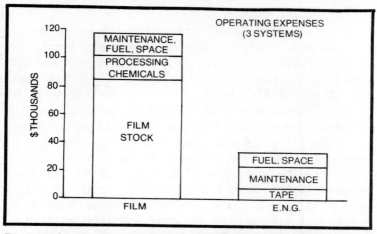

Fig. 6-16. An annual comparison of labor costs for three field crews of three electronic news-gathering systems. (Courtesy CBS television stations.)

$253.670 for a typical ENG operation. That's a difference of $113.288 for one year's operation. (See Fig. 6-17.)

In summary, although ENG equipment would cost about $113.000 more than comparable film equipment, a station could save the $113,000 in the first year's total operating cost alone. Very sophisticated financial analysis done recently on the cost of buying ENG equipment shows that a typical station could pay off the cost in three years, which leaves the station operator with a tax advantage on the capital investment.

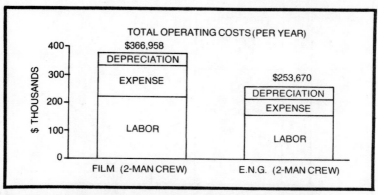

Fig. 6-17. A comparison of total operating costs for one year of comparable film and electronic news crews. (Courtesy CBS television stations.)

The study points out vividly that there are big savings in what is called "stock," film or videotape. According to the study, a typical hour of film costs $285 for processing and stock, while a typical hour of videotape, which can be reused, costs $28. (See Fig. 6-18.) There is some advantage in certain markets in labor costs because the operating union for electronic equipment may have a slightly lower pay scale than the comparable film union. But another big advantage is productivity. Even if the tape has to be transported, the time consumed in the final preparation for air is far less with tape because there is no processing time and because editing can be done more quickly. If a station invests in microwave equipment, the productivity per crew can increase as much as 50% over film. (See Fig. 6-19.)

These figures should drive home the point that electronic news gathering is here to stay, and modern reporters and producers will have to learn to make skillful use of these new tools. While the cost savings are important from the viewpoint of a station's management, they are important, too, from the viewpoint of everyone in the newsroom. They can mean doing

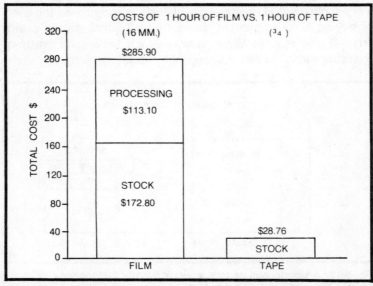

Fig. 6-18. A cost comparison for buying and processing one hour of 16 mm newsfilm as opposed to buying a like quantity of ¾ inch videotape. This does not inlcude the reuse of the tape. (Courtesy CBS television stations.)

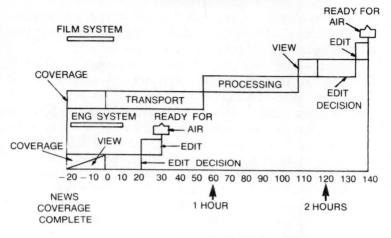

Fig. 6-19. A comparison of the time needed to prepare a news story on film or on videotape. Electronic news gathering (bottom of chart) takes far less time. (Courtesy of CBS television stations.)

more with the same budget, avoiding the crimps caused by inflation or, if policy so dictates, expanding the news coverage at reasonable cost.

FIELD REPORTING—FILM

So far I have talked about field reporting using the newest technology. However, the majority of stations are still using film, even though the trend to electronic news gathering is moving very rapidly. Now let's run through that typical assignment dealing with the proposed exit ramp off the interstate highway again—only this time it will be done on film.

After you make your morning appointment, the photographer checks the mobile unit and the equipment. Here, too, the batteries must be fresh, and a fresh supply of film must be on hand. If the camera operator hasn't already done so, several magazines must be loaded with film, an operation best done in the station's darkroom. The typical load is a 400 foot sound magazine, good for about 10 minutes running time.

Again, before you go downtown, you drive to the site of the proposed ramp and shoot silent film of the scene. Then you go

155

to your appointment. While you warm up the Council member, the photographer sets up a small set of lights, puts the camera on the tripod, and hangs microphones on you and the Council member to set up an opening shot. Then, after a few seconds work adjusting the lights and focusing the camera, the microphone is live and the camera is rolling.

You ask your questions, the lights are turned off, and the filming stops. The photographer then picks up the camera and tripod and moves to a location opposite you (the original shot was over your shoulder facing the council member). Then you do what are called cutaways. These are face-on or angle shots of you asking the questions, so that the editors will have some flexibility in putting the film together. By inserting you on-camera asking the question, the editors avoid the embarrassing jump which occurs on the screen when you go from one answer by the subject to another. If the subject has shifted position in the meantime, a jump appears on the film during editing.

Then you gather up the equipment, shake hands, and leave. Once you get to the mobile unit the photographer removes the film magazine you just used and labels it. Then a new magazine is loaded in the camera for the next assignment.

The assignment editor answers your radio call and tells you that you have the 1:30 p.m. interview with the Transportation Department official. Then you and the photographer (or crew) make a quick run by the station to drop off the morning film for processing. Next, you grab a bit of lunch and head for your interview. There you go through the same routine for filming the question-and-answer session.

As you are leaving City Hall you stop and film a "standupper" in the bright sunlight. The standupper is the opening to your report, a bridge to go between the two interviews and a closing. (See Fig. 6-20.)

If you had been asked to go cover the City Hall demonstration, as in the earlier example, you would have to treat the assignment differently. Unless it were extremely important to cover the demonstration live on the noon news, you would not get the story on that newscast. This is because all you could do would be to establish a live audio link by using your mobile unit's radio or a telephone and then to report from the scene while the station showed a slide or two on the screen. This does not look very good. Probably you would simply give

Fig. 6-20. A reporter doing a standupper as a bulldozer demolishes buildings in the background. The photographer is using a chest brace for the sound camera. The box hanging from the photographer's left arm is a power supply battery for the camera. (Courtesy WFMY-TV, Greensboro, N.C.)

the newsroom personnel some descriptive information about the demonstration, and a writer would write a short script for the anchorperson.

Then you should have the photographer shoot a little silent film (or sound film with only crowd noise) of the demonstration, and you would do a brief on-camera interview with the leader of the group. All this would have to be taken back to the station for processing and used on the 6 p.m. news.

Now you return to the station and drop off the afternoon film at the lab. Then, after you discuss what you shot and the questions you asked with the producer, you begin to write.

Since you were there when the film was shot and you have notes on the questions you asked plus some terse notes on the responses, you can begin to write a rough draft. If you are typical of many up-to-date television reporters, you have carried along a small audiotape recorder, and so you have a complete track of both interviews. This will speed up cutting since you know accurate word cues and times, and you will waste less time finishing up the final script.

In this case your job is easy. You have already written an open and close, so you consult your notes or your audiotape and decide what you think will be the best sound cuts from the interviews. Then write a lead-in for the anchorperson. This should be brief—probably about 15 or 20 seconds on the outside. Remember to do your opening as a "second-line lead" so that the studio lead-in will move smoothly into your piece.

Your brief opening should lead into an answer from the Council member and perhaps one or two questions and answers. While the interview is on the screen, if the interviewer gives you a proper peg (a reference to the highway ramp), put in instructions to the director to dissolve the video to the film of the proposed ramp site. (Dissolve means fading out the interview on the screen and fading in the scenes of the highway.) In this case you might let the scenes of the highway run through your middle piece of on-camera script (the bridge) and switch back just as the picture of the second interviewee comes up. At the end of the second interview, you add your closing.

An alternative way to open would be to show scenes of the proposed ramp location with your voice narrating over the silent film. If you were working with film and you did not have an audiotape of the soundtrack, any lapse of memory on your part would mean waiting until the film was processed in order to check what an interviewee said.

If your station was using portable videotape, you probably would have looked at the original tape while you were riding in the mobile unit. And if your station had invested in microwave, you would have the piece finished by now.

I will continue talking about film at this point, because editing videotape is somewhat easier from a reporter's point of view. Either you or a writer prepares a sheet of instructions, and these are approved by the producer. Then a technician does the final assembly, which can be easily and quickly reviewed. If your station has invested in highly sophisticated editing equipment, the process will be quite precise. If the equipment is less sophisticated, the precision will depend on the technician's skill at stopping the master tape at exactly the right spot. From the way the ENG technology is progressing, it looks as if reporters may be less involved in the final assembly process than they are when film is used.

The actual editing consists basically of playing the selected sections of the original tapes onto a new reel (dubbing) in the order you wish to have them used. The tricky part is getting the exact starting and stopping point you want. How you handle insertion of other picture or sound elements, such as scenes of an area the interviewee is talking about, depends on the type of equipment in use.

Your script will be the guide for editing. Getting the opening ready should not be difficult, unless you made mistakes and the editor has to listen and watch for good "takes." You should keep notes on the number of takes and which were good or bad.

The editor then cuts the City Council interview to your specifications, tying the two interviews together with the sound-on-film bridge you recorded. The editor may insert a "reverse shot" of you asking a question to bridge a cut in the interview film. If you don't do this you will end up in an embarrassing "jump" on the screen. After the film has been spliced and timed to meet your specification, the editor will add cue marks (little holes in the corner of frames) near the end of the film to warn the director when the film is nearly over. Then the editor cleans and lubricates the film so it won't leave dust or fuzz or hairs in the projector gate.

Once you have tidied up your script and checked the film, the producer will want to look at the finished product to see if there are any changes to be made. Whether you are using film or videotape, this is how your script might look:

Anchor	It looks as if the Mudville City Council is headed for a stormy session tonight ... as both sides in the interstate highway ramp dispute meet head on: Channel One reporter Eager Jones has been following this controversy ...
Sound on film	City Councilwomen Bernice Righteous will lead the opposition to a measure authorizing construction of the Catty Street ramp in downtown Mudville.
Reporter seen on screen for opening	Righteous says city streets won't be able to handle the increased traffic that would be generated by the new exit.

Sound on film. Righteous	(Sound on film. Righteous) (Tied to bridge and second sound on film)
Super (name)	
Seventeen seconds into interview roll B-roll silent on cue mark	
Silent film over sound from sound film	(Voice of reporter on sound track) Councilwoman Righteous places great stress on safety. City public works Administrator Hanibal Alp says Righteous is overemphasizing potential traffic hazards:
Take sound-on film	(Sound on film. Alp) (Tied to end of bridge)
Super (name)	
Alp is seen on screen, followed by reporter	(Reporter close) Administrator Alp faces tough questioning tonight when the City Council tries to once and for all resolve the highway ramp dispute. Eager Reporter. Channel One News. at Mudville City Hall.

You can readily see the amount of teamwork that goes into putting together a television newscast. This chapter has mentioned a news coordinator or assignment editor, the anchorperson, a producer, a reporter, a writer, a camera operator, film or electronic news crews, processing or tape technicians, and editors. Those not included are the director, technical director, floor manager, production assistants, studio camera operators, projectionists, video control technicians, make-up specialists, and the many people who have something to do with getting your story on the air.

THE PICTURE PART OF A NEWS STORY

You must have a basic idea of how film is shot so that you can talk intelligently with photographers and editors about their work. Motion picture film is really a rapidly moving sequence of still pictures, with each frame just very slightly different from the one before and the one after. The string of silent pictures is moved before our eyes just rapidly enough so that the eye cannot detect the change in the image between adjacent frames.

On modern newsfilm a thin strip of audiotape is attached on one side, and the sound is recorded there, just as it would be in an audiotape recorder. What the motion picture camera does is move the film in front of the lens, and just for a split second expose a small piece of film. As the film runs through the camera this series of subtle pictures becomes, to the human eye, motion.

As we said earlier, television newsfilm is usually shot on reversal stock (stock means raw film). When you process reversal film it comes out with the pictures positive and ready to project on a screen.

Film comes in two varieties for television news: 16 mm and 8 mm. Because the picture is bigger and the equipment more precise, the industry has been on the 16 mm film standard for years. However, the recent development of a lightweight, self-contained 8 mm sound camera has renewed interest in the use of 8 mm film by television stations. (See Fig. 6-21.) One of the major expenses of running a television newsroom is the cost of the film and the chemicals to process it. By using 8 mm film, which is smaller and shorter for the same amount of running time, a station can use less film and fewer chemicals.

While different brands of motion picture cameras vary in size and shape, most have the same basic elements. The camera must have at least one lens, some type of viewfinder so you know what it's aimed at, and a source of power to run it.

Hand-held cameras (the smaller ones usually used for silent filming) can have one, two, or three lenses mounted on some type of movable turret, or they may have only one fixed lens or one adjustable lens.

Fig. 6-21. A single-system, sound, super-8 news camera. This camera accepts 50 and 200 foot silent cartridge and sound, super-8 ones and has both manual and automatic exposure control, a zoom lens, and automatic gain control for sound recording. (Courtesy Eastman Kodak Company.)

The lens admits light into the camera and focuses the light entering the lens onto the film. The optical quality of the lens affects the amount of light that reaches the film and the sharpness of the focus.

The basic news camera usually has either three fixed focal length lenses or one variable length lens. Either way, the camera is usually equipped for taking what are known as wide angle, medium, and closeup pictures. As the names imply, the wide angle is for an overview of a scene, the medium for a view of several people or a general picture of what is going on, and the closeup shot for a blownup picture of one person or one object.

Some photographers carry a spare telephoto lens, which permits them to take close-appearing pictures of distant objects. It is very much like looking through a telescope: you are far away from an object, but the object is big and easy to see in the picture. Telephoto lens won't work well if jiggled, because every little vibration is overemphasized in the picture. Photographers frequently use a tripod or some sort of

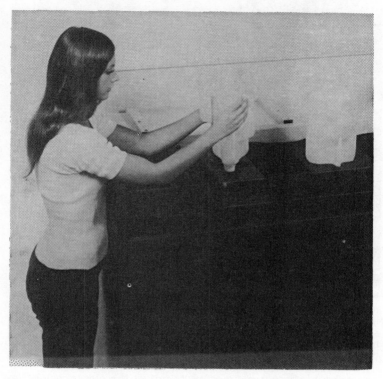

Fig. 6-22. A small motion picture film processor for use with super-8 film. The plastic bottles on top contain pre-mixed chemical solutions for the processor. (Courtesy Eastman Kodak Company.)

resting place for the camera when shooting with a telephoto lens.

Normally a photographer can brace the camera by holding it in such a manner that the upper arms become part of the rigid platform, or by resting it up against something. A seldom-used technique for supporting smaller cameras is a unipod—a one-legged support.

With the heavier sound cameras, a tripod or a chest pod (a shoulder and chest brace) is usually used to provide stability. (See Fig. 6-23). Occasionally a gunstock-type device is used with sound cameras.

The variable focus or "zoom" lens has gained almost universal acceptance for sound news photography. It is frequently awkward for the photographer to reach to the front of the camera and change lenses, but with a zoom, the

Fig. 6-23. The photographer (right) has an Auricon sound camera mounted on a chest brace. Note the film magazine on top of the camera, the earphones to monitor sound, the through-the-lens viewfinder on the side of the camera, and the audio mixer/amplifier attached to the chest brace. The reporter is carrying a small lavalier microphone. (Courtesy WFMY-TV, Greensboro, N.C.)

photographer just turns a crank to adjust the closeness of the picture. This system also allows for some quick but interesting effects such as opening an interview with a wide shot and then smoothly pulling in to show only the face of the interviewee.

This smooth, continuous altering of the picture is called either a zoom-in or a zoom-out, depending on which way you are going. The zoom lens is popular with news photographers because it allows one to use a number of different shots and to frame (the relationship of position, size of objects, and amount of space around the edges of a picture) shots precisely while working very rapidly.

Photographers use light meters to measure the relative amount of light available to their lens. There are a multitude of meters on the market. What is important is not the style of meter but the fact one is used. Measuring the amount of light available to a camera lens is tricky, and seldom does even an experienced photographer guess correctly. An exception is when you have a bright, cloudless, shadowless day. Then any photographer knows to close the lens (stop the lens) to its smallest aperture.

Photographers prefer to shoot in areas of maximum available light, since this improves the sharpness, quality, and color of their film. This is a prime reason for shooting outdoors whenever you can manage, as indoor lighting is always far less bright than a sunlit exterior. Besides, some indoor lighting distorts the color-reproducing characteristics of color film—a tendency which has to be accounted for by using translucent-colored material called filters in front of the lens or by using so-called "indoor" film.

Knowing how much light is available to the lens is important because each lens must be opened or closed to compensate for the amount of light. The more light, the smaller the lens opening; the less light, the greater the lens opening. The ideal situation is to be able to close the lens down, since this will improve the quality of the film, but newsfilm is seldom shot in ideal conditions. There is a bottom limit of relative darkness where you must either give up filming or substitute artificial light.

News photographers carry lighting equipment with them. One standard item is a single floodlight attached to a battery pack. This device is highly portable, although even with modern lightweight batteries, it can get to be a burden after it is carried for a while.

For static sound filming where electrical outlets are available the photographer will set up lights on lightweight folding stands. Usually an adequate set of lights can be packaged conveniently in a suitcase-sized carrier.

Lighting for television is a technical skill and cannot be adequately covered here. There are two main objectives: to light the front of the scene (the interviewee, for example) and to put light in back of the scene or person so that the images on the film are clear and sharp.

The viewfinder permits the photographer to preview approximately the scene to be shot. Older models of some cameras have externally mounted viewfinders which are not connected with the lens. When a camera has this sort of viewfinder, it must be adjusted in two ways: it must be set to correspond with the type of lens being used (close, medium, or wide), and there must be an adjustment for parallax. This means that the viewfinder must be aimed so that the scene you see through it and the scene the lens will take are exactly the same. Because an inch or two separates the viewfinder and the lens on the camera, it would be possible to set the two parallel and end up with a picture different from what you thought you were photographing. So this style of camera has an adjustment for distance, which compensates for parallax.

The newer lenses, particularly the zoom lens, have a mirror set up so that what you see in the viewfinder is exactly the same as what the camera lens is "seeing." This simplifies the photography, but it makes the lens far more expensive and delicate.

Cameras have two sources of power. Some smaller hand-held silent cameras are run by springs, which are wound after about 20 or 30 seconds of running time. Newer silent and all-sound cameras use battery power or occasionally electric power.

Silent photography can be learned quite rapidly by a beginner, especially if the photography is limited to outdoor daylight conditions. The use of lighting for dark interiors at night requires skill.

There are some definite rules to be followed in shooting newsfilm. One rule is to shoot in sequence. For instance, shoot a wide angle, then a medium shot, and then a closeup. Then perhaps you will return to a medium shot and another closeup. With some experience you will learn how to select shots so that what you shoot on the scene of a news story will tell the story with little or no need to rearrange (edit) the scenes.

In general, shoot 15-to-20-second takes for each scene until you are used to what you are doing. It's easy to shorten a scene, but it's impossible to lengthen it if you didn't shoot enough film.

Do not move the camera unless the motion is absolutely necessary. Camera movement—called a pan—is likely to disorient the viewer. A novice photographer should keep the camera stationary. If a pan must be done, it should be very slow and smooth and in one direction only.

Always shoot a couple of cutaways. They are out-of-sequence shots used for editing transitions. Say you are photographing the scene of a fire. You can turn around and shoot some film of the bystanders watching the fire.

If you are using 16 mm film, 36 feet of film are equivalent to 1 minute of running time. The majority of hand-held silent cameras use 100 foot rolls. This means you have about 150 seconds of total running time per roll. An experienced photographer can sometimes shoot two or even three simple stories on the same roll.

A word of warning: unless film is in extremely short supply, reload the camera when you have only a little film left in it. Loading a camera is something to do when you have time and are not under pressure. Putting a fresh roll of film in while you are in the midst of a fast-moving story can be nerve-wracking.

If you and your camera are the only equipment available in a situation where filming ordinarily wouldn't work, go ahead and shoot anyway and maybe you'll get lucky. For example, suppose it is night and there's a house on fire. You don't have one of those expensive portable lights. What do you do? First, open the lens to its widest aperature setting so you are letting in as much light as possible. Then slow the camera down to the next slowest speed below the standard 24 frames per second (probably 16 frames per second). What you are doing is holding each frame in the gate for a split second longer, thus increasing the amount of light it is exposed to. Then, tell the processing technician what you have done and adjustments will be made to "push" the development of the film. Maybe you will get usable film.

As another example, suppose you are jammed into a crowd as a convicted murderer is taken from the courthouse. You can't get a clear shot, so you hold the camera over your head and point it at the center of the action. You may have to open the lens an extra stop to allow for the relative darkness of shooting down. Then hit the start button and keep running. If you are lucky you may get a good closeup. When the crowd breaks you can more easily film the medium and long shots and the cutaways. Never say die—just keep that camera running.

Reporters infrequently shoot sound film, but for the sake of orientation, I will talk a bit about sound on film, or SOF as it's known. (See Fig. 6-24.)

Sound cameras are generally bigger and heavier than silent cameras. This is due to better construction, larger film capacity, larger lens capacity, and the addition of an electric motor and audio components.

Sound comes in two varieties. That which is recorded in the camera on the same strip of film is called "single system."

Fig. 6-24. A modern sound-on-film motion picture camera. A CO-16R/A 16 mm reflex camera is shown with a microphone and a focusing spotlight mounted on it. The camera has a variable-focus lens (note the crank to the "zoom" lens on the right). The camera can be carried without an additional brace by using the pistol grip shown below the lens. (Courtesy Cinema Products Corp.)

That which is recorded separately on another piece of film or on magnetic tape is called "double system." While some double system is shot for news purposes, the vast majority of newsfilm is sound on film using magnetic striped film (the film mentioned earlier with audiotape pressed onto it).

Sound cameras are usually operated with anything from a 400 foot (approximately 10 minutes) magazine to a 1200 foot (approximately 30 minutes) magazine. The 400 foot magazine tends to fit the customary, tightly controlled interview. Photographers usually have several of these magazines loaded and ready for use. But even with this advance preparation, changing film takes a little while, which is one reason for trying to do an interview on one magazine's worth of film. The magazines are loaded ahead of time because they must be loaded in the dark. In the field this is done with one's hands inserted in a lightproof black bag. It's a tricky procedure.

The audio amplifier for the sound camera may be part of the camera, or it may be a separate, plug-in unit. It will have at least two microphone positions with volume controls and may have more inputs or outputs (the outputs may be used to feed cartridge tape recorders among other things).

There are a number of possible microphone arrangements. The most sophisticated is the wireless mike. The wireless mike is used in situations where running a lot of microphone cable isn't advisable. Most local station reporters either use a version of the so-called pencil mike (a long, thin, tubular microphone) or a microphone which is hung around the neck on a cord or clipped to the clothing.

When work is done outdoors, most stations prefer the sturdy pencil mike with a "blast shield," which is a type of foam rubber material used to lessen the unwanted noises caused by wind blowing on the microphone.

Traditionally, the sound camera has been mounted on a tripod for most assignments. But in the last few years there has been a big swing to having the photographer carry the camera, using a chest brace or a gunstock-type support. This has been made possible by a considerable lightening of the cameras and of their audio mixers and power supplies.

Shooting sound this way gives a less stable picture, but it adds immediacy since the camera more nearly resembles the sensory inputs of the human eye and ear as it moves about following the action. The photographer also can work closer to fluid situations and be a little less obtrusive. The portable sound camera means for instance, that instead of having to pursuade a group of politicians to stop and come to a stationary location, you can interview them as they walk out of an important meeting.

The technique of shooting sound film has changed a great deal in recent years. It used to be that few local stations shot sound beyond doing sound interviews. The networks were the only news organization shooting wild sound (film with natural sound recorded simultaneously). Today this is standard procedure in most larger markets.

The result is a film report which imparts more action and more aliveness because the sounds which naturally accompany the pictures are included. However, in order to use this sort of technique successfully a station must have the capability of editing sound and silent film quickly, and then the ability to project or record more than one roll of film in order to combine all the parts into a finished piece.

Also, the reporter has to work very closely with the photographer to coordinate their efforts. For instance, you have to think about the type of sound that will be in the background if you choose to do the open and close on camera. If you are not careful, you can end up with an abrupt change in the background. Networks and major market stations often shoot sound film much as they would silent and then record a narration over the sound once the film is edited. The added work and time produces a truly superior report.

Film is edited in the same manner as audiotape. The part to be deleted is physically cut out, and then the film is rejoined by using either so-called film cement or tape. Editing permits the film to be rearranged to match a script, and for dramatic continuity. It also allows the precise timing of scenes.

At smaller stations you may do your own editing. In major markets editing is done by professional editors. In medium markets the photographers also may act as editors.

Without getting deeply into editing, there are a couple of points which are essential. There should not be too great a jump in continuity from one scene to another. The second common editing mistake is to change the direction of motion. If people are seen facing the screen to the right or moving to the right, then a shot taken from another angle may seem totally out of place.

The film can be rejoined by "gluing" the film ends together or by using a special adhesive tape. The sound track is optical (a rarity these days), it can be covered up with silver tape. If the track is magnetic, it can be erased with a magnet. But if you want fades or sound overlaps on the audio, you have to prepare more than one reel of film and, using more than one projector, produce a final mixture of the sound and picture sources, the same as was mentioned for visual cutting earlier.

The mechanics of film editing are best learned by the "hands-on" method of making splices until you are confident of your ability. There is one peculiarity of film editing which is important to remember. The audio on sound film precedes the picture, so as you begin a sound piece, you cut on the audio but you cut the end on the picture, which comes up 28 frames later than the final sound on magnetic film. If you want, you can cut on the final sound, in which case the sound will overlap with a new visual scene.

When you turn to electronic news gathering, many of the functions that have been described for film are taken care of automatically. Focus continues to be important, but the lens aperature may well be controlled within the camera. Also, you have the distinct advantage of being able to look at the camera viewer (or monitor) and see exactly what sort of picture you are recording.

Even if you should have to run the videotape recorder, it is similar in principle to an audiotape recorder and is simple to load, since many machines use preloaded tape cartridges. Just pop it in, and go to work. If your equipment is more sophisticated, you will undoubtedly have technical assistance and won't have to worry about the equipment.

Anyone seriously interested in taking up television news should try to keep up with the rapidly changing equipment and techniques involved in electronic news gathering, especially by reading on of the weekly trade publications.

Here is an excellent example of the fantastic capabilities of ENG: A heavily loaded passenger aircraft crashed on its approach to Kennedy International Airport in New York City. One of the major television stations had a two-hour block of news starting at 5 p.m. The plane crashed at 4:10 p.m., and because the station happened to be using its ENG equipment at a nearby location, it was able to get to the crash scene quickly. Within minutes it began transmitting live pictures of the rescue operation.

This live coverage of a tragic but dramatic story was available early in the first hour of the news and continued throughout the two-hour newscast and the evening. Competitive stations were trying desperately to get their film back to Manhattan, but air and road traffic were at a standstill.

While electronic news gathering offers untold new horizons for news departments, it presents problems for reporters. Television news has often been criticized for having a tendency to pick a visual event, assigning the first available reporter to it and, once the assignment is complete, sending the reporter off to another unrelated story. The reporter, of course, is expected to be an "instant expert." The criticism is legitimate in some cases, and the danger of taking this approach is increased with the flexibility of electronic news gathering. Since the equipment lends itself to covering a number of stories in rapid sequence and the cost of equipment tends to reduce the number of crews a station wants to employ, there is a risk of worrying about logistics than good journalism.

There is no doubt that reporters will continue to have to be at least as flexible with tape as they were with film and perhaps even more so. There certainly will be demands for better, faster, and more creative performance, which is a matter of training. But there has been a trend in the field toward larger news departments, staffed by both generalists and specialists. So there is a place for the specialized reporter, if he or she develops the qualifications.

Fortunately, with the exception of periodic economic retrenchments, television news departments have tended to gradually become larger and better equipped, so the risks of sloppy journalism that might result from the coming of ENG seem to be minimal. But the demands ENG places on reporters and producers seems to be maximal.

7
Delivering the News

Most broadcast reporters must be able to present the facts they have assembled in a clear, understandable manner. Today there is no such thing as a standard for broadcast reporters. Most of the old stereotypes have been thrown out. Gone are the legions of diction-perfect, resonant male voices. The voices of present-day broadcasters may be high-pitched, low-pitched, male, female, and even accented.

There is only one common denominator: broadcast reporters must be understood. Diction, pace, and interpretation all play important roles in the delivery of broadcast news.

Regardless of the quality of your voice, clarity of diction is essential in delivering news. Mumbled words or slurred syllables cannot be tolerated. Not only may people not understand what you said, they might even misunderstand a mumble and get entirely the wrong impression of what you were saying. Remember: you are giving information about topics which are frequently unfamiliar and therefore you must speak clearly.

Unfortunately, diction habits are often so ingrained that we do not hear them. Skilled criticism or a speech class and frequent practice with a tape recorder are helpful. Be alert to friendly criticism and comments from people who say they "didn't hear you" or "didn't understand you." These remarks are really hints that you may have poor speech habits. Most of all, make a conscious effort to speak clearly and with vitality, and you will be well on the way to doing a good job.

Pace has to do with the rate and variations of rate you use in speaking. The faster you speak, the higher your pitch is apt to be, the more likely you will be to stumble, and the harder it will be for your listeners to understand you. To some degree a faster pace imparts an atmosphere of excitement or urgency, but surprisingly these also can be implied by a slower pace.

Oddly enough, some newscasters who appear to use a very "punchy," fast, urgent style actually don't speak as fast as you think. They make extensive use of emphasis and inflection. A rough measure used in many newsrooms is that it takes 1 minute to deliver 135 to 150 words.

If you normally speak very rapidly, you may find you have to consciously slow down. And some people, especially persons from regions given to slow speech patterns, may have to speed up their rate of delivery.

Remember that no one gains if you are constantly out of breath. One of the most disturbing habits on-air people can have is gulping audible gulps of air between words or phrases. Pretty soon you find yourself listening to the gulps rather than to the words being spoken.

Good phrasing can be learned with coaching. But one of the best aids to good phrasing is writing good copy. This brings us back to the basic truth: good writing is essential to good broadcasting. The better you write what you read, the easier it is to deliver.

Interpretation means reading your copy so that what your audience hears is not words but thoughts. It takes practice for most people to read out loud in a manner that conveys the meaning and emotion contained in the written word.

This is one area in which you can gain valuable insights from a course in interpretation or from professional coaching. But remember, there is a difference between reading a dramatic script or a poem and reading news. Watch and listen as acknowledged professionals present the news. You will be conscious of two facts: (1) all the really good people interpret words, giving them emphasis and inflection even adjusting their pacing to fit the phrases and (2) there are vast differences in speech patterns and styles of acknowledged leaders in the field. In fact, some of the better known newscasters have unusual styles, but there is something about their delivery which causes people to listen.

For example, the famed broadcaster Paul Harvey imparts a feeling of drama and urgency through his rather unorthodox style. Another example is Hughes Rudd of CBS News who is known for his homespun drawl and the use of frank, common language to get across his point. Rudd would never say a government official "admitted to absconding with the funds." Rudd would say. "He admitted he stole the money."

Individualism is important. Never copy another person's manner or style. Learn to be as professional as you can in delivering your copy. and then impart your own personality—not one you've copied from someone else.

One thing all the top broadcasters do is impart feeling to their copy. You can't attract an audience or persuade a listener if your delivery is flat. boring. and without inflection or emphasis. You have to work to deliver a report or newscast; you have to consciously try to project feeling into what you're reading. You also must read well: no fumbling. no mispronunciations. and no sing-song delivery. These irritate and distract listeners.

Walter Cronkite has a fine, believable voice. so does Harry Reasoner. but listen to their copy—it's beautiful in its clarity and choice of words. Good writing shows.

If you are not sincere. it will be obvious. Think how many times you've listened to a well-delivered political speech—well delivered. that is. until the speaker stumbles over some phrasing and you realize he or she is reading something written by others to fit an occasion. This leaves you with a feeling of insincerity.

Above all. remember that life is sad. serious. gay. and whimsical. Don't impart a smile in your voice—or put one on your face—as you tell us about the five little children who burned to death. for example.

Know what you are talking about. The best way to seem credible when you deliver a newscast is to know your subject. Even if you don't write the copy. be informed about the background of the story. And pre-read the copy so you will have a chance to test the phrasing and to be sure that you understand what is being said.

If you write your own copy. it's just as important that you read ahead of air time. You will readily find out that the words and punctuation which looked so good coming out of the typewriter do not always sound right when you try to read them aloud

Knowing what you are talking about solves many of the problems involved in being a good on-air reporter. If you know your subject. you should be able to just begin talking about it off the cuff. using your notes only for dates. times. and numbers.

With the swing to electronic news gathering reporters are more than ever having to talk ad-lib: using the barest of notes and their own knowledge. More and more radio reporters are going live at the scene of a story. with no time to scribble a complete script.

There are individuals in the broadcast news business who don't pre-read their copy and who make no special effort to know what they're talking about. But they are the minority.

There's nothing better to fall back on when a film breaks or a tape cartridge doesn't play or a page of script is out of order than knowing enough about the subject matter to gracefully extricate yourself from the snafu.

Imagine being Walter Cronkite. and right in the middle of the 6:30 feed of the evening news you get a call from an old acquaintance. It's former President Lyndon Johnson's press secretary calling to say Johnson had died. What do you do? You come back on camera from the preceding material. holding the phone and talking to the press aide. Then you look squarely into the camera and tell your audience—ad lib—the news you have just learned. Next. you and your staff build a network newscast on the air. right in front of your viewers. And 60 seconds after you've finished the 6:30 feed. you go on the air again with a complete new show and a prepackaged obituary incorporated into it.

The ability to do this sort of thing comes from knowing the newsmakers. from talking with them. from reading about them. and from knowing what you are talking about. One network correspondent did a magnificent job on radio covering the funeral of former President Harry S. Truman. The reason he did such good work was that he sat down and reread as much as he could of the *Truman Memoirs* when he learned the former President was gravely ill. When Truman died. he knew he would be assigned to the funeral.

On your own scale. you should know your community and your state well enough to deal with an emergency situation with some ease.

REPORTING FOR RADIO

Radio is a fascinating medium. Human beings have unusual empathy for the human voice. With the skilled use of words and sounds. it is possible to arouse visual images in the minds of people. Just think how successful drama was on radio in the quarter-century that preceded television. A skilled speaker or a persuasive leader can evoke loyalty. hatred. and even hysteria in an audience.

Human beings seem to need the sound of other human voices. Only a few of us are willing to spend long periods in solitude. Most of us seek out others to talk to or listen to. How often have you been alone at home or in your car and flipped on the radio. put on a record. or turned on the television set just to hear another human voice?

The radio reporter faces the challenges of making what is said interesting and understandable without the support of pictures. And it can be done. through the imagery of well-chosen and familiar words. through colorful descriptions. and through the voices and sounds of the people and things that make the news. For example. you don't need a picture to have feeling for the sobbing wife of a man just sentenced to life in prison.

As a radio reporter you have to deal with facts and the emotional and physical setting of your story. You must convey the facts in language simple enough to be understood by people who may know or care little about what you are saying. And you must try to replace what might be seen on the television set with the sounds of the event. and in language which imparts the atmosphere and appearance of the surroundings.

Why say. "Jones's wife Matilda was in the courtroom throughout the trial"? You could say. "Jones's wife Matilda sat beside her husband throughout the trial chewing away her lipstick. This morning. when the verdict was announced. her lower lip bled." True. it took more words. but you gave your listeners some of the drama. the humanity. and the mood of the occasion. This is what radio is about.

Whenever possible. let others tell your story. It may be the factual accounting of a chief of detectives. or the emotional narrative of a welfare mother who is enraged because the school lunch program has been canceled. Even if you tell the story. try to tell it on location with sounds in the background. If the story is an outdoors one. record your report outdoors. If you have been attending a trial. record your spot in the echo-filled marble hallway outside the courtroom.

If your story is about protesting. let's hear some protesting in the background. Tell your story as you see or hear it.

Suppose the President is coming to your city to address a large civic gathering. You could simply wait for the President to arrive, observe what took place, and then dart into a telephone booth and report what you saw.

But this is a cermonial occasion. The President is going to save whatever news he's going to break for the civic gathering. So get as near to the band, the waiting crowd, and the plane as you can, and then turn on your recorder. Record some sound of the crowd and then, as the plane taxies to a stop, describe just what you are seeing. Pause when the band plays "Hail to the Chief" and insert a short excerpt of the Mayor's greeting. Then put a short, well-thought-out closing on the tape with background sound behind you. You will have a dramatic and meaningful report, and one which will make your listeners' ears perk up.

Think back, if you can, to the radio coverage of the Vietnam war. How many dramatic reports do you recall? News correspondents described just what a firefight is like in the mud and slime as automatic weapons chattered and close support bombers swooped overhead. Those reports did not necessarily tell you any startling facts. After all, it was a widespread, disjointed war, which couldn't really be summarized in a neat package like battle orders. But it was a war of people: millions of Asians whose land had been ravaged by war for decades. It was a story of teenage American youths recruited from midwestern farms and urban slums and sent to kill people without being given a reason.

This was the story the correspondents told as they crouched in ditches, trying to keep tape recorders and microphones dry. It was the human part of war, the part that everyone could understand.

And then there was the return of the American aviators held as prisoners in North Vietnam. The radio reporters didn't have scripts, just notes on who was supposed to be on the planes. They told what they saw while listeners heard color guards maneuver and ranking officers say words of welcome and praise. From a few of those tired, battered men was heard the overwhelming joy of their return to friendly soil.

Until recently it was rare for a radio reporter to do a live report. After the halcyon days of radio, live broadcasts, except for an occasional store opening or record hop, pretty much disappeared. But technology and the growth of news as a part of radio programing has brought back the live report.

Many stations have two-way radio equipment in their cars and find that doing a live report is easy. Others have added other devices such as small walkie-talkies and even telephones which plug into prewired receptacles.

These advances plus a growing aggressiveness in news departments and an informality of style which permits the reporter to call in and talk ad-lib or from notes are encouraging live reporting. The all-news stations particularly encourage their reporters to go to the nearest telephone or to the mobile unit and file a report just as soon as they can. In fact, the question-and-answer type of report in which the anchorperson asks the reporter questions is becoming increasingly common.

Live reporting is also receiving a stimulus from stations which permit greater flexibility in breaking into program material with an important story. Say there is a subway mishap in your city. Today's radio station would have the disc jockey or anchor reporter switch live to the mobile unit where one or more reporters would speak from the scene using some hastily prepared notes. Perhaps while one reporter was giving an introduction to what happened, another reporter would be cuing up a taped interview with a transit official. It would be played through the two-way radio. Then the anchorperson might ask the reporters a few questions, gathering their impressions of the scene. If an official were able to break free for a moment, one reporter might interview the official live using the mobile unit microphone while the other reporter tried to tape interviews with eyewitnesses.

How do you prepare for this type of thing? Know your topic, and practice talking ad-lib. Take a story you have just written and explain it without the use of a script into your tape recorder. Go for a walk and describe what you see into a tape recorder. Interview a few people in the park or some friends. Practice putting your thoughts together logically and fluidly. Work to get rid of bad habits such as saying "er" or "uh" between words, because this means you're still thinking of the next word. Learn to leave a split-second pause in your description rather than making primeval sounds. Play word games; they can be educational, and they help you to compose fresh sentences more quickly because they expand the vocabulary you have at hand.

When you are attending a lecture or a meeting, take clear, logical notes, not overly detailed but complete enough for you to reconstruct a report on what took place. Then make a quick outline of the main facts and, using this outline, explain what took place out loud or into your tape recorder.

Talk to people, even strangers, to build your confidence. Take a public speaking course. Accept responsibilities which require you to give talks or address groups. Build your own confidence by forcing yourself to talk off the cuff to groups. All of these tricks, even doing something which requires frequent and extensive use of the telephone, will help you.

Try doing some sportscasting if you're so inclined. It's excellent training ground. You learn how to perceive an event quickly, how to summarize while leaving out unessential moves, and how to lend color and drama to an unfolding event. One newscaster who originally made a name as a sports reporter eventually became anchorman of a major New York television newscast.

Practice interviewing. Pick some logical topic and go out with your tape recorder and interview people about it. If you write for a school newspaper, do your interviewing on tape, and then write your story from the tape. That way you can practice your writing and develop and critique your interviewing technique at the same time. If you are affiliated with a college radio station, volunteer to do student interviews on campus on current topics. This kind of experience is invaluable, both to teach you how to do random street interviews and to teach you to think on your feet and interact with strangers.

Do every interview assignment you can get. Good interview style develops only after practice and from constructive criticism. Learn to make your question short, to the point, intelligent, and understandable.

Ad-libbing comes a whole lot easier when you know what you are talking about. If possible, research your assignment, study any available copy covering it, check your station's morgue (file of clippings and scripts), and make phone calls. Keep up on the daily newspaper, the news magazines, and broadcast newscasts and spend a lot of time talking to people when you're not involved in reporting. You'll be calling on all of these mental resources if you have to go live with a report.

And keep calm. I remember my first experiences with tornado watches in the Midwest. The television and radio stations broadcast frequent reports on the progress of the storm and any tornado sightings. Pretty soon I found I could stand in front of a camera and talk off the cuff or use a map for a long time without becoming rattled or tongue-tied.

As you have been reading this book, you have noticed a constant emphasis on inserting sound or pictures into a story. Sound is for radio. When a reporter arrives at a story she or he should survey the situation for audiotape prospects. If you are attending a City Council meeting you probably have some permanent arrangement to record the session.

But what if the City Council takes a tour of the municipal jail? Well, you carry your handy battery-operated tape recorder. You record everything: the sounds around you, and the ambient sound or background noise. It may come in handy for editing or for a background to your voice report. Then try to record the comments of the jailer as the Council members are led around and their reactions. If you are permitted, record conversations between the Council members and the inmates. Record the inmates' remarks if you are allowed—and be careful because people confined behind bars often express themselves graphically and profanely.

Listen for and record obvious sound effects, like the clang of the steel doors. Record interviews with the participants after the tour. What you will have is a series of sound stories. You could do a straight narration, using the background sound. Or you could do a wrap—narration and interview inserts. You could feed the station actuality of your interviews. You could do a more dramatic piece using the sound effects and perhaps an exchange between a Council member and a prisoner. A tour of this sort should yield several stories to be used for several programs.

One important note about ethics: It is ethical to record a narration in the jail office and to ask the studio technician to blend that narration with the background sound you recorded in the cellblock. But it would be unethical to go back to the newsroom and recreate the scene.

Normally a recording with background sound is simply done by narrating with the sound in the background. In a jail, however, for a variety of reasons this might not be practical. Perhaps when you get back to the newsroom your news director will ask you to put together a more complicated piece involving sound, pro-and-con interviews, and the like. It might be used during the evening news block or next morning's drive time. You might even be asked to produce a 5-minute vignette on the conditions seen at the jail.

It's always a good idea in a situation like the jail tour to try to do one piece with a descriptive narration, ad-lib, as you walk through the place. Be sure to record a couple of closing lines, too.

Aggressive reporters come up with all sorts of ideas. For instance, you might walk alongside a jailer and the Council members and do a descriptive narration, interrupting yourself to pick up their conversations. You could do an introduction to your piece and the hold the microphone in front of the City Council president and pop a question like, "Judging by what you've seen so far, do you think the jail needs modernizing?" You are apt to get a more honest answer than you will get an hour later when the Council president is back in the outside atmosphere and has reassumed a cool cloak of public servant reserve.

Later this might happen: "Mr. President, do you see the problems here in the jail in the same light as you did, say, last week?"

"No, frankly I don't. I think we miss the human aspect. We aren't doing anything to stop crime by putting fresh paint on the walls. What we need to do is get these people back into their homes and working at worthwhile jobs."

At which point the jailer might say: "But Mr. President, we haven't enough guards now just to keep the place secure."

To which the Council President might reply: "Maybe you're too concerned about security. If you gave these people something to do, security wouldn't be such a big problem."

You see, you used your head and came up with an interesting confrontation of viewpoints which hit squarely on some of the issues that might be faced by the City Council. After you have recorded the rest of this confrontation, and while the group moves off to its next destination, you quickly record your closing with the same background—and you have a finished piece.

Think about closings. Don't just come out of tape. Have something worthwhile to say. For example: "The council is taking this tour at Council President Smith's suggestion after a dispute arose over the jailer's budget request for new guards and a complete paint job at the jail." Then add a good closing line: "This is Joan Hope, XYZ News, in Cellblock A at Mudville City Jail."

Use imagination in your closing. Even this element adds drama to your work. Note incidentally in the suggested closing it was said that the "Council *is*" taking the tour. True, it may be a couple of hours later when your tape is broadcast, but what you have is a slice of life, and of history, and the present tense is appropriate.

Some of the drama of this type of reporting is lost in a book's pages. You will learn a great deal by doing your own analysis of how the story was done, and by your personal critique of your final product. For comparison, listen to one of the clear-channel powerhouse stations that does a good news job—perhaps an all-news station. Hear how network and local reporters handle assignments similar to the one just described.

The tape recorder permits you to give a live quality to the news. You can record events as they happen and then play parts of them for your audience at their convenience. Tape has been used for years by reporters to get interviews and statements so that the listener can hear the voice and exact words of the newsmaker. But less than proper attention has been paid by many reporters to using sound creatively. So often sounds around us convey the subtleties of a story, especially the mood. You could do a piece on a protest by starting your recorder, taping some shouting, and then starting to record over the shouting. If your machine has automatic level, the shouting will be forced into the background. It's always wise to say a couple of words at the beginning that can be cut out if they came out less than distinct where the machine resets itself. For example, don't say a key name first because it might be distorted.

You could get close to some particularly agitated (*not* profane) demonstrator. Record a few of the demonstrator's shouts, and then try to interview the person. This is how it might work:

> *Demonstrator:* Boycott beef ... yeah stop the cattle barons ...stop the supermarket gougers ... yeah ...
> *Reporter:* Why are you so angry?
> *Demonstrator:* Because they're robbin' us blind ...
> *Reporter:* What's your name?
> *Demonstrator:* James Crossworthy.
> *Reporter:* What do you do for work Mr. Crossworthy?
> *Demonstrator:* (Pant, pant) I work on an auto assembly line.
> *Reporter:* So why are you so upset?
> *Demonstrator:* Look ... I make $350 for working 14 hours overtime plus my shift. The government takes 95 bucks, the state

30. so where does that leave me? Then I go in this supermarket and they want 4 bucks a pound for a half-decent steak. What am I supposed to do. eat lettuce? I work hard. my kids are growing ... I can't go without meat.

Reporter: Crossworthy was one of some 300 people ... men. women. even teenagers ... who blocked access to the supermarket for over an hour this morning. A leader of the demonstration says this particular supermarket was selected because it's beef prices were the highest in this week's grocery ads. I'm Alert Reporter. XYZ News. at the Wide Acres Shopping Center.

In a situation of this sort you're not really dealing with facts but with the emotions of the "common person." Of course, if you're going to do your job right, you should try for an interview with someone from the supermarket's management, the United States Department of Agriculture, or the cattle-raisers' organization.

All these suggested reports require editing, unless you are unusually lucky. In the last story you might need a splice between the yelling demonstrators and your opening (a fade would be better, but many news departments don't have the necessary production equipment). There would be a splice before and after the demonstrator who explained his plight.

It's a good rule of thumb to run your tape recorder every chance you get unless it is specifically prohibited. One thing good about audiotape recorders is that if you keep fresh batteries in them you should be able to record quite a lot of tape, assuming that you carry spare cassettes or reel tape with you. Tape is cheap and reusable, and most portable machines today give you a minimum of a half-hour running time per side before you have to flip the tape.

Do not become too reliant on the tape recorder. Take notes anyway, and keep notes on what you have recorded. Otherwise you'll waste hours trying to find the sections of the tape that you want to use.

A good reporter will find many uses for the tape recorder that have not been covered here. The main point is that as a radio reporter, you should try to tell your story in sound if at all possible. There are times, of course, when a straight voice report is the best choice, but you will find such occasions to be few.

REPORTING FOR TELEVISION

Prior to the mid-1970s few reporters had to worry about doing live television reports unless they worked for a network.

But the electronic news gathering revolution has changed all that. Now those little vans crammed with miniaturized equipment are fanning out across the countryside and more and more stations are switching to live or live-on-tape reporting.

The beauty of live coverage is that it permits the unfolding of the story to continue even as the newscast is underway. Say, for instance, the governors from your region are holding their semiannual meeting at your city's biggest hotel. Normally a station would film part of the proceedings and perhaps do a couple of interviews. Then the crew would probably return to the station. With live portable cameras, the news crew can record speeches. do interviews, send all this back to the station for preparation. and then stand by to do updates within the early evening news.

The report might go something like this: The anchor reporter does an introduction. and then up on the screen comes a wide shot of waiters setting tables for the conference's closing dinner. Reporter Jones walks into the picture and starts talking about what is going to take place.

Then the reporter says a few words to introduce and tie together excerpts from two of the day's best speeches. After the excerpts the reporter says that one Republican governor and a prominent Democrat both took exception to earlier statements. Then follows a taped interview with the Democrat and a live interview with the Republican. During the live interview the anchorperson interrupts to ask a question. And the piece ends with Reporter Jones signing off.

That is a slick. live presentation with some action and even a slight feeling of excitement because it is done in a room where something is going on. Because the story could be done live. the reporter had time to do a complete report. not only running excerpts of earlier speeches but running down and interviewing. both on tape and live. two dissenters. And if by some chance one of the other governors took exception to remarks made during the report. it would be possible to switch back to the hotel for a reporter doing another interview to further update the story.

Obviously the television reporter is under pressure to know something about what is going on and why and to appear relaxed and well informed on the air while confining the politician being interviewed to the subject at hand and keeping the interview brief. You have to play "heads-up ball" in this type of reporting.

The live camera is excellent for covering major trials. Courts (with minimal exceptions) do not permit cameras in courtrooms and, usually, not even in the parts of the courthouse closest to the courtrooms. So the only way to cover a trial visually is to have an artist sketch the major characters.

It is possible to interview outside the courthouse, and in major trials there's always a knot of reporters waiting outside when the participants emerge, hoping to get a few remarks from opposing sides. The live remote is good for this sort of coverage, because you can work close to the time of the newscast without any serious worries about getting the material ready for broadcast.

Another advantage of having the mobile live camera is that when the verdict becomes known the reporter can go outside, walk up to the camera position, and begin a report for the station's news bulletin.

The advent of new electronic equipment has changed the attitude of many television stations. Now it is possible to do a live cut-in on other programing anytime the news warrants it. Many stations realize that there is no reason to hold a story. If it's big and breaking, programing can be interrupted for a quick live report with visuals to support it. This technique informs an audience previously accustomed to listening to the radio for up-to-the-minute news, and builds audiences for the major television newscasts.

When you're working on tape or film, maintain as good eye contact with the camera lens as possible. You may have notes or a script. Try to memorize short scripts or at least long portions. Sometimes, when you're working with film, you can shoot your story by paragraphs with a periodic change of the picture. This device is particularly good if you are doing a straight on-camera story. It relieves the monotony.

Remember, you are performing. Be relaxed; use your body to help the story along—for instance, point to an object if it fits the story or walk if it's appropriate. Try doing your story from a setting, like sitting in the driver's seat of a piece of construction equipment. Let your face be natural: no smiles at grim news. Be expressive. Practice reading news stories in front of a mirror. Try a little amateur theater. One of your jobs is to make the presentation interesting. which means that you should not look stiff or sound dull.

Don't over announce. but remember that you are reading your copy for emphasis and expression. and no amount of visual activity is going to disguise a poorly read script. You must brief your camera operator on the story. You can't expect to get good pictures unless your support personnel understand what is going on. Remember. too. that you are dealing with professionals who are trained to visualize. You will get some sensational visual treatments for your stories if you put your camera operator and crew into the mainstream of the project.

Be on the lookout for visual and aural backgrounds. Be thinking how the parts of your story are going to fit together visually. You may not want to do your narration on camera out in the park if the rest of the story is going to be shot inside City Hall. It would make more sense to use the same or another interior location.

DELIVERING THE RADIO NEWSCAST

The day of the bass male voice delivering radio news is almost dead. There are still some around. and there are still radio station managers and news directors who wouldn't hire anything else. But listen to the networks. to the all-news stations. and to the music stations which have active news departments. The delivery is clean. understandable. and probably relaxed—even just a touch informal. Women aren't trying to sound like men. and men aren't trying to sound like they are in a large cavern. People are talking to people.

You must keep certain requirements in mind. Your audience must understand you. This means good diction. correct pronunciation. interesting and meaningful phrasing. good pacing. and an absence of extremes of accent or dialect. Beginners. especially young men. worry a great deal about the depth and maturity of their voices. In fact. a good many young people have ruined their voices by overprojecting to achieve bassiness.

Concentrate on good diction and on making what you read come alive; forget about the level of your voice. Practice conscious relaxation of your throat and breathing to achieve a pleasing voice within a pleasant pitch range. Worry about what you are saying and how it is being said. not about how deep your voice is.

Be honest. If for some reason you have noticeable speech difficulties, get professional counseling to see if corrections can be made. It may turn out that for one reason or another you shouldn't be a newscaster. This doesn't mean there aren't plenty of highly satisfying things you can do in broadcast journalism.

A few years ago station managers would become highly agitated at the suggestion that a woman read news. After all, people wouldn't be able to cope with hearing a woman do anything but women's features. Today that myth has been exploded. Women of every voice characteristic are on the air, sounding like themselves.

Perhaps the most difficult assimilation into broadcast news is made by persons who speak English as a second language or who come from a region with its own peculiar accent. Unfortunately, one reality is that these individuals must learn to speak in a manner which can be understood by a majority of their listeners if they are to be in the mainstream of broadcasting.

Anyone wishing to be an on-air newscaster or reporter should reasonably expect to need coaching or classroom training in speech and broadcast announcing. Everyone has bad habits and speech imperfections.

Start developing yourself right now. Read anything and everything out loud. Take the daily newspaper and record it, even if you use the cheapest little tape recorder. Play back what you have read and listen, and then do it over. Try to get skilled criticism from someone in broadcasting or from a speech teacher.

Be aware of your reading speed. Time yourself, and then find out how many words per minute you are reading. After you have settled down to an average, you can judge whether you need to slow down or speed up. Usually slowing down is what is needed because most of us have a tendency to speak fast in conversation.

Listen very carefully. Does your reading sound flat? If it does, try marking the important words in the copy and learn to emphasize them. Remember, sounding interested in the copy you're delivering is the result of being interested. Push your inflection and emphasis, and watch your phrasing until you are conscious that you are working hard at reading well. At this point you'll probably just be approaching an adequate delivery. Few newscasters can simply sit and read without exerting themselves. Most consciously try to read the copy so it makes sense.

Remember that there is a sense of mood to what you read. You are *not* a happy disc jockey. You are giving information, some of it joyful and some sad and most just serious. Be aware of the mood of what you are reading.

Correct pronunciation is important. Even if your newsroom doesn't have a special pronunciation guide, there is certainly a dictionary around. There are excellent guides on the market, and they are well worth using for practice. If you are working at a station, find out what standard is being used for pronunciations. There will be some variations from newsroom to newsroom.

The wire services provide pronouncers for the first use of new or unfamiliar words. You should post these in the newsroom for reference. People have a habit of using pronunciations of their names which will surprise you. Never assume the pronunciation of a person's name when it is possible to check it. Don't forget that people have a right to pronounce their names anyway they wish.

Breathing is an essential skill. You have to learn how to breathe. Sibilance is a serious problem which often requires professional help. However, you can avoid creating problems for yourself by not writing phrases which have a series of sibilant s-sounding sounds strung together.

Another annoying habit is a "popping" sound caused by expelling too much breath into the microphone as you form certain sounds. It is cured by moving farther away from the mike or by speaking at an angle to it.

A well-read radio newscast results not only from excellence of speech but from skillful writing and editing of what is read. If your copy is well written you are on the way to a well-read newscast. And if the copy is arranged in a coherent sequence, the whole newscast will sound better.

The old system of arranging news copy according to world, national, and local stories has been thrown out the window. Today's radio newscast is made up of news which should be of interest and importance to the station's audience at that time. The lead or beginning story will probably be what you or the editor feel is the most important thing that is happening at the moment without regard to where it is happening.

Determining a good lead takes practice, but equally important is putting the other items in the newscast in a sequence which gives it a flow. For instance, items which are related can be placed adjacent to one another. If the lead item is about the Secretary of State working on a Mid-East peace agreement, then it might be followed by an item about the Senate Foreign Relations Committee working on a new nuclear nonproliferation treaty.

While not all the items included in a newscast will tie together, you can watch for items which are seriously out of place. One would not put a story about a well-known movie star dying from a brain tumor next to a humorous closing item.

Many stations still adhere to the premise that any newscast should end with a humorous item or kicker. In fact, the wire services write their radio news summaries with a humorous or human interest item at the end. Putting a kicker at the end of a newscast should not be an unbreakable rule. A totally meaningless kicker just takes up time which could be better used for hard news. Besides, if you aren't a funny person, don't try to act like one. You don't have to apologize for all the bad news that might have happened—that's the way the world was that day.

Practice is essential to mastering any skill. And there's really no way you can become a proficient newscaster except by practicing. If you have stars in your eyes and absolutely must go on the air, then (1) practice hard (2) take courses or get tutoring, and (3) get on the air anywhere—the campus station, an overnight shift on a minuscule local station, or anything, just get a chance to be in front of that microphone where you work under pressure.

DELIVERING THE TELEVISION NEWSCAST

A television newscast differs a great deal from a radio newscast. Chances are you've seen the old cartoon about radio which shows a shirtless, unshaven slob sitting amid overflowing ashtrays and discarded coffee cups while introducing beautiful classical music. This has happened! But in television you are seen as well as heard. Everyone takes it for granted that you have a decent voice and can read the news. What both management and the audience want to know in television is how you look. By how you look I do not mean physical beauty. I am concerned about how relaxed you appear, the sort of eye contact you maintain, your self-confidence, and the way you adjust your mood to fit what you are talking about.

Forget about physical appearance. Yes, there are a lot of handsome, good-looking men and women on television. There are also a lot of people who couldn't by any circumstance be put in this category, and they're doing major market anchor assignments and network television newscasts. In fact, toss out the names of some major network anchorpersons at a party some time, and ask if people think they are good looking. You may be surprised at the reactions you will get. What these people do have is the ability to relate to an audience.

Generally, radio is a good training ground for television because you learn the basics of air presentation, including learning how to read news well. The problem with television is that people don't really expect you to read them the news off pieces of paper. You have to tell them the news by looking straight into the camera as much as you can, and by appearing relaxed and confident.

In recent years there has been a revolution in the way television newscasts are presented. It all started with what is now known in the field as "happy talk." Ever since the first television newscast was aired, the news department had sort of a formal, authoritative air. Then along came the ABC television stations, and they asked, "Why can't our newscasters be human?" It worked so well that everyone went overboard. The anchorpersons joked with each other, with the weathercaster, with the sportsperson, with the technicians, and with everyone. Unfortunately much of the banter was artificial and contrived.

But out of this came a radical change in newscasts. Now anchorpersons can be human. They stop and ask questions and discuss the news with their colleagues in the studio and, where ENG is used, with reporters in the field. A good many stations insist that the field reporters come into the studio and anchor their own reports. And, quite rightly, the newscast personalities mention little human things about each other, such as the birth of a child or a hole-in-one. After all, to most viewers these people come into the home via television several times a week, and they become, in a sense, part of the family.

Many newscasts have moved off the rigid formal sets to more fluid settings where people can move around and where more than one person can be seen at one time. Many stations have gone all the way and moved their newscasts into the newsroom. For some this is legitimate, because they have big, busy newsrooms and it is possible to change part of the newscast as it is being done. For other stations it's pure showmanship, because by newscast time they don't have the staff to fill a newsroom and most of the people seated off camera are props for the newscast.

Delivering news on camera requires eye contact. The ultimate device is a machine that unrolls the script, which is typed in large letters, and projects it onto a mirror directly in front of the lens of the taking camera. However, in smaller markets you won't have the luxury of reading off a TelePrompTer or other camera-mounted device. You will read from typed news copy.

But in most cases the copy will be typed in large letters with plenty of margin space. With practice you will learn to look up from the copy at frequent intervals, delivering much of the copy straight into the camera lens.

This is not quite as difficult as it sounds. Remember that television items are usually short, perhaps 20 seconds or less. The introductions to film and tape reports may be even shorter. So if you take time to study the script carefully before you go on the air, and if you reread what you will be saying next while reports or commericals are running, you will be able to present a remarkably large part of the newscast straight to the camera.

Familiarity with the script is essential for another reason: there is nothing quite as unconvincing as a television anchorperson who sounds as if the script were being read for the first time or who stumbles.

Your face has to do something; it is showing all over the screen. It should move, maybe wrinkle a bit, or show some emotion. In other words, relax and put your whole self into presenting the news. You are a person talking to other people. And people who talk to other people aren't usually flat, dull, or expressionless. But your facial and body motions must be natural. Nothing turns off an audience like a newscaster who appears to have memorized seven stock facial expressions to cover typical news stories.

You have to appear relaxed even if your stomach is doing flip-flops, because you must give your audience the idea that everything is under control. Just because the film has stopped in the projector, one camera has toppled, a dog is running through the studio, and an overhead light just burned out with a blue flash, there's really nothing seriously wrong. Again, being with people and appearing before people will help you to become relaxed and confident. Almost any activity which requires you to perform or appear before people is beneficial.

Being an on-camera news personality means performing. There is no way you can avoid this fact. If you don't do a good job of convincing the audience that you know what you are talking about and that you are relaxed and confident, then you haven't done your job. In fact, television is so performance-oriented that in the larger stations you will wear make-up. Oddly enough, this little bit of theater serves only one purpose: to make you look more natural on camera. Unfortunately, the lights used in television and the nature of camera tubes can make human beings look unnatural without make-up.

How do you dress? Well, the days of blue shirts and blouses have gone. The production personnel will give you some guidance as to colors and patterns. But today's television anchorperson dresses pretty much as business persons in the community would dress. Generally, one's appearance will be a bit more conservative than you might prefer. Television is a mass medium, and the audience in your area may not be ready for extremes in clothing. You will undoubtedly get solid guidance from the management on clothing standards.

In television you tell your audience the news, talk to them, remain cool and confident, look them straight in the eye, and try to be a warm human being.

8
Law and the Broadcast Journalist

Broadcasting is a regulated industry. This means that the broadcast journalist must operate within the limits of this regulation, while being aware of other legal restraints which apply to *all* journalists. This chapter will give you a general outline of the legal considerations faced by a broadcast journalist. It will *not* give you a definitive text on law. Anyone interested in broadcast journalism should at least read a good textbook on communications law and take a course in that subject.

In addition, the specifics of certain laws, such as libel and slander, differ from one place to another. This chapter will give you enough of an idea of the legal matters which might affect you and for you to be able to ask the right questions when the time comes. Never fear asking advice on any matter which appears to have legal aspects. Your management will probably know the answer and, if not, will refer the question to an attorney.

THE FIRST AMENDMENT

To a broadcast journalist, the single most important legal document affecting his or her occupation is the U.S. Constitution, specifically the First Amendment. The First Amendment contains four important guarantees: freedom of religion, freedom of speech and press, freedom of assembly, and freedom to petition the government for redress of grievances.

The First Amendment contains this directive:

> Congress shall make no law respecting an establishment of religion, or prohibiting the free exercise thereof; or abridging the freedom of speech, or of the press; or the right of the people peaceably to assemble, and to petition the Government for a redress of grievances.

The key words for journalists are "or abridging the freedom of speech, or of the press." Additionally, granting of the right to petition the government for redress of grievances allows journalists to sue when their rights are being infringed.

The freedom of speech right granted under the First Amendment is the source of the unusual power of the American press. Few countries have legislated such freedom, which allows the press to report a multitude of activities and comment freely on society and the government. Many people disagree with the liberality expressed in the First Amendment, and attempts to limit the rights it gives the press take place almost daily. Leading journalists and their professional associations devote a great deal of time to defending these rights.

Simply put, freedom of speech means freedom from censorship or other forms of interference. The news media does not have to go to the government for clearance of a story, nor does the government have the right to shut down a broadcast transmitter just because a news story was unfavorable to its conduct.

The law of broadcasting will be dealt with more later in this chapter, but there is one important point to be brought up now: When Congress drew up the legislation which regulates broadcasting, it specifically classified broadcasting as a form of communication covered by the word "speech" in the First Amendment. This eliminates any question as to whether the word "press" in the First Amendment might apply only to the written press.

The Fourteenth Amendment extends the actions prohibited in the First Amendment to include the states.

LIBEL AND SLANDER

If you turn to your dictionary seeking a definition for libel, you'll come up with something like this, taken from *Webster's New Collegiate Dictionary*: "Any statement, or representation, published without just cause or excuse, or by pictures, effigies, or other signs, tending to expose another to public hatred, contempt, or ridicule."

In broadcasting libel is referred to as slander, the oral form of libel. Libel and slander are defined somewhat differently in various jurisdictions, but there are a few general guidelines which can be safely applied to the problem. One of these is that in most jurisdictions, truth is an absolute defense against libel. In order words, if what you say is true, even if it causes a person hurt, you cannot be successfully sued for libel.

No reporter should set out to say or write something designed to do harm to another unless the facts are such that the public's need to know is paramount. One can do a great deal of harm to a public official by saying he has been indicted by a Grand Jury, but the public has a right to know that this official is held under serious suspicion of misconduct by a group of citizens called together to determine if the evidence warrants an indictment.

The news media has unique defenses when accused of libel and slander. The legal history of press libel decisions has developed the principle that fair comment by the media and the value of a free press to society outweigh the risk that an individual would be damaged due to the inaccuracy of facts.

However, one important guideline must be remembered: *there must be no malice involved.* Woe to the reporter who is found to have deliberately broadcast false information to intentionally harm an individual. Not only is it a gross violation of principles held by journalists, it's a neat way to end up with a civil judgment against you.

This question of accuracy of harmful information is precisely why journalists insist on attributing statements which characterize people. Always say from whom or what the accusation you are repeating stems.

There are a number of traps which open a reporter to accusations of having committed libel. Most have to do with police matters. Be careful to avoid libel by accusation. Always label the source of any accusatory statement. You must say, "Police say Samuels was allegedly stabbed by his uncle." Never say, "Samuels was stabbed by his uncle." It is possible Samuels was not stabbed by his uncle, and then where would you be? The word "allegedly" is written into most crime-related stories, even though it sounds awkward, as a way to fight off libel suits.

Be very careful in dealing with situations in which police say they have a "suspect." If you attempt to describe a suspect, don't be too specific about any one person. Forget about using pictures of "suspects" except for police composite drawings or, after checking, bank security-camera photos.

Tread with utmost caution on accusations of rape. First of all, substitute the word "assault" until an indictment is drawn accusing a specific individual of rape. And be certain to ascribe accusations of assault to some authoritative source, and even then make it an alleged assault.

Be nonspecific about apparent drunkenness. There are legal ways to define drunkenness, the most common being blood-alcohol analysis. Again, wait until an official charge is lodged.

Never assume the guilt of an individual. Police may say an individual admits guilt, and the physical evidence may point in that direction—such as his being found on the premises which has just been robbed. But until a charge is lodged, everything is "police say" and "alleged."

In some states a person may be arrested on "suspicion of" committing a crime. But in other states there is no such crime. Find out what the law is. And don't believe other press sources. The wire services make mistakes, particularly because they rely on local stringers of varying quality and because they shift staff members from state to state.

A person is not accused of a crime until he has been arrested, even if police talk to him or take him into custody. While I have talked mainly about police matters, remember that civil accusations of business misconduct or words like "illicit," "mismanaged," "corrupt," and "affair" all are potentially dangerous and must be attributed to someone else who makes a specific accusation which is reported by you as an allegation.

The journalist must take extraordinary care in writing and speaking about people who are not public figures. They are the most vulnerable to harm from a mistake (such as an incorrect fact about an alleged criminal record), and they have the strongest position in a suit. Public officials and public figures have fewer recourses, especially if they are held up to what they feel is public ridicule because of their actions.

In the famed *New York Times vs. Sullivan* case the U.S. Supreme Court decided that a public official could not recover damages in the case of a defamatory falsehood regarding his official conduct unless the falsehood had been broadcast with "actual malice."

The theory is this: The nature of American politics and public life allows for robust controversy and discussion of public issues. If an individual accepts a role in public life, then he or she must be willing to "take a few lumps."

Broadcast stations are further protected from certain libel and slander actions because they are forbidden to censor the broadcasts of political candidates over their facilities (this applies specifically to campaign broadcasts). Thus the stations cannot be held responsible for the content of these broadcasts.

In another important case, *Associated Press vs. Walker*, the Supreme Court said that the risks inherent in being a public official extend to individuals who are "public figures." In the AP case, the person seeking redress was an outspoken retired general.

Basically, the broadcast reporter should not knowingly repeat or utter falsehoods. You should check thoroughly accusations against people made by others, and delete them if you have any doubt as to their substance. It is easy to call up or interview an individual who is very upset over the proposed location of a new school and end up with that individual saying a school committee member has a financial stake in the real estate being considered for the school. You can't let this sort of statement slip by. You should confront the school committee member. If the person declines to confirm the accusation, you should then try to establish by other means if the accusation is true.

There are two ways to handle this sort of story. One is to delete the accusation on the grounds that it is unsubstantiated. The other is to try to prove the accusation and to confront the accused. There really is no reason to have extraordinary fear of libel or slander suits if you practice good journalistic procedures. You should check your facts and confront the accused as well as demand that the accuser support the accusation.

There will probably be times when angry newsmakers will threaten suits. Don't be scared off, but be smart, check with your management and with your firm's lawyers. You are in an especially good position if the threat to sue precedes use of your information, because then you have time to consult the lawyers. But if the threat comes after you have broadcast something, you should be able to rely on your common sense and professional ethics to have kept you out of trouble. After that, your firm's lawyers will probably calm down the whole affair when they remind the offended individual's lawyers of the various privileges accorded by the courts to the press.

PRIVACY

There is an area of law called privacy which you must be aware of. It is not always clearly defined in all locations. In general there are certain areas of life in which individuals have a right to be left to mind their own business. If you encounter a privacy question, it will probably have to do with documents or photographs.

Obviously one has to be cautious in the use of material from personal letters or other documents, and it would be unwise to use information overheard on a telephone line. It would be equally unwise to go onto private property with your camera and photograph or try to interview individuals unless you have been given permission to enter that private property.

On the other hand, if a person is in a public place you can photograph them with impunity. By public place is meant, for example, on a city street or in the public area of a government building. But you would have to get, in writing (as a rule), permission of a hospital patient, for example, before using that person's voice or image on the air.

Some photographers who feel they might be accused of invading private property will take their film or tape from a public street or sidewalk. You might run across the problem in a case where the police are taking someone into custody at a private home.

An incidental picture of a person at a public event is acceptable. Even if the person wasn't supposed to be where he or she was photographed and as a result suffers embarrassment.

If you have doubts about your rights to interview a person such as a class member at a school, protect yourself by asking the individual, while your tape or film is running, if it's okay to conduct the interview. Of course you should already have the permission of the institution's administrator before you start.

Radio reporters must always secure permission before recording telephone conversations. Occasionally someone you have interviewed on tape or film will complain about the content of the interview after it is complete. You are protected by the fact that the individual agreed to the interview—otherwise it wouldn't have taken place.

It is not at all unusual to get requests for deletion of certain materials from interviews, or for the prescreening of the final product. Any station worth its salt will politely decline this sort of request when it applies to hard news coverage. It may be that you will honor a request for deletion if there's a sound reason. but that is the station's prerogative. not the interviewee's.

COPYRIGHT

The average reporter will have only cursory need for understanding the copyright laws. Basically you cannot use news items from services to which your station does not subscribe or take an item from that service out of a newspaper. It's not likely you'll encounter many problems of this sort. since most stations have adequate wire service facilities. and usually newspapers are used just for reference and for background material.

It would be improper to steal a story off another station's air. but all good news departments listen to the competition. and if they find they are running behind on a story. then a vigorous effort is made to get the story from sources. But it would not and should not be stolen off the air of a competitor.

The courts also recognize that there are times when it is appropriate to use portions of a copyrighted work without obtaining the copyright-holder's permission. This is called "fair use." and in the case of a broadcast journalist might apply to a book or movie review. Or if you were preparing a feature on science or another specialized area. you might quote from a published work without obtaining prior permission. The premise of "fair use" is that your use would not detract from the value of the original work.

In the case of recorded music that you might wish to use to accompany a feature. check with the program department of your station to see if the music is licensed by one of the organizations which maintains blanket contracts with stations. such as the American Society of Composers. Authors. and Publishers (ASCAP).

FEDERAL COMMUNICATIONS COMMISSION

Broadcast journalists must live with the fact that they are working in a regulated industry. From the very earliest days of broadcasting in the United States. it was recognized there had to be some sort of government supervision of the airwaves. simply because the number of frequencies was limited.

The Radio Act of 1912 gave the Secretary of Commerce and Labor authority over radio broadcasting. The Secretary was given the power to grant licenses upon application. But what the law did not give the Secretary was the ability to *reject* applications.

The policy that evolved was to have all the infant radio stations share two frequencies. In no time the interference from the rapidly growing number of stations became intolerable. The transmitters didn't hold to the assigned frequencies well and, in some cases, the owners would change frequencies arbitrarily.

Out of this chaos evolved the Radio Act of 1927. This was the first legislation specifically designed to regulate radio broadcasting. The earlier laws had been aimed at maritime and telegraphic communication. The act established certain principles which still govern American broadcasting. They include the following:

The concept that the radio frequencies or television channels belong to the people.

The idea that this service should be distributed so that the signals available are equitably apportioned across the country.

The government has the right to regulate broadcasting, but this right is not absolute.

The right to use a broadcast frequency is not available to everyone.

Broadcasting is a form of expression protected by the First Amendment to the U.S. Constitution.

The Federal Radio Commission was given the job of implementing the act. Some of the problems the Commission dealt with included trimming down the number of stations on the air, setting up a legal mechanism, and developing engineering standards for the industry.

There was strong feeling in some quarters that the laws governing broadcasting needed further refining, including combination of wire and wireless communication under one jurisdiction. The eventual result was the Communications Act of 1934, under which broadcasting is regulated today.

The Communications Act contains the phrase "public interest, convenience and necessity," which plays an important role in the regulatory problems of broadcasters. It is a vague phrase, taken from legal precedents regulating public utilities, and the interpretations of this phrase have been many and varied in the history of broadcasting.

One of the key parts of the Communications Act of 1934 prohibits the FCC from censoring radio communications. Of course, there are subtle forms of censorship, such as the letters the FCC sends to station owners when someone complains about the content of a broadcast. The difficulty in answering these letters properly, superimposed on the owner's constant knowledge that the station's license must be renewed periodically, tends to make the station owner cautious.

There is one important provision in the act designed to prevent the holders of broadcast licenses from saying whatever they wish over the airwaves without someone having the ability to respond. The act contains a section, 315, which says that if one candidate for a political office is permitted to use the facilities of a broadcast station, then all the other candidates for the same office have that same right. The station management does not have to permit a candidate to use the facilities, but once one candidate appears, all others running for the same office may request time.

This section was amended to exempt certain broadcasts from this equal time requirement. They are a bona fide newscast, a bona fide news interview, on-the-spot coverage of a bona fide news event, and a bona fide news documentary (providing the appearance of the candidate is incidental to the subject matter of the documentary).

Further, Section 315a of the Communications Act contains one sentence which is very important:

> Nothing in the foregoing sentence shall be construed as relieving broadcasters, in connection with the presentation of newscasts, news interviews, news documentaries, and on-the-spot coverage of news events, from the obligation imposed upon them under this chapter to operate in the public interest and to afford *reasonable opportunity for the discussion of conflicting views or issues of public importance.*

This sentence (in italics) is taken by many as a legal precedent for the FCC's "fairness doctrine." What the section says is that if the licensee of a broadcast station allows a controversial issue of public importance to be aired, then a reasonable opportunity must be afforded for presentation of contrasting points of view. Unlike the equal time provision of Section 315, the FCC's own rules say that the Commission must not substitute its judgment for that of the licensee, but it can reasonably expect the licensee to demonstrate "reasonable judgments in good faith" in the handling of controversial issues.

In September 1975 the FCC modified its stand on equal time, saying both political debates and news conferences were exempt from equal times rules because they qualified as on-the-spot coverage of bona fide news events. There is an exception in the case of debates involving politicians. The event must be under the control of someone other than the broadcaster. In other words, if a radio or television station scheduled a debate between two candidates for an office, other candidates for the same office would be entitled to equal time. But if the local Junior Chamber of Commerce scheduled such a debate, the station could cover or broadcast it.

The FCC applied the equal time rule to political debates in 1962 and to political news conferences in 1964. This action is of particular importance because it appears to clear up some confusion over whether stations and networks should carry a news conference by an incumbent President who is an announced candidate for renomination or reelection. Shortly after the decision was announced, both CBS and NBC declined to cover live a presidential news conference, saying they felt the Commission's action did not relieve the equal time burden.

If the news department is doing a sound journalistic job there shouldn't be any problem for reporters. Good journalistic practice dictates that several aspects of controversial issues be explored. A good reporter or editor doesn't stick with just one side of an issue. He or she seeks out contrasting viewpoints from the known exponents of differing views and willingly discusses contrasting viewpoints with individuals and groups which bring those viewpoints to the attention of the news department.

In addition to normal coverage of known spokespersons, some news departments take certain controversial issues to the streets, getting interviews with members of the general public. A New York City television station has gone one step further. A panel of experts or opinion leaders is gathered in the studio, and then live remote units are stationed around the viewing area. Members of the public are encouraged to ask the panel questions about a specific topic, such as how to finance the public schools or whether probation is more effective than imprisonment.

There is one very sensitive area of the fairness doctrine; it is called "personal attack." When an individual is attacked in an editorial or in other programing, the station has an obligation to seek out the individual attacked and offer the opportunity for a personal reply.

The FCC requires that notice be given the individual attacked within one week along with a tape or transcript, and that time be offered for a reply. In the case of a station editorial which endorses or opposes a political candidate, similar steps must be taken within 24 hours. These requirements were first promulgated by the FCC in 1967 and were subsequently affirmed by the U.S. Supreme Court in its "Red Lion" decision in 1969. The word attack means an attack on the honesty, character, integrity, or like personal qualifications of the individual or group. And the individual or group must be identified.

The provisions of the 1967 FCC rules do not apply to attacks on foreign groups or foreign public figures. Nor do they apply to personal attacks made by legally qualified candidates or their authorized spokespersons or those associated with them in the campaign. And most importantly they do not apply to bona fide newscasts, news interviews, on-the-spot coverage of bona fide news events, and to editorials.

While each of these rules excludes bona fide news functions, you must remember that the overall balance of the station's news coverage can be questioned during the license renewal period, and it is increasingly being questioned by various pressure groups. One outstanding case is the New York City television stations which are consistantly being called to task by representatives of New Jersey, Connecticut, or suburban New York counties which feel that they are due more extensive news coverage.

The question of fairness is an important one which crops up frequently and serves as a constant reminder to the reporter that he or she should not accept one viewpoint without seeking contrasting ones.

FREEDOM OF INFORMATION

While the First and Sixth Amendments to the Constitution are supposed to insure a free press, the actual "freedom" of press can be and is sharply restricted. As a result the professional associations representing the press devote a tremendous amount of time trying to assure people that there is a free press with a clear-cut right to report and question freely.

Some of the issues of importance in talking about a free press are national security, public records and meetings, and agreements with sensitive groups.

National Security

There is a need to keep a limited number of government activities secret. The paramount question is how extensive is this need? During World War Two the broadcast industry cooperated under the voluntary Censorship Code. It prohibited broadcasting weather reports (except in emergencies) and contained an agreement to use only government-released information about military or naval activity.

But during peacetime the need to keep secret the activities of government is far more limited. There appears to be justification for keeping some secrets about military technology, keeping confidential some diplomatic negotiations (which for the most part are subject to review by Congress), and restricting access to legitimate security information.

However, there is an understandable tendency on the part of government offices and people who staff them to try to keep as much of their activities as possible from public view. After all, there is less latitude for public and official criticism if nothing is known about the conduct of government affairs.

Our system of government has a tendency to reduce this problem somewhat because so many people are involved in government. Someone always has an ax to grind, and so a good many "secrets" manage to "leak" out because people who hold opposing views or who have political motives divulge the information.

In recent years some excellent investigative reporting has been done by methodical reporters who have studied the political campaign funding reports the government requires of federal candidates. The information on violations is frequently suggested by these official reports, providing someone has the patience and skill to read them. Two major areas of concern are the government's procedures in classifying secret documents and the use of computers.

The government has classifications for documents which serve to restrict the number and categories of persons authorized to view them. Unfortunately the secret or classified stamp is often affixed to documents not to preserve legitimate national security information. but to keep them from curious eyes. This practice can only be limited by a combination of government rules (which are being tightened) and vigilant surveillance by the press and legislators.

Classified documents also need to be declassified when they no longer are secret or have a purpose which is served by secrecy. If for no other reason. these documents should be available for historical review after they have expired.

Data banks are increasingly being used at all levels of government. The legal and ethical question is just how much information the government should be allowed to assemble on an individual and to what use the government should put this information. The frightening thing is that the government has a great deal of information on everyone. And all that is needed to recover it in many cases is a social security number—an identification which is virtually nationwide.

The government has tax files. military records. birth records. security clearances. and various reports filed in conjunction with other activities (for example. if someone once lived with someone who had a security sensitive job). Through the computer the government agencies can call on motor vehicle records. court and police files. health notes. and other bits and pieces of information.

Having these records in most cases is neither improper nor illegal. But the question is. to whom are they given and for what purposes? These records have been assembled by interested government officials so that they could study the activities of people who were dissenting with government policies. The public is told that income tax records were searched by government officials seeking certain information. There have been reports of people being rejected for jobs because of activities which. while not illegal. did not agree with the predilections of government officials. Arrest records have been studied when they had no relevance.

All of this is frightening. and one way to control this sort of system is through the vigilant watchfulness of the press. which must work to expose improper use of the government's vast data files. The history of United States conduct of the Vietnam war and the famed Watergate affair amply illustrate the dangers inherent in the willy-nilly use of classification to conceal public documents.

You should be aware of Public Law 93-579: The (federal) Privacy Act of 1974. Here are some of the provisions of the act:

It covers personal data record systems kept by the federal government.

Federal agencies may collect only "relevant" data and must publish descriptions of their record system as well as keep the records timely and accurate. Among irrelevant items would be a person's politics or religion.

An individual has the right to inspect his or her records and to ask for deletions or corrections. Also, any agency may not disclose information from its files without the person's permission. Of course, there are exceptions. A major exception from the act covers investigatory, national security, and law enforcement files.

The act puts limits on the disclosure of social security numbers.

An individual may sue in a federal court if that person's rights under the act have been violated.

The federal government and many of the states now have laws which define just what documents are available for public inspection. However, it sometimes takes vigorous pursuit of these documents, a firm reminder about the law's requirements, and even court orders to get some documents dislodged. The federal law sets deadlines for the production of requested records.

Unfortunately there are a number of subterfuges public officials use to avoid producing documents. One, as Watergate demonstrated, is to shred or burn the documents. Another is to lose the files or "misplace" them or to send them to some remote point.

Obtaining the records of public departments and of public bodies is one problem and another is the courts. There are certain records which are clearly public, and others which fall under a cloud.

Land and zoning documents should be accessible. You should be able to go to the courthouse and figure out who (at least by name) owns a piece of property. The search itself may be complex, but the documents should be available.

Certain documents are filed in criminal and civil court cases which describe the accusations. You should be able to go to the court clerks and read the indictment in a criminal case or the documents outlining a civil suit. Once a case is adjudicated. the decision should be on file.

There are records that are legitimately confidential. The deliberations of a grand jury are secret. One reason this is not of great concern is that if a grand jury hands up an indictment. the whole matter will be recorded in court records anyway. The actual deliberations of the petite (trial) jury are secret.

Election records should be public. but this is one area in which the media have to be vigilant since there seems to be a natural tendency to distort the election process. One area which bears constant watching is the voter registration process. Voters can be encouraged or discouraged at registration time simply by the manner in which registration is handled. And in some areas one has to watch out for registration of unqualified voters.

Nowadays candidates are usually required to file documents having to do with the sources of their campaign funds and how these funds are spent. These records should be reviewed. because they sometimes give clues to discrepancies.

Most police departments have some method of permitting the press to inspect routine booking records and investigation reports. For the most part the reporter has to follow up these sketchy reports by personal contact with the officers involved. Much of the investigatory process is confidential, since the material is being gathered for possible introduction in a trial.

Federal authorities—such as the FBI, the Secret Service, and the Attorney General—are even more cautious about talking of investigations for fear of compromising the eventual trial. The best you can do is gain the respect of local federal officers. Then you will probably be given as much information as can be properly released.

Freedom of information laws are gradually being passed by the states. For example, New York State passed its law in May 1974. It covers records of public agencies, corporations, authorities. and commissions as well as state and local legislative bodies.

The biggest step forward has been in getting the clear right to inspect agency records. A great deal has been hidden over the years behind the bureaucracy of federal and state agencies. Generally the new laws require agencies to make their records available for "unimpaired access" by the public for inspection and copying.

Another requirement in one state is the publication of a list of the meetings of all boards, commissions, agencies, and committees which have regular meetings. The idea is that it then falls to the press and public to attend the meetings if they are interested.

One of the subterfuges used by public bodies is to neglect to reveal the time, place, and date of their meetings. Usually a little detective work and a lot of harsh publicity discourages recurrences of this practice.

One county welfare board used to try to conceal its meetings. When the local press discovered the practice and began attending meetings, the board would admonish the press that any action they took on cases was confidential by law. The press responded that, of course, it would abide by the confidentiality requirement but that applied only to client cases and not to board decisions on policy, expenditures, or programs.

Public boards often hide behind the "executive session." They usually say the matters being considered are personal or private and can't be discussed in public without doing some form of grievous harm. Most authorities on government agree that the only times public boards should meet in private is (1) to deal with personnel matters which might cause embarrassment to individuals if discussed in public and (2) to negotiate for the purchase of land where, if the intentions of the board were known beforehand, the price of the land might suddenly rise.

Agreements with Sensitive Groups

There are a number of areas in which there are sensitive legal problems encountered in routine press coverage. The courts provide one of the most trying areas. Another is hospitals, where the privacy of patients has to be protected while dealing with the problems of releasing information to which the public has a legal right.

The way the problems have been approached is to set up informal and formal agreements binding organizations representing both sides of an issue. Several state hospital associations have evolved guidelines in conjunction with groups representing the media. Typical guidelines require hospitals to make known to the media the names and phone numbers of authorized spokespersons for the hospital. They often define what information can be given to the press and what must be withheld and why.

For example, under one set of guidelines, a hospital must acknowledge admission of a patient and issue a general description of the patient's condition. Names of the deceased are revealed only after notification of next of kin. On the other hand, the guidelines prohibit hospital personnel from making any statement about intoxication, poisoning, rape, or morals crime. Most hospitals limit photographs or radio-television interviews unless the attending physician, the hospital administration, and the patient all agree to the interview or photographs.

The American Bar Association has done a great deal of work on an issue called "fair trial, free press." The purpose is to encourage the accurate and complete coverage of trials while protecting the rights of the victims and defendants.

The typical set of fair trial-free press guidelines are designed to discourage the release of certain defined types of information that would be inadmissible in court or might be prejudicial to the rights of the accused. Basically, the American Bar Association feels that the media has the right to know the facts including the identity of the accused along with pertinent information such as age, address, family status, and the circumstances surrounding the arrest. The ABA also feels that law enforcement officials should provide the identity of arresting and investigating officers (unless they have been working undercover) and the text of the complaint, indictment, or information.

What the ABA tries to prevent is the venturing of opinion on the accused's guilt or innocence or character. Other matters which the ABA thinks should be kept for revelation at a trial include alleged confessions, laboratory tests, and the nature of testimony which might be given by witnesses.

The association would like to prevent the release of the prior criminal record of the accused, but this information is usually a matter of public record and so becomes discretionary with the individual news organization. One argument is that each case should be treated in isolation. A contrasting argument says that a person's prior conduct may well be relevant to what is being considered now.

The ABA prefers more restriction then the media. In many states the two groups have come to agreement on ground rules. At the heart of the controversy is "pre-trial publicity" in which the defense would like to contend that everything said in the media about the defendant prior to or during the trial adversely affects the defendant's case. This is why it is so difficult to pick juries in cases that gain notoriety: there are few potential jurors who will not have heard or read something about the case.

The final ground rules in any case are set by the judge, and there have been some sharp clashes between bench and media over trial coverage and constitutional guarantees in recent years. The courts present a difficulty for electronic journalists because it is seldom possible to report a trial using customary electronic techniques.

The judiciary has historically objected to electronic equipment for three reasons: (1) the equipment is disruptive, (2) the participants in the trial may conduct themselves in a manner which they feel will reflect well in broadcast coverage, and (3) the editing of the report on the trial may distort the total conduct of the trial by using only appealing aural or visual sequences without regard to their relative importance within the total contest of the trial.

It has been shown on a number of occasions that the equipment can be installed so that it will not be disruptive and in such a manner that while the participants know the equipment is there, they have no way of telling if they are subject to the microphone's or camera's attention at a particular moment.

Judges are accustomed to working with lengthy briefs and total transcripts of trials. They are usually less harsh on the print media simply because a significant trial usually gets many column inches of coverage in the papers. But brevity is imperative in broadcasting, so the judiciary has to be convinced that the professional editorial judgment of the broadcast media would not distort a report of the day's events.

Of course, one could ask if electronic coverage of a trial is necessary at all. Electronic coverage outside the courtroom is limited by local rules. Federal courts often set specific boundaries, such as the entire courtroom floor of the federal building, while state courts very. If you have any question about law or legal aspects of what you are donig, ask someone at the newsroom or station who can advise you or refer you to the right source.

9
Documentaries and Public Affairs Programs

There are many reasons why radio and television stations broadcast documentary and public affairs programs. The first and foremost is the fact that the Federal Communications Commission looks very closely at the types and amount of public service programing done by a station. As a result, there is a strong economic incentive to do public service programs. A station cannot operate and make money without a federal license. and it can only keep that license by satisfying the FCC that the station has met its stated public service objectives.

As it happens. this type of programing can produce revenue. so many broadcast stations are eager to combine their compliance with federal guidelines with the profit motive. Some stations go far beyond any promises they might have made to the Commission because their owners firmly believe in the important contributions they can make within their audience areas.

DOCUMENTARIES

It is difficult to give a precise definition of a documentary, because many types of programs are called documentaries. In general a documentary attempts to take a deep view of some aspect of society. to explore different viewpoints, and to draw conclusions. In radio, where a 45 second report is common for hard news stories, a $2^{1}\!/_{2}$ minute feature might be called a minidocumentary. Although half-hour and hour documentaries have been common on television, the minidocumentary is now appearing within some extended evening newscasts.

One can safely generalize that a documentary will probably contain material gathered away from the station and will usually include interviews with a number of people. But this is a rule that can as easily be broken as followed. For example, one group of stations did a documentary on the Civil War which featured camera-animated sequences created by using series of Matthew Brady photographs taken at the battlefront.

Other examples of documentaries include the 30 minute and 1 hour news specials shown on television. Some, like the NBC White Papers, have been considerably longer. Some radio documentaries run a half-hour or hour, but more frequently radio documentaries consist of a series of shorter segments.

Many local television stations have adopted a practice of using the 7:30 to 8:00 p.m. (6:30 to 7:00 p.m. central time) period for local documentaries.

Radio documentaries vary considerably. They can run up to an hour. But with the development of all-news formats there has been a tendency to break up a major topic into segments. For instance, a series on violence in schools might be broken into five parts. Part one would be an introduction to the problem, with interviews of victims and educators. Part two might get into specifics of violent behavior; part three, solutions as seen by administrators and educators; part four, solutions as seen by teachers; and part five, a psychological view of violence and a wrapup of the topic.

Sometimes a series of this sort is programed vertically—over the course of one day. Or it can be programed horizontally, playing one segment a day for five days. Some all-news stations, feeling that their audience turns over frequently, will repeat the parts, sometimes mixing the vertical and horizontal scheduling of the segments. In any case, the segment usually ends with an appeal to listen for the next segment and a reminder when the next segment will be broadcast.

The CBS Radio Network has developed its own style for radio documentaries. The network pre-empts its regular feature schedule for a Saturday and Sunday of a weekend and replaces the features with 30 segments which are broadcast during the two days. The group of 30 segments has an overall title and purpose, and each is usually designed to cover one aspect of the topic. For instance, a series on medicine would devote one segment to organ transplants and another to heart disease. The length of an individual segment is determined by the length of the program which it replaces.

Some Techniques—Radio

The radio documentary has revived many nearly lost techniques as well as explored some newer ideas. Most radio documentaries rely heavily on interviews, but you also can hear sound effects, on-the-scene reports, and a number of other production techniques. Frequently long interviews are cut to very short segments in order to place various opinions or comments in a meaningful sequence.

Perhaps the basic way to produce a radio documentary is to do a number of interviews, edit them carefully, and tie the recorded segments together with a narration script to fit the program's time frame. This relatively simple technique works very well, providing that the narration script is well written so that the tape inserts fit smoothly and that those inserts are edited to advance the topic meaningfully without an excess of talk.

The major fault of this technique is that there often is a marked difference between the quality and background sound of the narration and that of the tape inserts, which are probably done in several different locations. Also, sometimes you want to tell your story better by including natural sound. A documentary about teenage problems in an urban community is apt to be more meaningful if the narration and the interviews include sounds of the city, streets, schoolyards, and the like.

A minidocumentary prepared by a network producer included the actual sounds of calves being born on a Montana ranch, sequences in which cowboys explained what was happening as they helped the mother cows give birth, and short excerpts from face-to-face interviews with cowboys. Then a narration was written to go with the sound. A great deal of mixing of sound was done to blend the raw material into a fast, smoothly moving segment. While this type of documentary requires very sophisticated production techniques, there is no reason why any radio station that has a portable tape recorder can't do a program with on-scene interviews and some background sound.

It's possible that a very interesting program might be done by talking with one person or one group of people in a setting that would be natural to them. The major thing to watch for is a background that is so noisy that it drowns out the interviews.

One of the sounds which enhances documentaries is music. Clever use of records or of music recorded during production of a documentary can be very effective. One producer used two country and western tunes sung by a federal prison inmate as a background for the concluding portion of a documentary on Christmas in prison. The performer was an amateur. but he conveyed the loneliness of a prison far better than might have been done by a professional recording artist in Nashville.

I have talked about narration in terms of an announcer sitting in a studio reading something which is written out to match a selection of tape inserts. But the narration might be the musings of a distinguished naturalist. interspersed with sounds of birds and the ocean and comments by other interviewees. Or the narration might be a poem read by the poet to the accompaniment of music or sounds which might be appropriate. or it even might be interview excerpts. There is really no limit to the possibilities. The limitations of radio documentaries are those of human imagination.

Most radio documentaries are short. because it has become common to run this type of programing in series. The producer has to think about the proper way to break down the topic. how to make each segment stand by itself. and at the same time how to interlock the segments so that they will relate to each other. One way to accomplish this is to incorporate a distinctive open and close into each segment so that they flow into each other.

Some Techniques—Television

Television is an excellent medium for documentaries because sight and sound can be combined to tell an important story in a dramatic and interesting manner. Most television documentaries include a mixture of interviews with film or tape which shows locales or actions that have something to do with the subject. Natural sound or sound effects can be combined to enhance the final production. Narration can be done over the visual material or on camera on location or on camera in a studio. Sometimes cameras are concealed (for example. a documentary on illegal gambling). Most often. the camera records human drama as it happens.

Almost anything can become the subject of a documentary. Delicate surgery at a medical center, run-down housing, crime, traffic, schools, recreation facilities, alleged mishandling of public property, the future of the city's industry, pollution—these are all topics that can be covered by any station anywhere.

Then there's the "instant documentary." Something big is happening—say the worst flood in a century—and it's too big to just be told on the regularly scheduled newscasts. The news staff is going full blast gathering material. Many stations on both radio and television seize on this type of situation and put together an instant documentary which gives the audience a more comprehensive picture of what is happening.

The visual techniques used in television documentaries are varied and virtually unlimited. Perhaps the most interesting recent development has been the use of portable videotape by independent producers and educational stations. These innovative groups have gone where heavier equipment wouldn't be welcome, and where some stations have been hesitant to go—for example, the ghetto—and have come back with dramatic, poignant statements on life and times in America. The reusability of tape permits the documentary producer to record far more material than is needed, thus relaxing the participants and often creating a feeling of sharing their lives with them.

The basic television documentary can start out just the same as a simple radio documentary: with a narrator or anchorperson providing continuity between interviews. Since it is simple to add visuals—either behind the anchorperson using rear screen projection or an electronic split screen or as the video portion of the program using slides, film, or videotape—most narrations are read with some sort of relevant visual material.

From this basic start, it is possible to travel in many directions. For instance, the picture and the sound do not have to be synchronous, as is the case when you see someone talking on the screen. A narrator or other people can be heard while you watch pictures of related activity. In addition, background sound can be mixed in to give more feeling to the program.

Instead of using motion pictures, you can use slides or still pictures in rapid succession to tell the visual story. As in radio, a poet or singer can carry a story forward, accompanied by appropriate visuals. In some instances, you could film or tape the narrator leading the audience through the experience of the program.

One documentary produced by a major market television station strung together poems written by school children in an urban elementary school. The children read their own poems. The producer selected visuals to accompany each poem. Some were scenes of the city shot on film, and others were still pictures, old newsreel clips, and children's drawings. The whole package of poems was given a narrative link to tie it together. The result was a program which showed adults how one group of children perceive the world about them.

Documentary production for television can be an exciting, challenging experience to the producer with an imaginative eye for visuals and a feeling for ways to tell a story which will drive a point home while making the audience pay attention. There are countless possibilities: documentary cameras have explored the surface of the globe and under the sea, poked into nursing homes, revisited France 25 years after the war, followed wheat farmers, followed a letter through the postal system, and traced human blood through the body's circulatory highways.

Research

Research is an essential part of documentary work. You need to develop a clear idea of what you are trying to explore and even make some preliminary observations on how you are going to go about your task. As in writing a book or term paper, producing a documentary is made much easier if you can start with an outline, a statment of what you want to investigate, some of the major areas which need to be covered, and how you are going to go about your job.

Your outline will change as you go along, but at least you will tend to keep yourself from going in a dozen different directions for no rational purpose. It is very easy in documentary production to finish the process of gathering raw tape or film and find that you have tons of material to audition and no clear idea how it should be used. This is why you need an outline. Once the topic is chosen and the areas to be covered are defined, you need to learn all you can about the topic by reading books and magazines, by library research, by saving clippings, and most important by talking to as many people as possible who are familiar with some aspect of your investigation.

You can obtain help from the public library and from groups representing various bodies of opinion in the field. For example, if you are doing a documentary on health care, there are dozens of organizations in the health care field, including the American Medical Association, the American College of Radiology, the American Hospital Association, the American Nurses Association, and their state affiliates who have gathered a great deal of material on almost any health topic.

Obviously each group represents certain sets of ideas and will do its best to present its own viewpoint. You will have to look for contrasting viewpoints. Oddly enough, the leaders of some of the major organizations will be quite frank in telling you the names of those who oppose their viewpoints. This information can be quite time-saving.

There are other ways to find contrasting opinions. If there is a legal matter involved, talk with the local civil liberties organizations. Such groups frequently get involved in issues of public concern. There are medical organizations with contrasting viewpoints. They include the newly formed physicians' unions and some of the groups which promote one specialized area of medicine.

You can also get a great deal of free help from legislators and government bureaus. Both collect data on a good many topics which they will provide, usually just for the asking. In addition, many topics which might be chosen for documentary treatment involve federal or state legislation or government rules. Examples include housing, transportation, medicine, and social service programs. It makes sense to consult with the people who make or enforce the rules to obtain background information and suggestions on whom to interview.

For example, if you were doing a program dealing with national health insurance, you would want to contact some of the leading senators and representatives. Several plans have been authored by individual legislators and by legislative subcommittees. The politicians and their staff members have data which would be important to you in addition to comparative studies they undoubtedly will have prepared covering other proposed legislation.

If the administration has a plan it is backing, you would be able to get assistance at the Department of Health, Education, and Welfare, which does much of the technical work on such legislation. There are also consumer groups which are interested in national health insurance and would be quite willing to provide data. And then, of course, there are the big health insurance companies which have their own specialists studying the various government proposals.

Once you have done enough research to determine what is known and thought about your topic, you have to begin defining what questions you want to ask and finding out whom to ask the questions of. Generally you can tell if you have delved into a documentary fairly deeply if you feel as if you have been through a learning experience.

Research sounds grim, but a quantity of reading and consulting with people who know something about the topic you're covering is necessary in order to do an effective job. If you were doing a documentary on drug treatment programs, for example, you would draw up a list of the programs in your area. Then you would begin collecting clippings about them. You would ask each program for descriptive information, and you would talk, probably on the telephone, with representatives of these programs.

You would read up on the theory of such treatment programs, research applicable laws, check municipal budget documents to find out what part of the taxpayers contribution is being used to support these facilities, and ask the regional office of the Federal Department of Health, Education, and Welfare for any data it might have available. This might include copies of fund grant applications for the programs.

You would talk with drug program leaders, ex-addicts if possible, active addicts, police officers, attorneys, social workers, and probation officers—anyone who might have some knowledge of drug programs. If there were a program to rehabilitate or assist ex-inmates, you might seek out participants who were familiar with the drug culture and talk with them.

Out of these contacts and your reading you would frame a set of questions which you felt should be answered and a list of sources (or interviewees). Your list of questions might be rather general:

What drug programs are available?
How do they differ?
How are they alike?

What kind of cure rate do they claim?

Where do they get their funds?

What is the known extent of the drug problem?

Who checks on the effectiveness and fiscal responsibility of drug programs?

Are the programs effective—and in what ratio to the money spent on them?

What needs to be done that isn't being done?

What can be done to accomplish the needed changes?

Some documentaries call for really deep investigative work. such as pouring through musty old documents in a courthouse. checking public records. and talking to people who may not be willing to reveal their identities. Then you must cross-check your whole body of facts with other sources until you establish what is to the best of your knowledge the solid factual story you are going to tell.

Other documentaries simply involve organizing facts so that some local issue is laid out clearly for further discussion by the community. If your community were getting ready to vote on revisions to the municipal charter. you might do a program or series of programs to illustrate the issues involved in the proposed revisions.

Gathering Material

Although no well-thought-out documentary should lead to the willy-nilly collection of raw material. you can expect to have far more material than you will be able to use in the final product. In order to get to the important questions. most documentary interviews consume a longer than usual amount of time and a greater than usual amount of tape for film. While a documentary interview should be well researched and thought out. it will most likely take some time to complete it in order to work the interviewee deeply into the topic.

In addition. you have to be thinking about production problems. For instance. should you audiotape or film sound and pictures of the surroundings where you are doing the interview? Is there some activity allied with the subject of the interview which requires taping or filming? Do you need to ask for charts or material for slides? Or do you need to arrange for further taping or filming at another time or at another location?

If you are relying on conversations with "average citizens" or if you are following some interesting people around. you should be prepared to use a lot of recording material. Don't put yourself in the position of having to turn off the recorder or camera just when something interesting is about to happen.

You may find yourself gathering a great deal of background material in order to have the flexibility of using your best production techniques to make your documentary interesting. In radio be sure to get sound related to the topic. and in television be sure to get all the pictures and sound you need.

The next problem is to catalog what you have gathered. This means listening to or viewing your raw material. You will find it helpful to take voluminous notes and to code the raw material so that you will be better organized as your project moves along. If possible. you may want to have some of your interviews transcribed so you can look at a precise record of what was said as you write and edit.

Usually the documentary writer/producer starts to write at this point. As a general rule it makes more sense to write a rough script and then see how the material you have fits in than to work on the tape or film first and then mold the script to it. This is one reason for having a transcript of the interviews so you can look at precisely what the person said and use exact quotes in your script. Of course. you may have to make some minor changes when you come to edit the interviews. because they read better on paper than they look or sound. but for the most part you will be pretty safe writing from a transcript. If you can't manage a transcript. listen to or look at the interviews and take very detailed notes on what is said and about how long key sections take. including exact quotes if you can. Even this will help you.

Then move to cutting the tape or film. Usually the basic portion which looks usable has been laid aside during the initial listening or viewing periods. Now the rough script and these materials are compared. and the film or tape editing begins. You pull out the responses from the interviews which seem to fit into the concept of your program and the rough script you have prepared. Later. you may go back and refine the excerpts. lengthening or shortening them or making production changes (such as cross-fades on audiotape) to smooth out the production values, but this is one of the last steps to take.

Then you revise the script again, and go back and recut the tape or film to fit the revision. Finally, you will review the rough program with others who may be involved, such as the management or the company lawyers. Afterward, you polish the production, inserting special effects, fades, dissolves, titles, and music to bring the program to the required time.

Documentaries are hard work, but they are a tremendous challenge to creative people since many of the constraints of day-to-day news coverage are absent. You have more time for production, more opportunities to do research and in-depth interviews, and usually more time on the air for your final product.

Let's run through production of two theoretical documentaries, one for radio and another for television.

A Radio Documentary

Let's say that you are going to do a series of 5 minute minidocumentaries on public housing for the elderly in your community. There will be five parts. The first segment introduces the topic, explains the facilities available, and talks about future plans. The second visits various facilities and talks with the residents, discussing their reaction to the housing and any problems they see. The third program deals with the overall need for public housing for the elderly, how many units are needed, and where the money comes from. The fourth program looks at alternative ways to serve the elderly from a housing viewpoint, and the fifth wraps up the subject, suggesting the most important areas for improvement—in other words, what ought to be done next.

You need to gather information on what facilities are available, so you ask the local housing authority to tell us what housing it has for the elderly, how many apartments are available, and where the facilities are located. One good step at this point is to get in your car and take a driving tour of the facilities so that you will know what the buildings look like and where they are located. You might contact the nearest federal office dealing with housing for the elderly and see if there are recommended standards for such public housing. The state may also have an office dealing with these matters. In many communities there are a number of citizens groups concerned with the elderly. These include public agencies, churches, welfare rights organizations, and coalitions of the elderly. Sometimes national groups such as retired teachers organizations or associations for retired persons put out policy papers on housing for the elderly.

Your research should include a check of your files for clippings and carbons of stories on local housing issues and a visit to the public library to check back issues of the newspapers. During this data-collecting process talk with as many relevant persons as you can, informally and without a tape recorder, so that you can become familiar with the important issues.

Ask the organizations you contact to put you on their mailing lists and to send you back issues of their literature. Also, get any studies or booklets they have published. This information will help you discover the issues and different points of view which are pertinent to your program. Another reason for getting on mailing lists is that you will have a constant input of ideas for future programs or features. Once you finish your housing documentary, you may want to do a followup sometime in the future.

The degree to which you carry on your research depends on whether your series will be an investigation of what facilities are available and how well they are meeting the community's needs or will be an analysis of specific faults, such as corruption in the handling of housing agency funds.

Now it's time to begin your interviews. If possible, use a high-quality, portable, battery-operated cassette machine. Make sure the batteries are fresh and use a reputable brand of cassette. Also, it's highly recommended that you replace the microphone which comes with the machine with a broadcast (studio) quality microphone. If you are going to interview outdoors or in noisy areas, fit the microphone with some type of "blast shield" to reduce the effects of wind and other extraneous noises.

A note on technique: When you begin your interview, run the machine for about 1 minute without anyone talking (that is, you or the interviewee). This will give you some background sound tape for editing. Frequently, when you are integrating interview tapes with narration, the change in background sound from the studio used to narrate to the location of the interview is very abrupt. By gradually adding background sound as the narration ends and the interview tape begins, you can reduce the effect of this jarring change in sound. Also, if you are integrating music or other sound effects, this trick helps.

Organize your questions logically. Ask all the questions you need to get thorough coverage of your topic, and don't be concerned if your interviews run long, providing they are producing useful background information. Think about ways to do the interview. If a certain type of sound setting is appropriate, then do the interview on location. For example, an interview with the recreation director of a housing project for the elderly might be better done in a corner of the recreation room rather than in a private office.

If you are on a walking tour, record the comments of the person taking you on the tour. And everywhere you go, record the ambient sounds for possible use as background to your narration or interviews. Keep good records of your interviews, both by writing down who, where, and when and by recording the same information on your interview tape. Get all your interviewees to pronounce and spell their names. This will save you a great deal of grief later. Be flexible, if a new opportunity for an interview crops up, go ahead and do the interview. It may end up being valuable for your program.

A legal note: Most lawyers advise documentary producers to obtain standard performance releases from persons interviewed, because an interview conducted in the preparation of a documentary is not regarded as spot news, which is usually exempt from the requirements for releases. The release protects your employer and you from being sued for using the person's talents for profit (in case your program is sponsored, for instance) or from being accused of using an interview for which you had not received permission.

As soon as you can, listen to your interview tape and make some notes or transcribe what is said. The sooner you listen, the quicker you can make up for any technical failures or omissions of important information. In addition you will have a clearer memory of the "context" and setting at the time of the interview, which can be important later when you are writing your documentary. Be sure to pay attention to details such as the time of day, where the interview took place, and the appearance of the person interviewed or that person's surroundings (for instance, how a resident's apartment looked).

Be sure to label your tapes carefully and to put corresponding information on your notes. If you have been using cassette tape, you will probably find it easier to dub all or at least the key parts of your interviews onto reel tape for eventual editing.

Group your information by program, and consider the possibility that you may use interviews on more than one program. One good trick when transcribing or taking notes on interviews is to use several sheets of paper and carbon paper so that you can put transcripts or notes of relevant portions of one tape in more than one program's folder when you start to plan how to use your interviews.

Then sit down and write a rough script, with suggested cuts of tape included. Listen to the audiotape and pull out the relevant sections. Cut them as precisely as you can, and time the cuts of tape you have selected. It is often convenient at this point to make a list of each cut you plan to use along with a precise transcript of what is said in the cut.

Now you compare the tape you have with the rough script, and make whatever changes are necessary, working all the time to bring the rough program close to the desired length it will run. The final time of the segment depends on whether it must fit in a precise time slot or just stay within certain limits, such as being close to 5 minutes.

Then record the narration, and begin editing the narration and the interview cuts together. After this has been done and you've trimmed the program down to length, you must work on sound effects and on polishing background sound. Your ability to do this will be somewhat limited by the number of tape recorders you have available, and whether you have a control board through which to mix your sound.

After you finish the technical aspects of production, you should gather together other people who have not been involved in preparing the features to listen objectively. Once you've done this, and the management and perhaps the lawyers have listened, you're ready to go to air. During this final stage, be sure to involve your station's publicity department so that it can promote your effort properly.

A Television Documentary

The ground-laying techniques for a television documentary are similar to those for radio. But through the planning you have to be thinking about pictures. You want to illustrate your documentary with the best and most meaningful visual material so that you will attract and hold the attention of the audience.

As in doing sound for a radio documentary. be sure to shoot plenty of visual material—preferably with sound-track—to go along with your straight interviews. Consider the visual technique you want to use. and if it is unique—such as following one individual around to view the subject through this person's eyes—then make sure all your taping or filming sticks to the basic visual concept. This would mean using the camera without a tripod. which will give you a more fluid view of the subject. but some scenes will be a little rough or jerky due to the jostling that occurs when you walk with the camera.

Your visual techniques can be very simple. for example. just interviews and a studio shot or interviews and silent film. Or they can be very sophisticated with beautiful camera shots or animation. Ask yourself. though. whether your visual material is helping to advance and tell the story. or is it pictures for pictures sake. If you come up with the latter answer. rethink your approach. Again. keep good notes on what you have shot. and view the tape or film as soon as you can after it is shot. laying aside the unwanted material.

Documentaries vary tremendously in style. What I have described is a fairly traditional pattern involving interviews and background sound and visuals. Some stations have done excellent documentaries using unique techniques. (See Fig. 9-1.) For example. the topic might be pollution. and the visuals might be examples of pollution. with a folksong taking up the whole sound track.

An educational station in Maine once told a story about that state's coastline and its people and their livelihood by having a well-known performer narrate in his New England accent as the camera followed him through the locales he was describing. The audience never saw the actor's face. but walked behind him as he wandered along. holding a conversation with an imaginary partner.

Sometimes a documentary will make extensive use of in-studio appearances. Or it may consist of an anchorperson who ties together a series of interviews. A recent network documentary used techniques which are available to most stations. The anchorman narrated from a studio desk set,

226

Fig. 9-1. A WQAD-TV team filming an open heart surgery documentary. The news director is on the left shooting silent cutaways with a Bell & Howell Filmo spring-wound camera with a three-lens turret. The photographer on the right is using a specially designed newsfilm CP-16/A sound camera with a single variable-focus lens. The microphone is mounted on the sound camera. (Courtesy WQAD-TV, Moline, Ill.)

while both still and motion picture visuals appeared behind him. There were cut-ins on both film and tape of reporters and of people being interviewed. Some of the reports had silent film or tape over their narration. At one point, a live cutaway was done to allow the anchorman to talk live with a leading political figure about the current status of legislation concerned with the program's topic. All these techniques are available to the majority of stations—the important factor is their skillful use to create a smooth-flowing program which logically covers the topic.

The point is to use sight and sound as best you can with the equipment and money available to tell an important story in a manner which will compel your viewers or listeners to remain with you throughout the broadcast. Documentaries give journalists a chance to expand from spot coverage of significant issues to a lot which cannot be stuffed into the typical report appearing in a newscast.

Legal Implications

Generally, reporters and other newsroom personnel pay little heed to legal issues which crop up with documentaries. Although I have already mentioned releases, it is important that you understand why you must obtain releases. Spot news coverage is protected by the First Amendment to the U.S. Constitution and its many interpretations. People who permit themselves to be interviewed or who are in public places or who are involved in newsmaking events generally cannot say their privacy has been invaded. But a documentary is not a spot event. Your interviews are usually planned in advance, and you are frequently working on private property where there is no news event in progress. The only way you can protect yourself and your employer from claims for damages due to invasion of privacy or from claims for compensation for using a person's voice or image is to have every person you interview sign a standard performance release. This procedure is cumbersome and will occasionally scare off a potential interviewee, but it is necessary.

There are some shortcuts. When you are dealing with institutionalized persons, check with your lawyer. You may be able to work out a release through the administration of the institution. When interviewing a semimilitary organization, such as members of a police or fire department, you may be able to leave a release with a ranking officer and have the officer take care of getting the signatures. But be sure you finally end up with the signed release.

Specifics of this problem must be taken up with your attorneys. Remember also that you are often working on private property or in institutions that are governed by laws and rules regarding privacy (for example, a mental hospital), which means you have to check ahead for ground rules.

It's a wise idea to have an attorney view or listen to the finished program if there are any legal implications. So if you are doing an expose' or a program which might be taken in a critical light by some organization, be sure you have stuck to all the rules by having your company attorney review the final product.

Promotion

When you're working in a newsroom you probably will pay little attention to the station's publicity program. However, when you are doing a documentary it is important to promote your effort fully. You want to insure the maximum possible audience for your effort, and if the program wins a prize or other recognition, you would certainly want to point out the superiority of your effort to what the competition is doing.

You are fighting entertainment programs for an audience when you air a television documentary. The same is true in radio, but of a lesser degree if the documentary segment is short. If it's long, you have precisely the same problem as a television producer in attracting and keeping your audience.

As far as on-the-air promotion is concerned, you should think about the parts of the actual program which might make catchy "teasers," which are short excerpts that arouse the curiosity of your audience. Make notes on possible teasers and, if you have time, make separate copies (dubs) of these segments so that you can go over them with the promotion department. Your knowledge of the subject matter and the expertise of the promotion department will get this done without bogging down your work.

Early in the development of the program, you must think about its theme and purpose and develop a description which is attractive but nonspecific enough so that you won't end up doing a program totally different from what your promotional material says. This has to be done because advertisements must be prepared well ahead of time if you are going to promote and air your program shortly after it is completed.

Be sure to keep an accurate list of the people you interview and their full names, titles, affiliations, and addresses. This information is invaluable in the external promotion of documentaries. The promotion department will list the names in the local media and also may arrange to provide information to house organs, specialized magazines, and association publications to give your publicity greater outreach. This not only stimulates an audience, it builds good will for future projects in a similar area and spreads the word that your organization is doing serious documentaries on important issues. This can reflect on the station's presentation to the Federal Communications Commission at license renewal time.

Reaping the Awards

There are countless awards given each year for programing on radio and television stations. Some of the most prestigious are the Sigma Delta Chi awards, the George Foster Peabody awards, and awards given by the Radio-Television News Directors Association. In addition, there are many awards given by specific groups interested in education, medicine, law, insurance, highway safety, aviation, and a diversity of other topics.

Many state wire service and broadcasters' associations give awards, as do local press groups in major cities. Awards are part of the way of life in documentary production. They are used by stations to promote their news and public affairs programs and to show that they have a superior staff. Awards can bring important benefits to the reputation of the producer and, occasionally, monetary benefits.

PUBLIC AFFAIRS PROGRAMS

The typical broadcast station does a great deal in the public service area. Not only will it produce documentaries on important subjects, it will donate a significant amount of free time for public service and community announcements. But a major part of the public service activity of most stations involves public affairs programs. Documentaries are public affairs programs, but the scope is much wider.

Radio and television stations frequently have regularly scheduled panel programs in which a person who is important to some aspect of the community's life is interviewed by a group of reporters. Wherever you go in the country you will hear and see local versons of the big-three network panel shows: Face the Nation, Meet the Press and Issues and Answers.

This type of program is fairly simple to produce, and it serves an important purpose. It allows reporters to question someone in public life at length about important issues. Most reporters relish a chance to get on this type of panel because they have the rare opportunity to pursue a line of questioning through several followup questions. This seldom happens during a news conference. The reporter might ask as many followup questions during an interview, but the time limitations of newscast will keep most of the questions and answers from being aired, and they are not likely to be aired one after another, as are the questions and answers during a panel show.

Many stations get additional mileage out of this type of programing by airing the whole program more than once. And others excerpt the most topical responses for inclusion within their newscasts. It's not too hard to get guests for panel programs, because many people in public life are looking for the exposure which comes with this kind of program. Politicians usually will risk having to answer a few tough questions just to be seen and to get a chance to talk at more length about some of their favorite topics.

Municipal, county, and state administrators find this type of program good because they get a chance to talk about what's on their minds without some of the constraints they face in public meetings or in short interviews. The panel-interview program is elementary to produce. Of course, the most important element is organization. You must line up important, interesting guests far enough in advance to be certain of their appearing. At the same time you must have the flexibility to change the guest if the nature of current news dictates a change.

For radio, all that is needed is a studio, enough microphones to insure that all participants are heard clearly, and a control room that is free so that someone can check the balance of the participants' microphones. For television, a simple set with comfortable chairs and a coffee table or a long desk will do the job.

There are a multitude of other ways to do public affairs programing. As mentioned earlier, some television stations which are equipped with the new electronic news-gathering equipment are allowing opportunities for the public to engage in two-way conversations with panels of experts or newsmakers.

This technique has been a part of radio for a long time. The telephone call-in show follows this basic idea. Some of these programs are designed to be frivolous and entertaining, but others deal in significant matters and call upon a variety of experts to answer questions from the public. There are a number of variations on this technique. Some all-news stations work a call-in segment into one part of the day's programing and either rotate guests or have an expert on one particular topic in the studio to take questions from the audience. For example, one major all-news station had a psychologist on tap during the late morning each weekday for several months so that parents could call in and discuss their children's problems.

Sometimes the call-in period follows a series of informational programs. For example, a station might run several weeks of features on how to stop smoking and then schedule a call-in period one day to discuss how smokers and ex-smokers in the audience are dealing with their problems. Other topics that have been discussed include medical questions and income taxes.

Sometimes a broadcast station will open up a public meeting to its audience. A radio or television station may take its equipment to a municipal building, for example, and actually broadcast a public meeting so that its audience can see exactly what goes on in these meetings.

A variation used by some radio stations is to hold their own town meeting. This seems to work well in big cities where a station can announce that it will broadcast from a hall in a certain part of town. Then the station gathers together a group of community leaders to answer questions from the audience. and the whole session is broadcast live.

Then there's the whole category of informational programs in which a station dishes out material which should be of interest to major portions of the audiences. Both television and radio stations do this. inside and outside of regular newscast periods. You can think of many of these programs. For March to mid-April a large number of stations carry income tax tips. Many stations carry programs which talk about education or medicine. Often these features turn out to be highly saleable. In fact, some are successful enough for the radio networks to offer a limited lineup of programs which inform the audience on matters related to a specific topic, such as consumer news, education, or finance.

There is really no limit to the variety of ways a station can perform a public service. For the most part the extent of these

Fig. 9-2. A lightweight Philips television camera being used to broadcast a rodeo. Similar equipment is used for news special events remotes. (Courtesy Philips Broadcast Equipment Corp.)

programs need only be limited by the imagination of their planners. (See Fig. 9-2.) Interestingly enough, many good public affairs programs are not expensive to produce, and often they bring in enough revenue to at least defray their costs.

SUMMARY

Public affairs programing is a growing area in broadcast journalism. Many stations have dragged their feet and are just beginning, with the FCC's prodding, to do the sort of jobs they are capable of doing. Sometimes the motivation has been economic; other times it has been out of fear of the unknown.

The cure to the worry over the cost of public affairs programing is to remember to keep it simple and within the equipment and personnel capabilities of the station. There also may be unexploited sources of income waiting for development by creative salespersons who are willing to sell an intangible such as a documentary or a call-in feature.

The simplicity rule also can overcome the fear of the unknown. It's true that some well-financed major market stations drop thousands of dollars producing documentaries, but it is possible to do a workmanlike job with facilities available in almost any broadcast station.

For example, a rural television station could do a documentary about the ugly trash heaps that dot the local countryside. All that is needed is some good silent film to illustrate the problem. Then, depending on the station's budget, selected interviews could be done with farmers, county sanitation officials, public officials, etc. Or the silent film could simply be used to introduce a program, and then a studio panel could be assembled to discuss the problem and possible remedies.

A small radio station could do the series on housing for the elderly that was outlined earlier. All that has to be done is to go out and get the necessary interviews covering many viewpoints on the topic and then to tie together key parts of the interviews with a well-written narration.

Any television station can do a guest interview if it has even one live camera. A radio station at minimum effort can at least record a city council meeting for playback later in the day. And from these humble beginnings can come far more sophisticated programs.

The beginning newsperson should be aware of public service programing. It offers excellent possibilities for learning, for doing challenging assignments, and for advancing professionally. You may find yourself wanting to specialize in the fascinating area of documentary production. Or you may get to be the host of an interview-panel show. In any case, you will find intellectual challenge and career opportunities in this developing aspect of broadcast journalism.

10
Editorializing

For a long time the concept of editorializing over broadcast stations was subject to intense debate. Since broadcast stations are franchises granted by the government for limited periods of time, many people felt that the stations should not be vendors of the owners opinions. Newspapers were regarded as different because they operated entirely in the private sector and looked back upon a long history of editorializing and observance of the First Amendment right to freedom of speech.

HISTORY

Historically, in the early days of radio few stations showed any interest in taking sides on public issues. Gradually radio developed commentators, who were mostly the columnists who appeared in the newspapers of the time. The newspapers resisted this incursion into their domain just as they had resisted the broadcasting of news. But the dramatic setback came in 1941 when radio station WAAB in Boston applied for renewal of its license.

The Federal Communications Commission then became aware that WAAB had been broadcasting editorials. The station had given its support to candidates for political office and had taken stands on various public issues. The Commission told WAAB that its license would be renewed but that the station would have to stop editorializing. In its decision, which became known as the "Mayflower Decision," the FCC said: "A broadcaster cannot advocate." The Commission ruling applied only to spokespersons for the station licensee and not to commentators whose broadcasts were heard over the station.

The Mayflower Decision remained in effect throughout World War Two, but in the late 1940s the National Association of Broadcasters zeroed in on the decision. On July 1, 1949, the FCC reversed the Mayflower Decision, ruling that stations could editorialize if they maintained overall balance or "fairness" in their broadcasts.

Even after editorializing by broadcast stations became legal the practice spread only slowly. It takes a great deal of courage for a broadcast station's ownership to approve editorializing. Taking a stand means becoming accountable for your opinions and your actions. And you can be certain of irritating business people, political leaders, and other community powers who it would be better to pacify from a commercial point of view. In addition, broadcast stations can be called to account for their performance at license renewal time and at other times, so a timid licensee would avoid editorializing.

Fortunately, there are an increasing number of broadcast station owners who look upon editorializing as an important community service. They feel that a free flow of opinion is part of the structure of a democracy. Some owners feel that their communities deserve another source of opinion and comment than the local newspaper.

Today editorials are being broadcast by large and small stations across the nation on topics ranging in significance from an appeal to reduce highway driving speeds to an outright statement on drugs or birth control. Stations usually take one of two approaches in presenting editorials. Some vest the authority of spokesperson on the station's chief executive. Others hire a person who is known as an editorial director and spokesperson. A few use both, favoring the chief executive to speak on important issues and the editorial director to speak on less controversial issues.

Many stations have followed the pattern of newspapers in forming an editorial board to help frame station editorial policy. This is one of the ways editorializing comes home to the newsperson. If you assume that someday you will move into management, you should think a bit about how you would react to some of the questions which have to be resolved by the editorial board. And as a senior reporter or management person, you may be asked to write editorials, probably for airing by someone else. In stations that employ writers, one or more of the experienced writers often prepare editorials.

GROUND RULES

When the FCC did away with its restrictive Mayflower Doctrine it began a trend to what is now known as the "Fairness Doctrine." The first descriptive statement on the Fairness Doctrine was promulgated by the FCC in its *Report on Editorializing by Broadcast Licensees*, which was issued in 1949.

In a 1974 report by the Commission, the Fairness Doctrine was described as having two essential duties: "(1) The broadcaster must devote a reasonable percentage of this broadcast time to the coverage of public issues; and (2) the coverage of these issues must be fair in the sense that it provides an opportunity for the presentation of contrasting points of views."

The FCC has clearly stated that it puts the burden on the station as to who speaks for different viewpoints, the shades of viewpoint expressed, the subjects considered, and the format within which the presentation takes place.

There are certain obligations the FCC puts on stations when they editorialize. For example, the Commission says: "If a licensee fails to present an opposing viewpoint on the ground that no appropriate spokesman is available, he should be prepared to demonstrate that he has made a diligent, good-faith effort to communicate to such potential spokesmen his willingness to present their views on the issue or issues presented." Then the Commission continues; "There may well be occasions, particularly in cases involving major issues discussed in depth, where such a showing should include specific offers of response time to appropriate individuals in addition to general over-the-air announcements."

What the FCC means is that if a station is going to broadcast its viewpoints, then it must make time available to others to express their viewpoints. But what the first quote says is that stations must make a positive effort to locate spokespersons for contrasting viewpoints.

So if your station does an editorial in which it takes sides in favor of publicly supported day-care centers for low-income working mothers, it must make time available for responses by spokespersons for groups which may oppose this idea. Most stations maintain mailing lists, which include all basic community opinion leaders, and also special lists for certain topics. But on top of this the station must actively seek out spokespersons for groups not included on any list.

If you were doing an editorial on day-care centers, for example, you would routinely send a transcript to political leaders, civic leaders, parent groups, educational groups, minority groups, and the like. But you would also want to check with individuals representing aspects of the civil rights controversy, perhaps the American Civil Liberties Union or the Welfare Rights League.

Remember, if you write an editorial or supervise editorial activities, make certain that all the interest groups of which you are aware are told about the editorial, and be sincere in your efforts to discover new groups. The purpose of this seeking-out process is for these groups to have an opportunity to use your station's air time to respond to the editorial. Remember that dissenting groups are to be given no less of an opportunity to speak their piece than the station took to make the original statement. This means "equivalent" not "equal" time. You should provide the same length of time and the same number of exposures in similar periods of the day, but not necessarily the exact same time periods.

The FCC gives the station management a tough mandate when it comes to deciding who will speak. The FCC expects the station to permit all major viewpoints to be heard on an issue and leaves to the station the determination of which are major and which are minor viewpoints.

There is another aspect to the Fairness Doctrine that must be considered when talking about editorials—that is how the doctrine applies to editorials about political issues and personalities. The main point is that if a station endorses a candidate or attacks an individual, then it should be prepared to offer time for response to opposing candidates or to the individual attacked.

What is a personal attack? Here's what Section 73.123, Chapter I, of Title 47 of the Code of Federal Regulations says:

> (a) When, during the presentation of views on a controversial issue of public importance, an attack is made upon the honesty, character, integrity or like personal qualities of an identified person or group, the licensee shall, within a reasonable time and in no event later than one week after the attack, transmit to the person or group attacked (1) notification of the date, time and identification of the broadcast; (2) a script or tape (or an accurate summary if a script or tape is not available) of the attack; and (3) offer of a reasonable opportunity to respond over the licensee's facilities.

The above-mentioned section has some exceptions:

(b) The provisions of paragraph (a) of this section shall not be applicable (1) to attacks on foreign groups or foreign public figures; (2) to personal attacks which are made by legally qualified candidates, their authorized spokesmen, or those associated with them in the campaign, or other such candidates, their authorized spokesmen, or persons associated with the candidate in the campaign; and (3) to bona fide newscasts, bona fide news interviews, and on-the-spot coverage of a bona fide news event (including commentary or analysis contained in the foregoing programs, but the provisions of paragraph (a) of this section shall be applicable to editorials of the licensee).

All that legal mumbo-jumbo has within it something which should have made your journalistic eyes sparkle. It says that as far as your day-to-day functions as a reporter are concerned, you don't have to worry about demands for equal or equivalent time. There are exceptions: (1) no station worth its salt is going to go with a one-sided story unless the other side refuses comment and (2) your station would be asked to prove that over all it maintains balance in the variety of opinion and news coverage it offers. But if you are out interviewing a political candidate and his opponent's manager comes running up and demands equal time, you can politely and respectfully decline on principle.

The preceding legal citation contains another section of interest to journalists. It reads:

(c) Where a licensee, in an editorial, (1) endorses or (2) opposes a legally qualified candidate or candidates, the licensee shall, within 24 hours after the editorial, transmit to respectively (1) the other qualified candidate or candidates for the same office or (2) the candidate opposed in the editorial (a) notification of the date and time of the ditorial; (b) a script or tape of the editorial; and (c) an offer of a reasonable opportunity for a candidate or a spokesman of the candidate to respond over the licensee's facilities: *Provided, however*, that where such editorials are broadcast within 72 hours prior to the day of the election, the licensee shall comply with the provisions of this paragraph sufficiently far in advance of the broadcast to enable the candidate or candidates to have a reasonable opportunity to prepare a response and to present it in a timely fashion.

CONTROLLING EDITORIALS

In considering editorials, keep firmly in mind that editorializing has its place, and that place is within the station's editorial presentations or within the commentary of authorized commentators.

There is *no* place in straight news coverage for editorializing. Your opinion is not newsworthy. Your function as a reporter is to marshal as many facts as possible and to present as even-handed a report as possible. The same obligation is placed upon any decent news department. That is not to say that certain stations haven't been known for slanting the focus of their news (by either commission or ommission) to favor certain viewpoints, but professional newspersons wouldn't want to be associated with that sort of operation.

As long as you are a reporter you will have to put aside your opinions and make a sincere effort to discover and report the facts as an impartial observer.

Appendix A
The Radio Code, National Association of Broadcasters Eighteenth Edition, January 1974

News

Radio is unique in its capacity to reach the largest number of people first with reports on current events. This competitive advantage bespeaks caution—being first is not as important as being right. The following standards predicated upon that viewpoint.

1. *News Sources.* Those responsible for news on radio should exercise constant professional care in the selection of sources—for the integrity of the news and the consequent good reputation of radio as a dominant news medium depend largely upon the reliability of such sources.

2. *News Reporting.* News reporting shall be factual and objective. Good taste shall prevail in the selection and handling of news. Morbid. sensational. or alarming details not essential to factual reporting should be avoided. News should be broadcast in such a manner as to avoid creation of panic and unnecessary alarm. Broadcasters shall be diligent in their supervision of content. format. and presentation of news broadcasts. Equal diligence should be exercised in selection of editors and reporters who direct news gathering and dissemination. since the station's performance in this vital informational field depends largely upon them.

3. *Commentaries and Analyses.* Special obligations devolve upon those who analyze and/or comment upon news developments. and management should be satisfied completely that the task is to be performed in the best interest of the listening public. Programs of news analysis and commentary shall be clearly identified as such. distinguishing them from straight news reporting.

4. *Editorializing.* Broadcasts in which stations express their own opinions about issues of general public interest should be clearly identified as editorials and should be clearly distinguished from news and other program material.

5. *Coverage of News and Public Events.* In the coverage of news and public events the broadcaster has the right to exercise his judgment consonant with the accepted standards of ethical journalism and especially the requirements for decency and decorum in the broadcast of public and court proceedings.

6. *Placement of Advertising.* A broadcaster should exercise particular discrimination in the acceptance. placement. and presentation of advertising in news programs so that such advertising should be clearly distinguishable from the news content.

Reprinted from The Radio Code. published by the Code Authority. National Association of Broadcasters. Eighteenth Edition. January 1974.

Appendix B

The Television Code, National Association of Broadcasters Eighteenth Edition, June 1975

Treatment of News and Public Events

General

Television Code standards relating to the treatment of news and public events are. because of constitutional considerations. intended to be exhortatory. The standards set forth hereunder encourage high standards of professionalism in broadcast journalism. They are not to be interpreted as turning over to others the broadcaster's responsibility as to judgments necessary in news and public events programing.

News

1. A television station's news schedule should be adequate and well balanced.
2. News reporting should be factual. fair. and without bias.
3. A television broadcaster should exercise particular discrimination in the acceptance. placement. and presentation of advertising in news programs so that such advertising should be clearly distinguishable from the news content.
4. At all times. pictorial and verbal material for both news and comment should conform to other sections of these standards. wherever such sections are reasonably applicable.
5. Good taste should prevail in the selection and handling of news:
   Morbid. sensational. or alarming details not essential to the factual report. especially in connection with stories of crime or sex. should be avoided. News should be telecast in such a manner as to avoid panic and unnecessary alarm.
6. Commentary and analysis should be clearly identified as such.
7. Pictorial material should be chosen with care and not presented in a misleading manner.
8. All news interview programs should be governed by accepted standards of ethical journalism. under which the interviewer selects the questions to be asked. Where there is advance agreement materially restricting an important or newsworthy area of questioning. the interviewer will state on the program that such limitation has been agreed upon. Such disclosure should be made if the person being interviewed requires that questions be submitted in advance or if he participates in editing a recording of the interview prior to its use on the air.

9. A television broadcaster should exercise due care in his supervision of content. format. and presentation of newscasts originated by his station and in his selection of newscasters. commentators. and analysts.

Public Events

1. A television broadcaster has an affirmative responsibility at all times to be informed of public events and to provide coverage consonant with the ends of an informed and enlightened citizenry.
2. The treatment of such events by a television broadcaster should provide adequate and informed coverage.

Reprinted from The Television Code. published by the Code Authority. National Association of Broadcasters. Seventeenth Edition. second printing. January 1974.

Appendix C

Code of Broadcast News and Ethics, Radio Television News Directors Association

The following Code of Broadcast News Ethics for RTNDA was adopted January 2, 1966 and amended October 13, 1973

The members of the Radio-Television News Directors Association agree that their prime responsibility as journalists—and that of the broadcasting industry as the collective sponsor of news broadcasting—is to provide to the public they serve a news service as accurate, full, and prompt as human integrity and devotion can devise. To that end, they declare their acceptance of the standards of practice here set forth, and their solemn intent to honor them to the limits of their ability.

Article One

The primary purpose of broadcast journalists—to inform the public of events of importance and appropriate interest in a manner that is accurate and comprehensive—shall override all other purposes.

Article Two

Broadcast news presentations shall be designed not only to offer timely and accurate information, but also to present it in the light of relevant circumstances that give it meaning and perspective.

> This standard means that news reports, when clarity demands it, will be laid against pertinent factual background; that factors such as race, creed, nationality, or prior status will be reported only when they are relevant; that comment or subjective content will be properly identified; and that errors in fact will be promptly acknowledged and corrected.

Article Three

Broadcast journalists shall seek to select material for newscast solely on their evaluation of its merits as news.

> This standard means that news will be selected on the criteria of significance, community and regional relevance, appropriate human interest, service to defined audiences. It excludes sensationalism or misleading emphasis in any form; subservience to external or "interested" efforts to influence news selection and presentation, whether from within the

broadcasting industry or from without. It requires that such terms as "bulletin" and "flash" be used only when the character of the news justifies them; that bombastic or misleading descriptions of newsroom facilities and personnel be rejected, along with undue use of sound and visual effects; and that promotional or publicity material be sharply scrutinized before use and identified by source or otherwise when broadcast.

Article Four

Broadcast journalists shall at all times display humane respect for the dignity, privacy, and the well-being of persons with whom the news deals.

Article Five

Broadcast journalists shall govern their personal lives and such nonprofessional associations as may impinge on their professional activities in a manner that will protect them from conflict of interest, real or apparent.

Article Six

Broadcast journalists shall seek actively to present all news the knowledge of which will serve the public interest, no matter what selfish, uninformed, or corrupt efforts attempt to color it, withhold it, or prevent its presentation. They shall make constant effort to open doors closed to the reporting of public proceedings with tools appropriate to broadcasting (including cameras and recorders), consistent with the public interest. They acknowledge the journalist's ethic of protection of confidential information and sources, and urge unswerving observation of it except in instances in which it would clearly and unmistakably defy the public interest.

Article Seven

Broadcast journalists recognize the responsibility borne by broadcasting for informed analysis, comment, and editorial opinion on public events and issues. They accept the obligation of broadcasters for the presentation of such matters by individuals whose competence, experience, and judgment qualify them for it.

Article Eight

In court, broadcast journalists shall conduct themselves with dignity, whether the court is in or out of session. The shall keep broadcast equipment as unobtrusive and silent as possible. Where court facilities are inadequate, pool broadcasts should be arranged.

Article Nine

In reporting matters that are or may be litigated, the journalist shall avoid practices which would tend to interfere with the right of an individual to a fair trial.

Article Ten

Broadcast journalists shall not misrepresent the source of any broadcast news material.

Article Eleven

Broadcast journalists shall actively censure and seek to prevent violations of these standards, and shall actively encourage their observance by all journalists, whether of the Radio Television News Directors Association or not.

Appendix D

The Society of Professional Journalists Sigma Delta Chi

THE SOCIETY OF PROFESSIONAL JOURNALISTS
SIGMA DELTA CHI
(Adopted by the 1973 national convention)

The Society of Professional Journalists. Sigma Delta Chi. believes the duty of journalists is to serve the truth.

We believe the agencies of mass communication are carriers of public discussion and information. acting on their Constitutional mandate and freedom to learn and report the facts.

We believe in public enlightenment as the forerunner of justice. and in our Constitutional role to seek the truth as part of the public's right to know the truth.

We believe those responsibilities carry obligations that require journalists to perform with intelligence. objectivity. accuracy. and fairness.

To these ends. we declare acceptance of the standards of practice here set forth:

- **RESPONSIBILITY**: The Public's right to know of events of public importance and interest is the overriding mission of the mass media. The purpose of distributing news and enlightened opinion is to serve the general welfare. Journalists who use their professional status as representatives of the public for selfish or other unworthy motives violate a high trust.
- **FREEDOM OF THE PRESS**: Freedom of the press is to be guarded as an inalienable right of people in a free society. It carries with it the freedom and the responsibility to discuss. question. and challenge actions and utterances of our government and of our public and private institutions. Journalists uphold the right to speak unpopular opinions and the privilege to agree with the majority.
- **ETHICS**: Journalists must be free of obligation to any interest other than the public's right to know the truth.
1. Gifts. favors. free travel. special treatment. or privileges can compromise the integrity of journalists and their employers. Nothing of value should be accepted.
2. Secondary employment. political involvement. holding public office. and service in community organizations should be avoided if it compromises the integrity of journalists and their employers. Journalists and their employers should conduct their personal lives in a manner which protects them from conflict of interest. real or apparent. Their responsibilities to the public are paramount. That is the nature of their profession.

Politics of Broadcast

PN 4784
T9
A1
A 43
1971-72

PN 4784
T9
A1
A 43/X
8th

88/

Broadcast Stuff

PN 4784
B75
R69 x
1986

PN 4784
B75
I=3
1985

* PN 4784
B75
M.24
1987

PN 4784
B75
E38
1986

3. So-called news communications from private sources should not be published or broadcast without substantiation of their claims to news value.
4. Journalists will seek news that serves the public interest. despite the obstacles. They will make constant efforts to insure that the public's business is conducted in public and that public records are open to public inspection.
5. Journalists acknowledge the newsman's ethic of protecting confidential sources of information.

- **ACCURACY AND OBJECTIVITY**: Good faith with the public is the foundation of all worthy journalism.

1. Truth is our ultimate goal.
2. Objectivity in reporting the news is another goal. which serves as the mark of an experienced professional. It is a standard of performance toward which we strive. We honor those who achieve it.
3. There is no excuse for inaccuracies or lack of thoroughness.
4. Newspaper headlines should be fully warranted by the contents of the articles they accompany. Photographs and telecasts should give an accurate picture of an event and not highlight a minor incident out of context.
5. Sound practice makes clear distinction between news reports and expressions of opinion. News reports should be free of opinion or bias and represent all sides of an issue.
6. Partisanship in editorial comment which knowingly departs from the truth violates the spirit of American journalism.
7. Journalists recognize their responsibility for offering informed analysis. comment. and editorial opinion on public events and issues. They accept the obligation to present such material by individuals whose competence. experience. and judgment qualify them for it.
8. Special articles or presentations devoted to advocacy or the writer's own conclusions and interpretations should be labeled as such.

- **FAIR PLAY**: Journalists at all times will show respect for the dignity. privacy. rights. and well-being of people encountered in the course of gathering and presenting the news.

1. The news media should not communicate unofficial charges affecting reputation or moral character without giving the accused a chance to reply.
2. The news media must guard against invading a person's right to privacy.
3. The media should not pander to morbid curiosity about details of vice and crime.
4. It is the duty of news media to make prompt and complete correction of their errors.
5. Journalists should be accountable to the public for their reports. and the public should be encouraged to voice its grievances against the media. Open dialogue with our readers. viewers. and listeners should be fostered.

- **PLEDGE**: Journalists should actively censure and try to prevent violations of these standards. and they should encourage their observance by all newspeople. Adherence to this code of ethics is intended to preserve the bond of mutual trust and respect between American journalists and the American people.

Glossary

Ampex—type of tape recorder: this firm makes both audiotape and videotape recorders

Beat—Series of locations regularly visited or telephoned by reporter

Beeper—audible warning sound on a telephone line: also news slang for telephone interview

Blast Shield—foam rubber cover to protect microphone's sensitive inner parts from effects of wind and extraneous noise

Carting—recording material onto a cartridge for easier handling

Chest Pod—chest harness and brace for sound camera

Control Track—thin ribbon of audiotape down opposite side of magnetic-track sound film

Correspondent—term usually applies to senior and better paid station and network reporters

Cover Shot—shot taken of action other than primary activity to be used in editing film or tape

Double System—sound and pictures recorded on separate reels

Dubbing—copying from one tape to another

ENG—electronic news gathering

Feed—transmission of a story or group of stories

FPS—film term meaning frames per second

Kicker—short. humorous or human interest story at end of newscast

Lead-In—introduction to film or tape

Locked Up—all finished. wrapped up

Magnetic Stripe Sound Film—motion picture film with narrow stripe of audiotape down one edge on which audio is recorded

Mix—the combination of elements into a single element. i. e.. combining background sound with narration into one piece

Natural Sound—background sound natural to a location

Parallax—optical inclination of two parallel lines to apparently merge in the distance: in photography. a mechanical adjustment which must be made if camera lens and viewfinder are separate. parallel components

Pencil Mike—long. thin tubular microphone

Radio Circuit—Special broadcast quality hookup ordered through domestic or overseas telephone companies

Reversal Stock—film which develops positive without having to print a positive from a negative

Reporter—newsperson

Single System—audio and video recorded simultaneously on the same film or tape

Spotmaster—brand of cartridge recording and playback machine

Stock—raw film

SOF—sound on film

Super—meaning superimposure: optically or electronically superimposing writing on the television screen

Take—a scene. series of actions. period camera is turned on

Telephoto Lens—lets you take closeups from a distance

Take Out—complete. major story

Unipod—one-legged support for camera

Videotape—speaking without being seen over film or tape

VTR—videotape recorder

Wild Sound—background sound

Wrap—introduction and closing narration around interview or insert of newsmaker

Zoom—lens capable of continuous focus from closeup to wide angle. taken from brand name Zoomar; also. to zoom

Index